lonely planet

JOURNEY

Iceland's Ring Road

Anthony Ham, Eygló Svala Arnarsdóttir,
Alexis Averbuck, Jade Bremner

Iceland's Ring Road is a road trip that must be taken. One of the world's most beautiful drives, it encircles an elemental landscape forged by volcanoes and glaciers that still bring the Earth alive here, with thundering waterfalls, deep canyons and bubbling geothermal springs. Along the way, you'll pass through a world of small towns and even smaller farms, of fine foods and sub-Arctic wildlife. But this is, above all, a journey across an epic landscape worthy of the most magical Icelandic sagas.

Contents

Plan Your Trip

- My Ring Road 4
- Land of Glaciers 8
- The Wild Coast 14
- Cool Cities, Small Towns ... 18
- The Earth on Fire 22
- Icelandic Food 26
- 6 Ways to do Iceland's Ring Road ... 30

Go to p32 for the full route map

The Drive

SOUTHWEST ICELAND

- Reykjavík City Guide 36
- Reykjavík to Selfoss 48
- Detour: Golden Circle 62
- Selfoss to Vík 78

SOUTHEAST ICELAND

- Vík to Skaftafell 100
- Skaftafell to Höfn 116
- Höfn to Stöðvarfjörður ... 140
- Stöðvarfjörður to Egilsstaðir 152

Grjótagjá cave (p187)

NORTH & WEST ICELAND

- Egilsstaðir to Reykjahlíð 170
- Reykjahlíð to Akureyri ... 182
- Akureyri City Guide 194
- Akureyri to Hvammstangi 200
- Hvammstangi to Reykjavík 218

INSIGHT ESSAYS

- The Road That Changed Iceland 44
- Iceland's Storied Landscapes 94
- Elemental Iceland 132
- Slow and Solo on the Ring Road 166
- Iceland's Real-Life Hobbit Homes 216
- Ring Road Roulette: A Family, a Motorhome and No Clue ... 232

Toolkit

- First Time 236
- Money 237
- On the Road 238
- Packing 244
- Where to Stay 245
- Responsible Travel 246
- Access, Attitudes & Safety 248
- Language 249

Previous page: Stöðvarfjörður (p149)

My Ring Road

Anthony Ham anthonyham.com; @AnthonyHamWrite

I just can't stay away from the Ring Road. Each time I return, I take a different detour, or stay in my favourite places just a little bit longer. As I go, I read the sagas and lose myself in the landscape. I particularly love the Ring Road in winter, when the roads are quieter, snow carpets the landscape, and there's often a red glow on the horizon at night. And when the Northern Lights appear, I become convinced again that Iceland really is nature's greatest show on Earth.

Anthony wrote the Plan and Toolkit chapters and the route chapters from Vík to Höfn and Egilsstaðir to Akureyri. He is an Australian writer who writes about the wild places of the planet, from Africa and the Amazon to the Arctic. He writes for the New York Times *and has written more than 150 guidebooks for Lonely Planet.*

MY BEST VIEWPOINTS

Dyrhólaey
Along a black-sand beach running west to eternity, with puffins in the foreground. p90

Seyðisfjörður
From the approach down off the high pass or around the harbour with the church floodlit at night. p163

Km97 Lookout
Between Egilsstaðir and Myvatn, layer upon layer of mountains are possessed of wild and desolate beauty. p175

Eygló Svala Arnarsdóttir
@eyglosvala

I love travelling my own country and making new discoveries. The stretch of Ring Road that goes through East Iceland is not long, but it's lined with surprises, and even though I've visited the region many times, it's always a different experience. Once, in whimsical spring weather, I cancelled hiking due to snowfall but went skiing instead. I returned in summer, hoping for the legendary East Iceland heat wave, but caught the infamous Eastfjords fog instead, which completely blocked the view. It did add a veil of mystery, though. It's best to travel with an open mind and be flexible.

Eygló wrote the two East Iceland legs, from Höfn to Egilsstaðir, and the Reykjavík and Akureyri city guides. She has written for Iceland Review, Kinfolk Travel *and Lonely Planet, among other travel publications.*

MY BEST STRETCHES

Höfn–Djúpivogur
Notice the colours of the mountains; walk on Fauskasandur beach. p144

Streitishvarf
One of the most geologically interesting parts of the route. p148

Reyðarfjörður
I like to stop for the view after the tunnel and think of my grandfather who was stationed there with the allied forces. p157

Jade Bremner
@jadeob @jadebremner

One of my first ever travel-writing assignments was in Iceland, and I was tasked with driving the Ring Road. Looking back, I had no idea what I was getting myself into. Ring roads in my native England are concrete monstrosities, but their Icelandic namesake was a mesmerising display of epic scenery and gawk-worthy sights. Every turn was close to some kind of geographical wonder: a deep volcanic crater or iceberg-covered lake, an enormous waterfall or rugged sea arch shrouded in legend. I vowed to return to discover everything I'd missed. Two decades of visits on, I still haven't seen it all.

Jade wrote three legs from Hvammstangi to Vík. She has authored more than 80 Lonely Planet books, and has edited for and contributed to Time Out, The Independent, The Telegraph, Radio Times, The Times, CNN, Newsweek *and* Outside Magazine.

MY BEST SPOTS

Jökulsárlón
Seals swim by and icebergs crash into the water; ethereal experience. p128

Þórsmörk
Sculpted by eruptions so dramatic it's named after Þór (Thor). p84

Skógafoss
Not the biggest waterfall, but one of the most perfectly formed. p87

Skógafoss (p87)

DANIEL DORSA FOR LONELY PLANET

Alexis Averbuck alexisaverbuck.com

Every time I land in Iceland, zipping towards Reykjavík through lavafields that stretch to the far mountains, my heart soars. The noise of the world subsides and I immerse myself – strolling between brilliantly coloured houses, buzzing cafes and wildly creative museums and galleries. Then, when I head into the countryside, along the Ring Road, I face a wonderful dilemma… what to choose? Thrilling open-air hot pots, the jagged inspiration that is the rift valley Þingvellir, or the adventures through monumental volcanoes, waterfalls, glaciers and shores. I love finding moments alone in these spaces, feeling joy and awe in every direction.

Alexis wrote the Golden Circle detour. She paints and writes about her adventures – from living in Antarctica to crossing the Pacific by sailboat – for Lonely Planet, National Geographic UK and other international outlets.

MY BEST PASTRIES

Hafið Bistro
Relax in Djúpivogur, waterside, with homemade *ástarpungar* (love balls) and a coffee. p145

Beitarhúsið Café
You don't expect great cardamom *kleinur* (doughnuts) in a highland lavafield, but there they are! p177

Lauren Breedlove @girlwanderlist

I fell for Iceland's otherworldly landscape on my first trip nine years ago, and have been back seven times since. I love letting word of mouth recommendations from locals or other travellers guide my Icelandic adventures. Visiting well-known spots at sunrise is my favourite; I've often had them to myself. I specialise in remote and offbeat travel, outdoor adventures, and authentic culinary and cultural experiences. My work has been published in *National Geographic, Travel + Leisure, Food & Wine, AFAR* and others.
Lauren wrote the Slow and Solo essay (p166).

Daniel Dorsa @danieldorsa

Iceland is probably the most accessible place you get to see raw, untouched beauty, and the windshield becomes the best screen you could ask for. There's so much to recommend, but in the east you can see puffins at Borgarfjarðarhöfn and have a luxurious spa experience on the river at Vök Baths. I'm an LA-based photographer whose work explores the relationships between people, the environments they inhabit and the landscapes that connect them.
Daniel's photographs can be seen throughout, including the Elemental Iceland photo essay (p132).

Emily Lethbridge @emilylethb

Following in the footsteps of ancient saga characters all around Iceland has been a passion of mine for nearly two decades. Take some time to find a sheltered spot outdoors somewhere during your trip – tune into Iceland's beauty on a micro-scale, as well as admiring the magnificent vistas. I'm a researcher at the Árni Magnússon Institute for Icelandic Studies in Reykjavík, and I'm fascinated by the roles that Iceland's past literary traditions and places play in modern society.
Emily wrote Iceland's Storied Landscapes (p94).

Thomas O'Malley

I took on the Golden Circle and the southern stretch of Iceland's Ring Road in a bus-sized RV with a pregnant partner and our toddler. It was my first time driving anything bigger than a small car – what could possibly go wrong? If you're planning something similar, stock up on beer and wine at Keflavík airport on arrival: Iceland's in-country prices are ruinous. I'm a travel writer based in Scotland and have contributed to more than 20 Lonely Planet guidebooks, from Denmark to Mongolia.
Tom wrote the Ring Road Roulette essay (p232).

Zoë Robert

I've lived in various places, but call Iceland home. Over the past 20 years, I've travelled the Ring Road in all seasons but prefer the long midsummer days with camping gear in tow, allowing for more flexibility and unexpected adventures. Based in Reykjavík, I've covered Iceland for local and international publications including Reuters, CNN and *Iceland Review*, where I was also managing editor.

Zoë wrote The Road That Changed Iceland (p44).

Luke Waterson lukeandhiswords.com

I was first attracted to Iceland's Ring Road for its hiking but fell for its sights rich in legends and its charismatic turf houses. I love Northwest Iceland, especially the area around Skagafjörður, north of the Ring Road's Varmahlíð: this is Iceland's farming heartland and it glimmers with greenery and history. I specialise in adventure travel writing, have contributed to 80+ Lonely Planet titles, and also write for the BBC, *Telegraph, Britain* magazine and DK.

Luke wrote Iceland's Real-Life Hobbit Homes (p216).

James Gulliver Hancock
@gulliverhancock

The Ring Road is one of many iconic journeys I've taken. It was the middle of summer and I travelled with my dad, who couldn't sleep because of the midnight sun, so we'd go on wanders over mossy green hills and black beaches at all hours of the night that felt like day. The showers smelled like rotten eggs as the water all came from geothermal springs! I'm an illustrator for Lonely Planet and *My How Things Work* series spans subjects from space stations to trains.

James drew this title's illustrated map.

Reynisfjara (p91)

Land of Glaciers

Iceland: the name says it all. You're never far from a glacier here and there are countless ways to experience them.

A Country of Glaciers

Each glacier tells its own story, and we'll come to that. But in Iceland, it's the whole that is its own natural epic. Glaciers and ice caps envelop a remarkable 11% of the country's land mass. Much of that is the work of Vatnajökull (p115), which alone takes in 8% of Iceland – look at a satellite map of the country and you'll get an idea of its extent. If you leave aside the North Pole and Antarctica, Vatnajökull is the world's largest ice cap, or the largest in the Earth's inhabited realm.

Why so many glaciers? Most date back to a cooler period – a mini Ice Age, if you like – that began around 2500 years ago. Ice caps form when piles of snow accumulate and freeze, building up over millennia in an area that never warms sufficiently to melt the ice. As it slowly compresses, it grows in weight, pressing down upon the landscape beneath it.

As for the ice cap, so too for glaciers. The immense glittering weight of an ice cap may seem immovable, but around its edges, slow-moving rivers – glaciers – flow imperceptibly down the mountainsides. Like rivers, glaciers carry with them pieces of stony sediment, which they dump in cindery-looking moraines at the foot of the mountain, or on vast gravelly outwash plains such as the Skeiðarársandur (p110) in Southeast Iceland. And for long sections of Iceland's south coast, the Ring Road takes you within touching distance of these ice rivers.

Volcanoes and their lava and debris flows may help shape the earth, but the relentless crush of glaciers carries similar power – glaciers were instrumental in shaping the Iceland we see today.

Skaftafellsjökull (p113)
DANIEL DORSA FOR LONELY PLANET

The View from Afar

There are almost as many different ways to experience the Icelandic ice as there are glaciers. The easiest (yet still intensely pleasurable) way is to admire the glaciers from afar.

When glaciers retreat, they often leave behind lakes or lagoons at their base, and these promise some of the most spectacular and accessible glacier experiences on the planet. As ice breaks off (or calves), it forms icebergs that float on the water. Nowhere is this more evident than at Jökulsárlón (p128), where pieces of Breiðamerkurjökull (p123), one of Vatnajökull's largest galciers, float right past you on their way out to sea.

You can also see lagoons with icebergs at Fjallsárlón (p123), Kvíárjökull (p122) and Skaftafell (p113).

Up Close & Personal

You can, of course, do far more than just admire glaciers from a distance.

One possibility is to hike right up to the glacier's tongue or snout, and there are places where you're close enough to touch the ice. At both Skaftafellsjökull (p113) and Svínafellsjökull (p120), you can be within touching distance less than an hour after parking your car. Apart from feeling dwarfed by the sheer immensity of the ice wall towering over you, you'll also hear the glacier as it groans and creaks like a living being.

MICHAL BALADA/SHUTTERSTOCK

JÖKULSÁRLÓN LAGOON

The Jökulsárlón lagoon is the best place in Iceland to see those luminous blue pieces of ice that are extremely old: they were created by centuries of compression squeezing out the air bubbles that give ice its usual silvery-white appearance. Light refraction also causes that intense blue colour. These glorious shapes, every one of them different, set against the glacier backdrop, are breathtakingly beautiful and a symbol of the ice's great age and fragility.

EXPLORE THE ICE

The Sagas of the Icelanders (preface by Jane Smiley; 2000)
Available across Iceland, *The Sagas of the Icelanders* is a weighty tome that includes old stories from this landscape.

Lonely Planet's Iceland (14th edition, 2026)
Lonely Planet's *Iceland* guide includes detailed recommendations across the Ring Road and beyond.

Guided Ranger Walks
Join one of the guided ranger walks at Jökulsárlón at 11am from June to mid-September to learn more about the Breiðamerkurjökull glacier.

Fjallsárlón (p123)

Another excellent way to commune with the ice is to take a boat, with three main options. At both Jökulsárlón and Fjallsárlón, Zodiac or inflatable boats zip around the lagoon; while the engine noise can be distracting, they get you really close to the wall of ice that rises from the water.

Another favourite option is to join a guided kayak tour out onto the lagoon. Travelling in this way is a real pleasure. While you may not make it to the actual glacier – in part for safety reasons – you will get very close to some of the icebergs. This is an option at both Jökulsárlón and Heinabergsjökull (p130).

The final way to get up close on the water are the Jökulsárlón-only amphibious boat, a truck-boat that drives along the lagoon shore and then converts into a boat to enter the water. It's a method of transport high on novelty, but, in our view, there are better ways to see and draw near to the ice.

And then, of course, there are the glacier hikes where – only with a guide and the proper equipment – you can walk up onto the glacier. It's a brilliant way to get a feel for the ice. Also excellent are winter-only tours to ice caves beneath the glaciers. A handful of recommended operators (p129) offer small-group tours.

Ice Rivers
(Jemma Wadham; 2021)
Although not specific to Iceland, this study of glaciers is an excellent primer on how glaciers work and the threats they face.

The Future of Ice
(Gretel Ehrlich; 2004)
Another lyrical evocation of ice-bound landscapes and the position they occupy in the human psyche.

I'll Show You
(Justin Bieber; 2015)
The music video for Justin Bieber's 'I'll Show You' shows the singer at Fjaðrárgljúfur and taking a dip in Jökulsárlón lagoon.

BEST GLACIER VIEWS

Sjónarnípa (p115)
Hike from Skaftafell Visitor Centre to the lookout at Sjónarnípa for unrivalled views over Skaftafellsjökull.

Kvíárjökull (p122)
Hidden from the road, this superb glacier comes down off the heights into a sweeping natural amphitheatre.

Fjallsárlón (p123)
Views of the glacier at Fjallsárlón are prettier (and quieter) than at Jökulsárlón. Both are magnificent.

Blautakvísl (p104)
This pristine stream has a roadside stop with glorious views of the Mýrdalsjökull glacier.

The Future?

Advancing and retreating has always been a part of glacier ecology, but Iceland's glaciers are in trouble. Its major ice caps – Vatnajökull, Mýrdalsjökull in the southwest, and Langjökull and Hofsjökull in the highlands – have been melting at an unprecedented rate since 2000. Glaciologists believe the ice cap Snæfellsjökull in the west (with an average ice thickness of only 30m), as well as some of the outlet glaciers of the larger ice caps, could disappear completely within a few decades. In 2025, satellite images showed Skeiðarárjökull had retreated by 1km in just eight years. Iceland's Office of Meteorology also warns that, as global temperatures rise, the country's glaciers are losing close to ten billion tonnes of ice every year.

The well-worn tourism mantra of 'see it before it's too late' has never been more apt.

Snæfellsjökull (p228)

HIGHLIGHTS

❶ Svínafellsjökull (p120)
Leave crowds behind and walk to the tip of the glacier tongue and listen to it moan. There are lots of places where you can do this, but most, including Skaftafell, are much busier.

Ice-Cave Tour, ❷ Jökulsárlón (p129)
These winter-only tours take you under the glacier and into the world of ice. This is where you'll really get to see the blue ice and marvel at the magic.

Glacier Hike, ❷ Jökulsárlón (p129)
Step onto the glacier and get an unrivalled understanding of its textures and perils. The best place is around Jökulsárlón, but there are numerous spots to do it in the south.

LAND OF GLACIERS

Zodiac Tour, ❷ Jökulsárlón (p128) or ❸ Fjallsárlón (p123)
Get in the fast boat and zip across the lagoon to where Breiðamerkurjökull calves into the lagoon. This is as close as you can get to the glacier in a boat.

Kayak Tour, ❹ Heinabergsjökull (p130)
We love this way to explore glacier lagoons – no engine noise! If the crowds are starting to get to you at these magical places, this is the antidote.

❺ The View from Höfn (p130)
Take a walk out the southern end of Höfn and look out across the water for epic views of the looming Vatnajökull ice cap and its glaciers.

The Wild Coast

The Ring Road hugs the coastline for much of its route around Iceland. It takes you within reach of whales, seals and puffins, to add to the natural drama already at large in Iceland.

Watching Whales

Iceland is an important feeding ground for the whales of the North Atlantic, and they come to feast in the country's krill- and plankton-rich waters from June to September. This is true of most of the whale species, including the most commonly sighted, the humpback, which is known to breech, dive and otherwise swim close to whale-watching boats; they can be over 12m long and weigh 40 tonnes.

Whales are especially drawn to Skjálfandi, the large, long inlet off the northern town of Húsavík (p192), a small town that is the epicentre of Iceland's whale-watching industry and an easy detour off the Ring Road. There are a handful of excellent boat operators set up to take you out in converted fishing or whaling vessels (some of which are electric-powered), or a Zodiac or inflatable boat.

On a boat trip out onto the water, you might also see harbour seals and playful white-beaked dolphins, while whale species can include minke, fin, sei, pilot and sperm whales. If you're incredibly lucky, you might see a blue whale, the largest mammal (nearly 30m long and up to 80 tonnes) on the planet. Sightings of blue whales are rare – your best chances are different to other species, in April and May, or October to December.

Whales can sometimes be seen swimming offshore elsewhere around the coast, including at Ingólfshöfði (p124) or off the Vatnsnes Peninsula.

Seals

Unlike whales, seals are year-round residents in Icelandic waters, and can be seen in many places alongside or not far from the Ring Road. These

Whale breaching off Húsavík (p192)
TATONKA/SHUTTERSTOCK

include the Eastfjords, on the Vatnsnes Peninsula (p214) in Northwest Iceland, in the Mýrar region on the southeast coast, in Breiðafjörður in the west, and in the Westfjords; seals are commonly seen feeding and frolicking among the icebergs in the lagoon at Jökulsárlón (p128). There's also a seal centre, Selasetur Íslands (p212), and seal-watching tours at Hvammstangi (p212) in North Iceland, around halfway between Reykjavík and Akureyri.

There are two seal species to watch out for – the grey seal and the harbour seal. The latter, with its distinctive markings, is the least shy and most commonly seen of the two. For such a large species (they can be 2m long and weigh 100kg) they're remarkably agile in the water. Stay well away from seals on the beach – mothers leave their pups to fish, and may not return if humans get too close.

Puffins & Other Birds

Puffins are the biggest draw for the average traveller – you'll find them at many places near the Ring Road, including Ingólfshöfði (p124) and Borgarfjörður Eystri (p162) from about May to early August.

But birders have so much else to look forward to. Millions of seabirds nest on coastal cliffs and islands from May to August. Most impressive for their sheer numbers are gannets, guillemots, gulls, razorbills, kittiwakes, fulmars and puffins. In smaller numbers, you might see wood sandpipers, Arctic terns, skuas, Manx shearwaters, golden plovers, storm petrels and Leach's petrels. Watch also for the many species of ducks, ptarmigans, whooping swans, redwings, divers and gyrfalcons, and two species of owl.

THE BLUE WHALE

Perhaps the greatest prize of all in the waters off Húsavík (p192) is the opportunity – in April and May, or October to December – to see a blue whale, the largest animal on earth. Year-round, you can see an intact blue whale skeletons on earth in Húsavík's Whale Museum (p193). The blue whale is listed as endangered by the International Union for the Conservation of Nature (IUCN), which estimates numbers worldwide at between 10,000 and 25,000.

WHALES & COASTAL LIFE

North Sailing (northsailing.is)
This Húsavík whale-watching outfit has an excellent rundown on local whale species you can see; click on 'Whales & Birds'.

Ice Whale (icewhale.is)
The Icelandic Whale Watching Association runs campaigns to encourage visitors to go whale watching rather than whale tasting.

Trapped (Baltasar Kormákur; 2015)
This murder mystery series set in Siglufjörður shows the other side of Iceland's coast, set in a remote fishing town cut off by a snowstorm.

HIGHLIGHTS

1 Whales, Húsavík (p192)
Arguably the best of Iceland's wildlife encounters: you can see humpbacks, seals and puffins in summer, with blue whales possible either side of summer.

2 Whale Tours, Reykjavík (p36)
Although you're unlikely to see whales off the capital itself, it's possible, and boat tours out of Reykjavík give you a good chance.

3 Puffins, Ingólfshöfði (p124)
Take a tractor trip and climb up onto an eerie headland in search of puffins and other seabirds in a great day out.

4 Seals, Hvammstangi (p212)
Head out to sea in an old fishing boat under the midnight sun to look for seals and other wildlife in one of the least-known, but most rewarding, of Iceland's wildlife tours.

5 Seals, Jökulsárlón (p128)
There's so much else going on at Jökulsárlón that the seals play second fiddle – but it's one place that sightings are near-guaranteed.

6 Reindeer, East Iceland (p159)
Watch for Iceland's wild reindeer as you drive one of the wildest and loneliest stretches of the Ring Road from Höfn to Stöðvarfjörður.

Cool Cities, Small Towns

Reykjavík is surely one of Europe's coolest capitals, but Akureyri's a quiet gem, and small-town Iceland is one of the joys of travel here.

Reykjavík

Some cities don't have to try too hard. Effortlessly cool Reykjavík is just such a place. Quite apart from its spectacular location, this is a city of designer boutiques, Scandi-cool galleries and sweet small-town architecture masquerading as a big city. Contributing to its uniquely Icelandic legacy is the minimalist work of Guðjón Samúelsson (1887–1950), arguably Iceland's most famous 20th-century architect. He is responsible for the Hallgrímskirkja (p38) that crowns the city and draws every eye heavenward, as well as the thought-provoking nearby swimming pool, Sundhöllin (p38).

From left: Reykjavík (p36); Akureyri (p194)

Akureyri & Beyond

Akureyri is Reykjavík's alter ego. Both are beautifully situated along a dramatic stretch of Icelandic coastline, but where Reykjavík is big and international, Akureyri has a compact centre and a long waterfront, and gives the impression that it's going quietly about its business whether tourists pass through or not. Its older quarter begins near the waterfront, then climbs the hill past the strangely compelling Akureyrarkirkja (p196) to the city's excellent Akureyri Art Museum (p198).

Of the Ring Road's other larger towns, Vík (p91) may first appear to be a roadside service funnel for Ring Road travellers. But climb the hill above its church for stellar views and detour southwest into an old quarter lined with wooden cottages, and you may be forced to rethink.

And while Höfn (p130) is unlikely to win any style awards, its location – on a peninsula with glorious views west across the water to the Vatnajökull ice cap and along the coast – gives you a front-row seat to the superb south coast. After long kilometres between towns, arriving in Höfn feels like an oasis, and it is something of a minor culinary capital – you'll eat well here.

Icelandic Villages

For all the hype surrounding Reykjavík, for many Icelanders it's the villages and small farms that

are the quiet heartbeat of the nation. The further you get from Reykjavík, the smaller the settlements – charming villages like Breiðdalsvík (p148) and Kirkjubæjarklaustur (p109). Elsewhere, Húsavík (p192) sits on a rise, looking out across the waters of Skjálfandi towards snowcapped ridges.

Village of the Arts

About as far as you can get by paved road in Iceland and not fall into the sea, Seyðisfjörður (p162) has long been something of an artist's favourite. Wrapped around a tight harbour in the shadow of high mountains, Seyðisfjörður has the stately white Skaftfell Art Center (built in 1907, but with a focus on contemporary art). On a hill above the town is *Tvísöngur,* a sound sculpture by German artist Lukas Kühne that replicates the traditional Icelandic singing style *fimmundarsöngur*. But nothing symbolises Seyðisfjörður more than its quaint blue church and rainbow-painted street; the Blue Church Summer Concert series *(blaakirkjan. is)* is held annually, with Icelandic and international musicians performing weekly throughout summer. In winter, Seyðisfjörður falls softly to sleep, only to be roused from its slumber in February with the List í ljósi festival *(listiljosi.com)*, which illuminates Seyðisfjörður with glowing artworks.

TURF-ROOFED HOUSES

Turf-roofed structures (p216) are common across Scandinavia, and they're considered a Viking invention. They're even credited with inspiring the hobbit homes in *The Lord of the Rings*. Aside from their ability to keep the warmth in, they were also favoured because they used readily available and inexpensive materials. But for all their positives, they came at a cost – turf-roofed homes were damp, often filled with smoke, and extremely dark.

DIVE INTO ICELANDIC DESIGN

A Guide to Icelandic Architecture (Dennis Johannesson; 2000)
Published by the Association of Icelandic Architects, this book covers 250 Icelandic buildings.

Iceland Design Centre (honnunarmidstod.is/en)
If Icelandic design has piqued your interest, visit Reykjavík's outstanding Design Centre, which takes a deep dive into the subject.

Design March (honnunarmidstod. is/en/honnunarmars)
The Design Centre runs this annual event, during which it inaugurates hundreds of exhibitions and open workshops to the public.

HIGHLIGHTS

❶ Hallgrímskirkja (p38)
Climb boutique-lined Laugavegur to Hallgrímskirkja, the church that looks like an iceberg or ice palace and came to symbolise the city's offbeat charm.

❷ Akureyri (p194)
Check out the museums and architecture – but be sure to just walk along the waterfront to enjoy the sub-Arctic air in a city bathed in clear sunshine or buffeted by icy winds (possibly on the same day).

❸ Seyðisfjörður (p162)
Stay longer than you planned in this utterly delightful harbourside hamlet. It's not difficult to see why so many artists call it home, and its church may be Iceland's most photographed outside Reykjavík.

❹ Hofskirkja (p122)
Tucked away off the Ring Road and too often overlooked in the rush between glaciers, Litla Hof's tiny turf-roofed church has a bright interior and is one of the world's cosiest places to worship.

❺ Glaumbær (p206)
A wonderfully well-preserved turf-roofed complex (now a museum) where you can get a sense of what a medieval Icelandic community looked like and how they lived.

❻ Keldur (p85)
Visiting a turf-roofed home is one thing, but sleeping overnight in the oldest surviving example of the genre when the wind's whistling outside will make you a convert to all things Viking.

The Earth on Fire

The uniquely Icelandic complement to glaciers is its wonderful world of volcanoes. See them live in all their glory, and see what they leave behind.

Iceland's Volatile Volcanoes

Not many countries can lay claim to having a thriving volcano tourism industry. But, of course, this is Iceland, a country whose Eyjafjallajökull eruption paralysed Europe for a week in 2010. Over recent years, near-constant volcanic activity along the Reykjanes Peninsula has drawn – and continues to draw – tourists in ever-increasing numbers.

While a volcano's outbursts – and the enduring consequences – are spectacular, the causes of eruptions generally lie hidden from our view, kilometres beneath the surface. That said, scientists are always watching and monitoring, not to mention becoming better at predicting when an active volcano is getting ready to blow.

Fissure eruptions and their associated craters are the most common type of eruption in Iceland. The still-volatile Lakagígar crater row around Laki mountain is the classic, if extreme, example. When it erupted in the 18th century, it produced the largest lava flow in human history, covering 565 sq metres to a depth of 12m. An eruption on that scale today would be catastrophic.

Iceland's most active volcanoes hide beneath glaciers. When they erupt, the meeting of molten lava and glaciers, fire and ice, has spectacular consequences. That was the case in 2010 with the Eyjafjallajökull eruption, which caused massive flooding that damaged the Ring Road and a famous ash plume that grounded Europe's aeroplanes.

Recent eruptions in Iceland have tended to create less dramatic outcomes – they're often called 'tourist eruptions' because their fountains of magma, electric storms and dramatic ash clouds make striking photos but cause relatively little damage. Then again, it's all relative: eruptions that began in 2024 partially swallowed the town of Grndavík.

The Icelandic Met Office *(Veðurstofa Íslands; vedur.is)* keeps track of eruptions and the earthquakes that tend to precede them, plus the emissions that follow. As of 2018, the volcanoes to watch are Katla, Hekla and Öræfajökull, all well overdue for eruption.

Live Volcano Experiences

There's always some kind of volcano erupting in Iceland, and in recent years, conveniently, at least for tourists, there's a near-constant series of eruptions happening along the Reykjanes Peninsula near Reykjavík.

Things change with exciting regularity, but local tour operators will know the latest and be ready to take you there. Possibilities include hiking into some sections of the eruption zones

BEST VOLCANIC EXPERIENCES

Reykjanes Peninsula
Fly in a helicopter over the latest volcanoes to blow.

Fagradalsfjall and Litli-Hrútur near Reykjavík
Hike through newly formed lavafields from the 2021–23 eruptions.

Þríhnúkagígur (p57)
Descend to the floor of Þríhnúkagígur volcano to feel like you're in a Jules Verne novel.

Vestmannaeyjar
Walk to the top of Eldfell, the volcano that formed in the 1973 eruption.

Hverfjall (p187)
Climb the ash-grey tephra ring of Hverfjall that perfectly resembles an extinct volcano.

Fagradalsfjall

(sometimes with a distant view of the spectacular eruption) and flying over fresh lavafields. Depending on your timing, you may be able to fly over a volcanic eruption on a helicopter tour and see bubbling, flowing lava.

A Volcanic Landscape

Most of Iceland was shaped by the upheavals caused by its subterranean geology. But there are some places where those origins are plain for visitors to see.

In some places, you can climb to the crater of a dormant or extinct volcano and look down into the magma chamber. One such volcano – with multiple calderas and eerily hued lakes – is Askja, in the highlands; you can visit on a super-jeep tour out of Möðrudalur (p176). Another option is the walk around Kerið crater along the Golden Circle route (p77), the descent into the crater of Þríhnúkagígur (p57) or the climb to Hverfjall (p187) near Mývatn.

LAVA & MOSS

Active volcanoes might get everyone excited – and rightly so – but so many of Iceland's most stirring landscapes were formed by volcanoes and tell stories of past eruptions. One of these is the expansive Kristnitökuhraun Lavafield (p53), an otherworldly landscape that is purely volcanic in origin, with its craters and other lava formations colonised by great fields of moss that appear luminous in certain light.

Kerið crater (p77)
©RON WATTS/GETTY IMAGES

WORLD OF VOLCANOES

Icelandic Meteorological Office (en.vedur.is/earthquakes-and-volcanism/volcanoes)
Maintains an active map of current volcanoes. At last count Iceland had 32 active volcanoes.

Vatnajökull National Park (vatnajokulsthjodgardur.is/en)
The national park's website has useful information about the park, including its geological history and practical information.

Eurovision Song Contest: The Story of Fire Saga (David Dobkin, 2020)
This American musical rom-com takes Eurovision and Icelandic volcanoes as inspiration.

Icelandic Food

Back in the day, Icelandic food was fermented and dried – functional. Now it's all organic, high-end and one of the country's great pleasures.

Traditional Icelandic Food

If there's one dish that everyone knows from Iceland, it's *hákarl* (fermented shark). The thing is, you won't find it on menus, nor will you see *harðfiskur* (a dried haddock snack) or *svið* (a boiled sheep's head cut in half). Even horse was on the menu (and occasionally still is). However, these foods remain very much a part of Iceland's culinary landscape. That manifests in a repackaging of old staples – you can now find dried fish snacks and other dried foods sold as novelty snacks. *Hverabrauð* (rye bread), cooked over a hot spring, is now sold as artisan baking.

But these echoes of the past remain important because Icelanders still remember what life was like before the modern era, when they eked out an existence in an unforgiving landscape on a remote edge of Europe. Winter lasted for most of the year, and they had to survive on what little they had. Salt and fermentation were critical to making food last as long as possible, and people ate every part of every creature.

Modern Icelandic Food

The Iceland you visit today couldn't be more different, but that's because Iceland is riding a wave of prosperity hitherto unknown in its history. Yes, it's expensive, but it's also innovative and an emerging culinary star. You should make the food here a centrepiece of your journey.

What was once a drawback – the landscape more likely to explode than yield crops – has become an advantage. In a world where organic is a mark of quality, Icelandic food is some of the freshest and purest in the world. Animals don't need to be fed hormones, and use of antibiotics

A dish at Friðheimar (p67)
DANIEL DORSA FOR LONELY PLANET

is rare. Instead, animals lap fresh spring water and feed on grass and grains. And because Iceland is so far north, there's little need for farmers to use pesticides or herbicides, and geothermal greenhouses mean they can grow vegetables year-round in an entirely natural process.

Put another way, modern Icelandic cuisine is farm-to-table dining at its finest. Fresh fish, locally foraged berries, organic vegetables – it's hard to believe it if you were here 50 years ago, but Iceland's chefs are now the envy of Europe. Put those ingredients at the service of professionals, and Michelin stars multiply. And even casual dining can be exciting here – have farm-fresh ice cream at a dairy, try cake made with fresh *skyr* (yoghurt-like dessert), or stop for a famous Bæjarins Beztu (p38) lamb hot dog.

Where to Eat

Reykjavík is obviously the best place to eat in Iceland – the choice is simply marvellous. Plan to try at least one high-end tasting menu in the capital. It's now as much a part of the Icelandic experience as glaciers and volcanoes.

But you'll also find fine foods elsewhere. Höfn's emerging culinary scene means you can try many of the highpoints of the country's cooking, from lobster (actually langoustine) to organic lamb, all washed down with sheep-dung-smoked Icelandic whisky (p131). And that's just at one restaurant...

FOOD FESTIVALS

Festivals are a great way to sample traditional foods. In February, Þorrablót is a traditional midwinter feast of dried fish (pictured), boiled sheep's head, dung-smoked lamb and pickled ram's testicles. Reykjavík's spring Food and Fun Festival *(foodandfun.is)* draws celebrity chefs from around the world – they're given the quintessentially Icelandic challenge of creating affordably priced gourmet menus using only Icelandic ingredients.

RECIPES & INGREDIENTS

North: The New Nordic Cuisine of Iceland (Gunnar Karl Gíslason, 2014)
A cookbook that helps you to recreate those special Icelandic meals when you return home.

Icelandic Flavors: A Journey Through the Land of Fire and Ice (Babel Boost, 2025)
Recipes, stories (including from Viking times) and lavish photographs get to the heart of Icelandic cuisine.

Icelandic Seafood
Atlantic cod, Arctic char (best when caught wild), wolffish (sweet and meaty white fish) and langoustine (small lobster) are Icelandic mainstays.

Sign in front of Bæjarins Beztu (p38)
ALEKSANDRA TOKARZ/ALAMY

BEST ICELANDIC FOOD EXPERIENCES

Lamb Hot Dog
It's become an internet sensation: the lamb *pylsur* (hot dog) at Bæjarins Beztu (p38).

Icelandic Meat Soup
There's no better place to try it than roadside stop Beitarhúsið Café (p177).

Lobster (Langoustine) Baguette
The best street food in Iceland? It's certainly a prime candidate, from Hafnarbúðin (p131) in Höfn.

Icelandic Lamb
Try it anywhere that it's on the menu – it could just be Iceland's most-loved dish.

Dill
Take an incredible culinary journey at Iceland's first Michelin-star restaurant (*dillrestaurant.is/en*).

Ways to do Iceland's Ring Road

The Ring Road is a 1322km epic, a loop around some of the most spectacular landscapes in Europe. Do it clockwise or anticlockwise, take every detour or stick to the main road – there are no bad choices on this magical route.

1 The Full Experience
Time *10–14 days*
Best for *Those who want it all*

Taking 10 days or – better still – two weeks to drive the Ring Road makes for one of Europe's best road trips. It means that you can take every detour – go whale watching in Húsavík, for example, or take the best detour of them all: the Golden Circle. And everywhere along the Ring Road itself, it's waterfall, after glacier, after hot spring, after black-sand beach and so much more.
Possible overnights Reykjavík, Hvammstangi, Akureyri, Mývatn, Egilsstaðir, Höfn, Vík, Selfoss

2 The Quick Version
Time *6–7 days*
Best for *Those with little time and on a tight budget*

A little over 200km per day may not sound like much, but Iceland packs a lot into every kilometre of road – you'll find yourself stopping often. You may not get to take many detours, but there's still plenty to see and do right by the roadside, from ice caves in winter to boat journeys among the icebergs all year round.
Possible overnights Reykjavík, Vík, Höfn, Egilsstaðir, Akureyri

See p32 for the full route map

3 Clockwise for a Change
Time *7–10 days*
Best for *Those who like to save the best until last*

It really doesn't matter in which direction you drive the Ring Road – both ways work just as well. The major attractions that occur in quick succession along the South Coast work in this case as a crescendo as you near the end of your circumnavigation of the island, and the quieter roads of the north may be a more gentle introduction to driving in the country.
Possible overnights Reykjavík, Hvammstangi, Akureyri, Mývatn, Egilsstaðir, Höfn, Vík, Selfoss

Northern Lights over the Ring Road

Húsavík (p192)

For essential trip tips, see p235

4. South Coast & Back
Time *3–5 days*
Best for *Those looking for the highlights*
We met lots of travellers who planned to do the whole Ring Road, but decided on a shorter, more concentrated version. None left disappointed. Just focusing on the South Coast (with the Golden Circle thrown in) means you can really immerse yourself in the wonders of Skaftafell, Fjaðrárgljúfur, Jökulsárlón, Ingólfshöfði and the landscapes of Dyrhólaey and Reynisfjara around Vík, quite apart from allowing time to fall in love with Reykjavík.
Possible overnights Reykjavík, Selfoss, Vík, Höfn

5. Navigating the North
Time *5 days*
Best for *Second-time visitors*
If you've been to Iceland before, chances are you've been south – most visitors head straight for the road as it unfolds between Vík and Höfn. The north is almost like a different country – and the drama of the natural world extends seemingly to every far horizon. Watch whales, take a super-jeep tour into the highlands and follow waterfalls through Jökulsárgljúfur.
Possible overnights
Hvammstangi, Akureyri, Húsavík, Reykjahlíð, Egilsstaðir

6. Reykjavík & the Golden Circle
Time *3 days*
Best for *Those short on time but looking for a taste*
Whether you visit the Golden Circle as one big day trip (or as part of a series of day trips) from Reykjavík, this is like a condensed version of the Ring Road and an essential part of any visit to Iceland. You can swim and snorkel between two continents, bathe in geothermal springs and follow the sagas that tell the story of a nation.
Possible overnights Reykjavík, Selfoss, Hella

WHEN TO GO

Dec–Feb
Winters can be surprisingly mild, but beware of wind chill and snowstorms. Highlights include ice caves and the Northern Lights.

Mar–May
The spring thaw can be lovely, with fewer crowds before the summer onslaught. Many attractions (and hiking trails) remain closed until May.

Jun–Aug
The high season: everything's open, car parks fill fast, whales and puffins are around, and you might get sunshine, rain or even snow.

Sep–Nov
September is like a bonus summer month, with similar weather but fewer visitors. Days are shortening, it's getting cold, and some businesses close.

The Drive

A stage-by-stage, kilometre-by-kilometre account of the route. Your journey begins here.

SOUTHWEST ICELAND
Reykjavík to Selfoss, p48
Golden Circle Detour, p62
Selfoss to Vík, p78

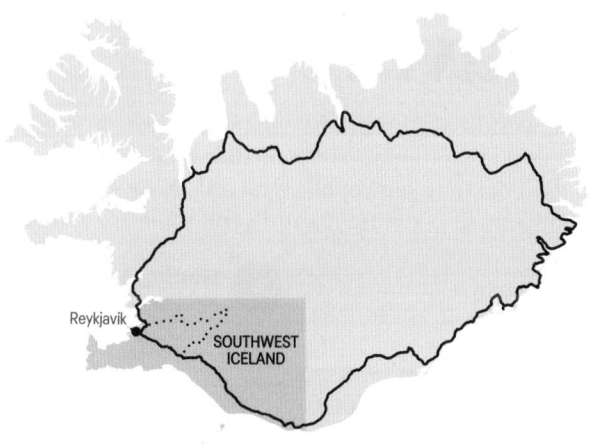

SOUTHWEST ICELAND

The Southwest is where most people get their first taste of the Ring Road and Iceland's geographic phenomena. From the Blue Lagoon, with its turquoise healing waters, drive through farmlands to lesser-known bathing corners, climb into deep craters and cool down in the pools of misty cascades lit with rainbows. Don't forget a detour into the Golden Circle – with tectonic plates to dive between, steam rising from volcanic fields and water exploding from the earth. Buckle up – you're in for one hell of a ride.

Gullfoss (p72)
DANIEL DORSA FOR LONELY PLANET

CITY GUIDE:
Reykjavík

View of Reykjavík and Hallgrímskirkja (p38)

Welcome to the world's northernmost capital and Iceland's only city. With fewer than 150,000 inhabitants, it's far smaller than most other capitals, but to Icelanders it's a bustling metropolis with a thriving art scene, concerts and cultural happenings, exciting nightlife and top-class restaurants.

WORDS BY
EYGLÓ SVALA ARNARSDÓTTIR
Eygló is a travel writer from Iceland.

Arriving
For most people travelling the Ring Road, Reykjavík is the start and end point. Rte 1 goes through the city's east.
Plane Keflavík International Airport is a 50-minute drive from the capital via Rte 41 to the southwest. Reykjavík Domestic Airport services destinations in Iceland and Greenland.
Bus BSÍ Bus Terminal in the city centre is where the airport shuttle arrives *(flybus.is)* and the starting point for bus tours. The Mjódd public bus terminal *(straeto.is)* in Kópavogur is for connections in and outside the capital region.
Car There are many car rental outfits in the city, particularly around BSÍ, but for road-trippers, it's usually most convenient to hire a car at Keflavík International Airport.

HOW MUCH FOR A

Cup of filter coffee **750kr**

Hot dog with everything **740kr**

Ticket to Reykjavík Art Museum **2430kr**

Getting Around
Orientation Most landmarks, restaurants and activities are in the city centre.
Driving To park in the city, the Parka or EasyPark apps are useful. Meters are sometimes card only. Find convenient garages by City Hall, opposite the National Theatre and underneath Harpa Concert Center. There are four tariff zones; for P1 in the centre, the fee is 630kr per hour for a maximum of three hours.
Taxi There are taxi stops in the centre, but queues may be long at night on weekends. Uber does not operate in Iceland; taxi companies include Hreyfill *(hreyfill.is)*.
Bus Download the Klappið app *(klappid.is)* for tickets and find schedules and more information on *straeto.is*.
Cycling Bike and e-bike rentals include Reykjavík Bike Tours *(icelandbike.com)* and Borgarhjól *(borgarhjol.is)*. The city has a network of cycling paths.
Scooters Rent an electric scooter with the Hopp, Bolt or Zolo apps. Be careful with curbs and in slippery conditions.

For schedules and trip planning, go to visitreykjavik.is

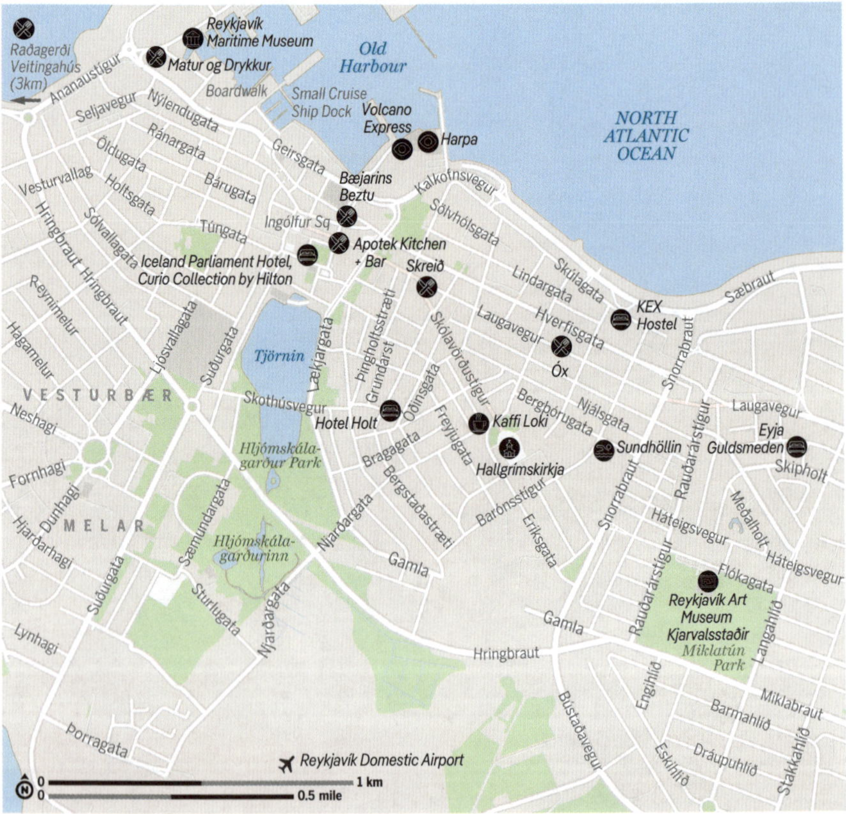

A DAY IN REYKJAVÍK

 Have a morning swim with the locals in **Sundhöllin** (reykjavik.is/stadir/sundholl-reykjavikur), designed by Guðjón Samúelsson. Walk over to his **Hallgrímskirkja** (hallgrimskirkja.is), and admire the view from its tower. Afterwards, have brunch at a nearby restaurant, perhaps flatbread with smoked lamb or trout at **Kaffi Loki** (loki.is).

 Browse the shops in the town centre, then visit **Harpa** (harpa.is) concert centre with its striking geometric glass facade by Ólafur Elíasson. Check out an exhibition, maybe the **Volcano Express** (volcanoexpress.is), then continue along the harbour. Join a whale and birdwatching boat tour, or continue to **Reykjavík Maritime Museum** (borgarsogusafn.is).

 Dine at Michelin-listed **Matur og Drykkur** (maturogdrykkur.is), which offers a seasonal 10-course dinner with optional wine pairing (booking advised). For a simpler option, try the famed hot dog at **Bæjarins Beztu** (bbp.is) in the city centre. End your evening with an artisan cocktail at **Apotek Kitchen + bar** (apotekrestaurant.is).

Where to Stay

From camping to five-star hotels, Reykjavík has options for all price ranges. Stay centrally for easy access to the nightlife (p40), or seek peace and quiet on the outskirts. Generally, you can get better deals off-season. Keep an eye out for packages from hotel chains located around Iceland, such as Íslandshótel (*islandshotel.is*) and Berjaya Iceland Hotels (*icelandhotelcollectionbyberjaya.com*).

BEST PLACES TO STAY

KEX Hostel €€
Hip and simple comfort. Centrally located with a lively atmosphere. *kexhostel.is*

Eyja Guldsmeden Hotel €€€
Cosy boutique hotel near the city centre with a view of the city and Esja mountain. *hoteleyja.is*

Iceland Parliament Hotel, Curio Collection by Hilton €€€
Luxury and historical ambience in the heart of downtown. *icelandhotelcollectionbyberjaya.com*

Hótel Holt $$$
Built in the 1960s as one of Reykjavík's first hotels, this artsy institution is decked out with original paintings, drawings and sculptures. *holt.is*

Where to Eat

Central Reykjavík is lined with eateries and cafes of all kinds, ranging from hot dog stands to Michelin-starred restaurants – not forgetting all the food halls. Most of the finest dinner options can be found in the immediate downtown area, Laugavegur, Hverfisgata, Austurstræti and the surrounding neighbourhoods. The most affordable dinner options include fish and chips in the harbour area. Many restaurants offer economical lunches.

REYKJAVÍK SPECIALITIES

Reykjavík is Iceland's biggest harbour city, and the seafood here is fresh – make sure to order fish while in town.
Kleinur Twisted doughnut (pictured), beloved with coffee. You'll find it almost everywhere.
Pylsur The Icelandic hot dog; a mix of lamb, beef and pork. The most famous is **Bæjarins Beztu** (*bbp.is*) in the city centre.

Rolled pancakes with sugar Served as an afternoon treat on weekends. Icelandic pancakes are crêpe-like, and also served filled with cream and jam. Available in **Kaffivagninn** (*kaffivagninn.is*) by the harbour.
Flatbread with smoked lamb The typical portable lunch, great for travelling and hiking. Available in **Kaffi Loki** (*loki.is*) and other traditional eateries.

BEST PLACES TO EAT & DRINK

Ráðagerði €€
Not strictly in Reykjavík, this atmospheric restaurant is found on the tip of Seljarnarnes, near the Grótta lighthouse. *radagerdi.is*

Skreið €€
Spanish-inspired cuisine in the heart of downtown. Inventive tapas with Icelandic seafood. *skreid.is*

ÓX Restaurant €€€
Let Michelin-star chefs lead you on a magical culinary journey where nothing is as it seems. Book well ahead. *ox.restaurant*

Árbæjarsafn museum

GUNNAR FREYR STEINSSON/ALAMY

Tour Reykjavík with One Card

Get the pass that gives you access to the city's buses, swimming pools and a selection of museums, and start exploring! It's great to begin the day with a swim. Take bus 5 to Árbæjarlaug pool, then walk to Árbæjarsafn museum to learn more about life in the Reykjavík of the past. Take bus 12 to the Laugardalur area, and walk through the valley to the Botanic Gardens and Reykjavík Family Park and Zoo, where you can see seals, reindeer and foxes. Visit Ásmundarsafn sculpture museum, then take bus 11 to the Kjarvalsstaðir gallery before heading back downtown (*visitreykjavik.is/reykjavik-city-card*).

REYKJAVÍK MUSIC SCENE

Reykjavík has long been a party town. During WWII, when Iceland was occupied by the allied forces, soldiers and locals got together in the city centre for dancing. In the '60s, Glaumbær was the hottest venue, where bands such as Trúbrot gave iconic performances. Friðrik Þór Friðriksson's 1982 documentary *Rokk í Reykjavík* captured the alternative music scene that spawned Björk and other artists.

From its humble beginnings in 1999, festival **Iceland Airwaves** (*icelandairwaves.is*) has become a fixture on the international music calendar. For a long weekend in November, music lovers hop between venues to see their favourite bands or make new discoveries.

Innipúkinn Festival (*facebook.com/Innipukinnfestival*), held in the first weekend of August, is lower key, highlighting local musicians, while in late August, jazz lovers from around the world crowd the annual **Jazz Festival** (*reykjavikjazz.is*).

Live music is performed in venues such as **Gaukurinn** (*gaukurinn.is*) and **Hús máls og menningar** (*facebook.com/husmalsogmenningar*), while legendary DJ Andrea Jónsdóttir keeps people rocking through the night at **Dillon** (*dillon.is*) on weekends. For something classical, catch the Icelandic Symphony Orchestra at **Harpa** (p38) concert centre.

Along the Way We Met...

KASIA DYGUL I've lost count of how many times I've driven Iceland's Ring Road, but it still feels like an adventure every single time. One moment you're on black volcanic sands, the next you're winding through lush fjords or past towering ocean cliffs – and thanks to our wild microclimates, you can see all four seasons in a single afternoon. Reykjavík combines the warmth and ease of a small town with the culture, food and energy of a lively capital.

Kasia is a Reykjavík resident, foodie and storyteller who loves sharing Iceland's hidden gems. @lifehobbyist

KASIA'S TIP: Pack a swimsuit – in Iceland, the pools are where life happens.

Hike Öskjuhlíð Hill to Perlan

On a green hill near the city centre perches the glass dome of one of Reykjavík's landmark buildings. The forested hill has a system of paths, popular for walking, running and cycling, leading to WWII remains and a geothermal beach.

HOW TO

Getting there: Take bus 18 or 13 to stop Perlan and find the path between the trees. If you're driving, park by Reykjavík Natura Hotel or Nauthólsvík to enjoy the walk up Öskjuhlíð, or drive straight to Perlan and park there.

Admission: For current pricing and the opening hours, see *perlan.is*. Free for children under six.

More info: Details and bookings on *perlan.is*.

Take a walk through the woods on the chain of paths that lead to **Perlan - Wonders of Iceland**. Signs indicate the remains of the allied occupation during WWII.

Built in 1991, the dome sits on six water tanks, some of which are still in use. We'd recommend visiting Perlan before or after your Ring Road journey to learn more about Iceland's natural landscape, fire and ice. There's a captivating exhibition on volcanic activity, and a human-made ice cave that allows you to explore glaciers from within. View a replica of a bird cliff and listen to whale song, while discovering fascinating facts about Iceland. Be sure to catch the aurora show in the planetarium and marvel at one of the world's wonders. Walk out to the viewing platform, then have refreshments in the cafe and restaurant at the top of the building and admire the view of Reykjavík – at certain times the dome rotates.

Make your way back down to **Öskjuhlíð**, and if you have time, drop by **Nauthólsvík**, the geothermal beach. Have a dip in the cold sea or soak in the hot tub if it's open.

Exhibition on volcanic activity at Perlan - Wonders of Iceland

Explore Viðey Island

It's so close that you can almost touch it. In the past, pre-phones, islanders used to shout over to people on the other side of the channel. The ferry ride from Skarfabakki is only five minutes, but it feels a bit like travelling to another dimension.

Getting there: Skarfabakki ferry and cruise terminal is a few minutes' drive from the city centre, or you can take bus 16 (stop Skarfagarðar), walk or cycle.

When to go: Visit in summer for plants and birds, in winter for the illuminated *Imagine Peace Tower* (9 October to 8 December). Viðeyjarstofa restaurant and cafe opens according to ferry schedules.

Tickets: A return ferry ticket costs 2400kr and can be bought at the terminal and online. Hourly departures from 15 May through August, weekends in other seasons. Scheduled departures run from the Old Harbour June to August. See *elding.is* for tickets, schedules and package tours. Tours and events are available on *reykjavikcitymuseum.is*. Ferry tickets are included in the Reykjavík City Card; see *visitreykjavik.is*.

Oldest Stone Building
Stately **Viðeyjarstofa** is the oldest building in Reykjavík and Iceland's oldest stone building. Skúli Magnússon, who ruled Iceland under the authority of the King of Denmark, had it built as his residence in 1753 to 1755. Now it serves as a cafe, restaurant and venue for various events. Have a cup of coffee and a waffle with jam and cream – be sure to sit outside if the weather is nice. Then take a walk around the island.

Admire Outdoor Art
The *Imagine Peace Tower* by Yoko Ono was unveiled on Viðey in 2007. Walk around the white foundations into which the words 'Imagine Peace' have been engraved in numerous languages. The tower is lit on 9 October, John Lennon's birthday, until 8 December, the anniversary of his death, and on special occasions each year – the blueish beam of light is clearly visible from Reykjavík. Outdoor artwork *Áfangar* by Richard Serra is also located on Viðey.

Visit a Ghost Village
Skúli was far from the first inhabitant of Viðey – a monastery was operated on the island from 1225 to 1550. Later, it was the site of a leprosy hospital. The island was also the site of a printing works, a large dairy farm and a fisheries company. In its heyday, as many as 240 people lived permanently on Viðey, but the village was abandoned in 1943. The old school building remains, as a museum, but the other houses are gone; only the concrete foundations are left.

FROM TOP: DANIELE CAROTENUTO PHOTOGRAPHY/GETTY IMAGES, JACOB BOOMSMA/SHUTTERSTOCK

CITY OF LITERATURE

In *Reykjavík: A Crime Story* by author Ragnar Jónasson and former Prime Minister of Iceland Katrín Jakobsdóttir, a teenage girl disappears from Viðey without a trace. They're not the only authors to take Reykjavík as a setting – on the mainland, join a Reykjavík City Library literary walk (usually on Thursdays at 8pm in summer; *borgarbokasafn.is*), or trace stories on your own with the Reykjavík Culture Walks app. Read up on Reykjavík with Hallgrímur Helgason's *101 Reykjavík* or Einar Kárason's *Devils' Island* (both have been filmed). For book lovers, **Reykjavík International Literary Festival**, *(bokmenntahatid.is)* held biennially in spring.

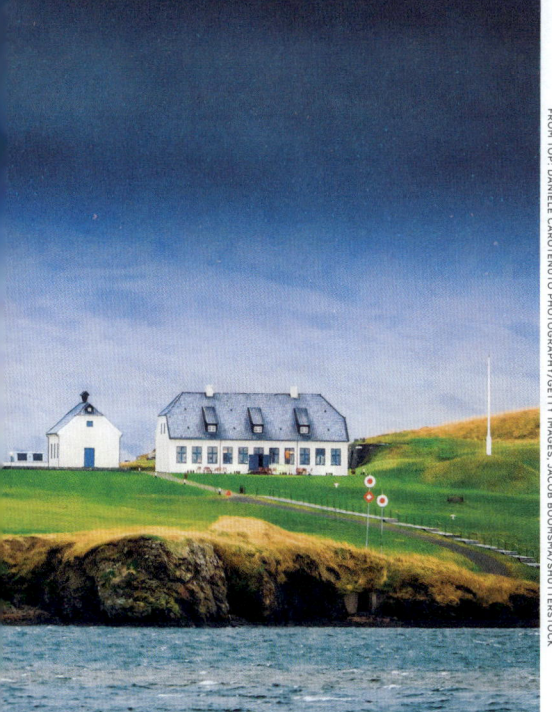

From top: Viðeyjarstofa; Viðey Island

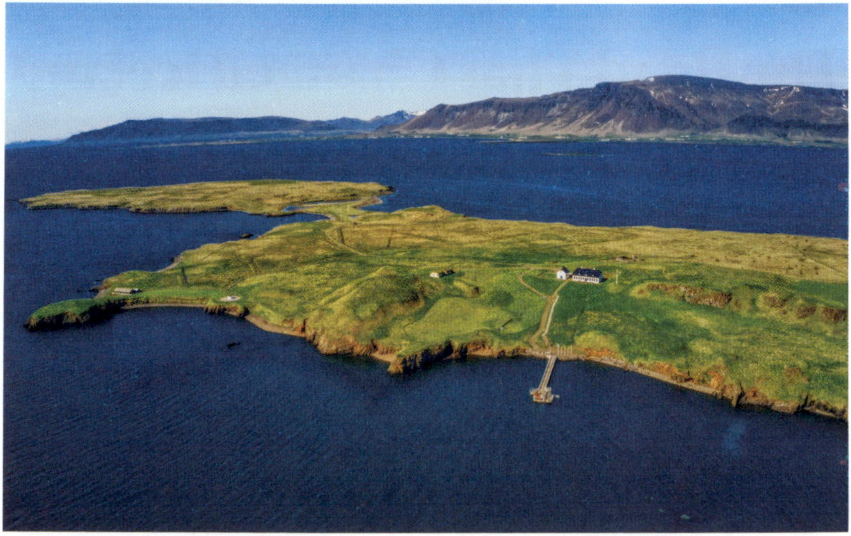

The Ring Road crosses the Jökulsárlón glacier lagoon (p128)
ELROCE/SHUTTERSTOCK

INSIGHT

The Road That Changed Iceland

Completed just over 50 years ago, the Ring Road has gone on to transform life in Iceland, says Zoë Robert. In the face of floods and icebergs, it has opened up once-remote regions and now offers visitors the road trip of a lifetime.

WORDS BY **ZOË ROBERT**
Based in Reykjavík, Zoë has covered Iceland for Reuters, CNN and Iceland Review.

THE RING ROAD formally opened in 1974, on the 1100th anniversary of Icelandic settlement, with the unveiling of a roughly 900m bridge over Skeiðará glacial river in the south. The bridge – at the time the country's longest – was the final piece needed to connect the country's road system, with local newspaper *Morgunblaðið* hailing it the 'nation's birthday gift to itself'.

G Pétur Matthíasson of the Iceland Road and Coastal Administration remembers it well. 'Icelanders were very excited about the completion of the Ring Road and a large number drove the circle during the first year.' As a kid living in the south, his family were previously unable to reach the east of the country without driving in the opposite direction towards Reykjavík and north via Akureyri before finally heading east. 'So it changed things a lot.'

A Different Life

Before the construction of roads and the arrival of motor vehicles – the first came in 1904 – travel in Iceland was mostly by horse or on foot, and cargo transported by ship. Vera Roth, who has researched and written about old travel paths in South Iceland, explains that the completion of the Ring Road changed everything. 'People no longer needed to wade through glacial rivers, there was increased communication between communities – and very importantly, increased access to food.

'Previously, people had to be completely self-sustainable,' she says. 'People went to the store perhaps once a year – in the spring – and it took up to three weeks back and forth, and they could only transport what they could carry on horseback. Once the bridges and roads were built, people started to live a completely different life, so it was very positive.' The first journey from Höfn in the east to Reykjavík by car was in 1932.

As for the completion of the Ring Road, the only issue was the cost, Matthíasson explains. 'It was, of course, a hugely expensive project. I remember the government having a sale of bonds and a lottery for the public to help fund it. The state couldn't afford it otherwise.'

Floods, Ice and Mountains

While road conditions have greatly improved since those early days, there are still challenges in keeping the road open – namely, strong winds and snow, Matthíasson says. Glacial outburst floods are another challenge, and floodwaters and icebergs have occasionally destroyed bridges, leaving temporary gaps in the Ring Road. 'But they happen much less often. In 2011, we had to build a roughly 150m bridge over Múlakvísl river in six to seven days, because the bridge there was totally destroyed,' he recalls.

Photographer Páll Stefánsson estimates that he has driven the Ring Road hundreds of times since he began his career in 1982. 'Driving conditions are better with the road now sealed and there are tunnels through more mountain passes, which were often closed in the winter,' he says. 'But there's of course a lot more traffic now.' The increase in rental-car traffic, especially the increase in drivers unfamiliar with local conditions, means that the Ring Road needs to be closed more frequently, says Matthíasson. 'Otherwise, we can end up having a lot of people in trouble because what happens when there is heavy snow and low visibility is that small cars start to get stuck. Very quickly, the snow accumulates around the cars and fills the road. So we have learnt to close the roads earlier so we can then open them again earlier, too.'

In recent years, there has been much discussion of the need for improved road maintenance. Sections of the Ring Road need to be rebuilt to cater to the volume of traffic. 'But this is a huge project. We have been focusing on replacing single-lane bridges, which can be dangerous for those not used to them, and continue to work on other aspects too,' explains Matthíasson.

> 'People went to the store perhaps once a year – in the spring – and it took up to three weeks back and forth, and they could only transport what they could carry on horseback. Once the bridges and roads were built, people started to live a completely different life...'

Towns Transformed

Journalist Egill Bjarnason and his wife Sigrún run Skúlagarður Country Hotel and Grös bistro at Ásbyrgi (p178), around 50km off the Ring Road. Before taking over management of the hotel, they lived in the nearby town of Húsavík (p192). Fifteen years ago, it was still a typical small fishing town, but tourism has brought positive changes, Bjarnason says. 'Today, it is very dynamic, lively and warm – it's a lot more open. With so much focus on the service industry, it has become really welcoming. And it is the same in many towns and villages around the country.' The economic impacts are visible too. 'Now, when you drive into these towns you see that people have done up their houses, fixed their windows. Towns which were almost dead before are now brimming with life.'

Roth agrees. 'The increase in visitors travelling means that people can continue to live in smaller communities by selling accommodation and catering to tourists.' The challenge for Bjarnason and his family has been extending the season beyond the summer months, especially with Rte 862 – the most direct route to the hotel from the Ring Road – not currently being cleared during winter. 'For many reasons, it is important that we have year-round tourism. Rather than having people who work in the industry for just a few months a year, the industry offers a real career opportunity.'

More visitors are travelling to the North during the winter, though. 'Fifteen years ago, Iceland's tourism industry was more seasonal. I find it incredible that selling people the idea of coming to Iceland during the winter months – when it is dark for around 20 hours a day – has worked,' he says with a laugh. 'But of course people want to see the Northern Lights, and one way to do that is to stay in rural locations, away from the city lights.'

Tourism's Impact

As for the impact tourism has had on the country as a whole, you don't need to look further than the first Lonely Planet guide to Iceland (published in 1991), says Bjarnason. 'There was an international cuisine section listing the few such restaurants which existed in Reykjavík at the time. You can see how much just this aspect of life in Iceland has changed over the years, both in Reykjavík but also in smaller places around the country.' Tourism has transformed Iceland, becoming the largest industry, he adds. 'However, for a long time its growth was not treated as a priority. That led to a lack of public investment in infrastructure. Today, we are doing a much better job protecting nature from overwhelming traffic and encouraging travellers to go beyond the most popular parts,' he says.

As for veering off the beaten track, Roth says there is renewed interest in returning to use the old travel routes. He is publishing a guide to help people do just that. 'People today are living such fast-paced lives, but many people want to actually slow down.' Rather than sticking to the most popular spots, visitors can reconnect with nature and discover more-hidden sites. And this goes for driving the Ring Road too. Learning about the history and spending more time in each location can help people get a better understanding of these places, she concludes.

Hvalnes Nature Reserve and lighthouse (p144)
FOKKEBOK/GETTY IMAGES

Reykjavík

This section of the Ring Road starts just beyond Reykjavík's city limits. The highway here could have been plucked from any city suburb, with petrol stations, supermarkets and busy intersections. But persevere – when driving south, Iceland's dramatic beauty is soon to reveal itself. Scenery turns greener, with flat pastures as far as the eye can see, and roads get emptier as mountains appear in the distance. Closer to Hveragerði, black lava rocks are punctuated by rich green moss, and the landscape becomes rife with geothermal activity. It's possible to drive this section of the Ring Road in conjunction with the Golden Circle route, or to use that route to skip this leg entirely.

Hveradalir Geothermal Area (p56)
MUMEMORIES/SHUTTERSTOCK

Jade Bremner

Selfoss

71.5 KM
1 HOUR'S DRIVE

THIS LEG:

- Reykjavík
- Árbær Open Air Museum
- Rauðhólar
- Vífilsfell
- Kristnitökuhraun Lavafield
- The Geothermal Exhibition
- Hveradalir Geothermal Area
- Hveragerði
- Ölfusá River
- Selfoss

Driving Notes

At certain times of day, the Ring Road near Reykjavík is not a fun drive. Drive the city suburb section outside rush hour when possible. A few kilometres south, the road starts to clear and it's all freewheeling from here, with gorgeous scenery. If you're planning on driving the Golden Circle (p62), you'll have to either double-back along this leg or skip it entirely.

Breaking Your Journey

The most natural place to stop on this very short leg is the town of Hveragerði, which is around two-thirds of the way through the drive. It has fuel, terrific food and plenty of accommodation options – plus the chance to relax in natural geothermal baths or get a spa treatment in the town's superb wellness centre.

Jade's Tips

BEST MEAL Tryggvaskáli (p53), for fine dining in the oldest house in Selfoss.

FAVOURITE VIEW The vast expanse of Kristnitökuhraun Lavafield (p53), with craters and moss-covered formations.

ESSENTIAL STOP Hveragerði (p56), a hot springs town, where you can soak tired limbs in naturally heated water.

ROAD-TRIP TIP Book big experiences, including the Blue Lagoon and the Þríhnúkagígur Volcano, in advance.

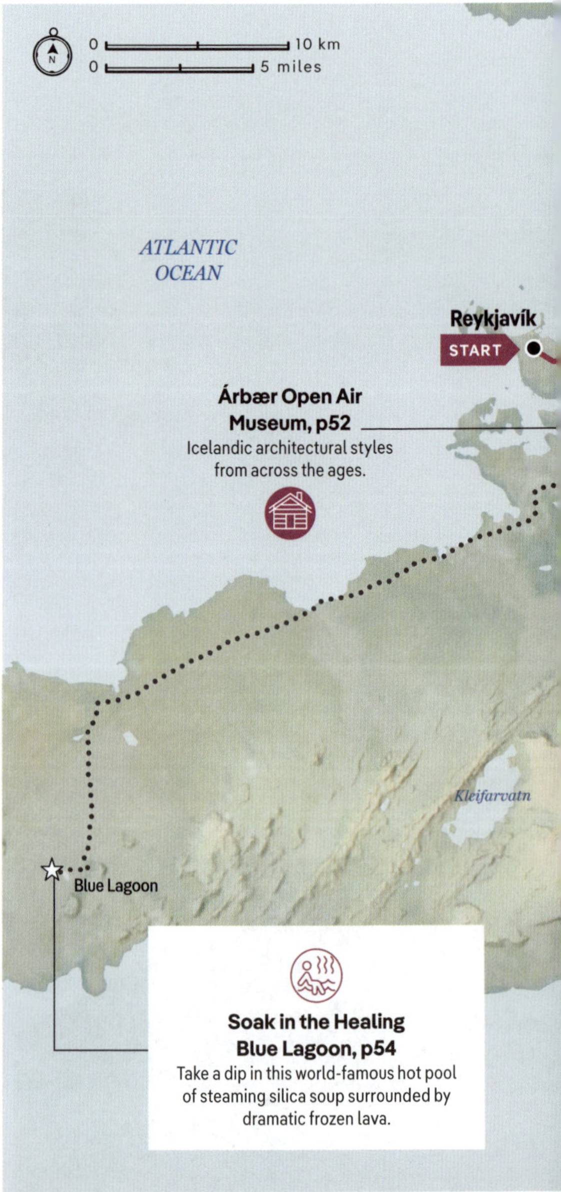

Árbær Open Air Museum, p52
Icelandic architectural styles from across the ages.

Reykjavík START

ATLANTIC OCEAN

Kleifarvatn

Blue Lagoon

Soak in the Healing Blue Lagoon, p54
Take a dip in this world-famous hot pool of steaming silica soup surrounded by dramatic frozen lava.

PREVIOUS STOP This route begins just before the Ring Road on the outskirts of busy Reykjavík (p36). If travelling directly from Keflavík International Airport, it's a 45-minute (50km) drive along Rte 41 to the first stop. Alternatively, you may choose to make the nearby Blue Lagoon (p62; 22-minute drive/23km) your first port of call, rather than doing a later detour.

Árbær Open Air Museum

Around 4km southeast of Reykjavík city centre, the **Árbær Open Air Museum** (*borgarsogusafn.is/en/arbaer-open-air-museum; adult/child 2450kr/free*) showcases numerous Icelandic architectural styles with around 20 old buildings that have been transported here, from 19th-century homes to stables and a turf-roofed church. In summer, staff dress up in clothing from past eras. It also runs arts and crafts demonstrations and has rotating exhibitions, on everything from life as a primary-school child in Iceland in the 19th and 20th centuries to the various cart designs used across the country. Guided tours take place every day at 1pm, year-round (no booking required).

Rauðhólar

Driving southeast out of the suburbs, passing Lake Raudavatn to the north, the landscape becomes more open, then volcanic. Part of the Heiðmörk Nature Reserve, established in 1950, **Rauðhólar** ('red hills') is right off the Ring Road. This striking cluster of pseudo-craters, also known as rootless cones or rootless craters, formed as the byproduct of flowing lava from an eruption 5200 years ago. The area is great for stretching the legs – walk among Sitka spruce and volcanic terrain forming part of the Elliðaárhraun lavafield. It's free to visit and open 24 hours a day.

Vífilsfell

Around 11km east of Rauðhólar, **Vífilsfell** mountain will come into view, rising 655m above the volcanic plateau of Hellisheiði. Stop in the parking lot (named 'Litla Kaffistofan' on maps) to take in the views of the peak, which is snowcapped most of the year. From here, a challenging hiking trail (6.7km, roughly two to three hours) goes up the slopes for soaring panoramic views. The trail is not for the faint of heart, with steep ledges and stairs. Be aware

FROM LEFT: SIGGA_KOLLA/SHUTTERSTOCK, BADA/SHUTTERSTOCK

Rauðhólar

Reykjavík — 9.5km — Árbær Open Air Museum — 6km

Cruise Rte 49, the busiest road in the country, to hit the Ring Road.

Árbær Open Air Museum

of rock or ice fall, and avalanches if attempting it in certain weather.

Kristnitökuhraun Lavafield

A little more than 6km east of the Litla Kaffistofan car park, the vast volcanic landscape of **Kristnitökuhraun** unfolds. Looking like another planet, the plateau was formed during an eruption in 1000 CE, the same year Iceland became a Christian nation. Local legend holds that this place, dotted with craters and peculiar rugged, moss-covered, jet-black lava formations and fields,

continues p56

BEST PLACES TO EAT

Kaffi Krús, Selfoss €€
Cafe and restaurant in a charming old orange house on the main road, serving freshly made Icelandic and international dishes. *(kaffikrus.is; 11am-9pm Mon-Fri, noon-9pm Sat & Sun)*

Tryggvaskáli, Selfoss €€€
Fine dining in the oldest house in Selfoss, with intimate dining rooms (some with river views) and dishes using local produce, including salmon, duck and lamb mains. Terrific cocktails too. *(tryggvaskali.is; 4-9.30pm)*

Old Dairy, Selfoss €
Inside the first dairy factory in Iceland, this food hall serves up tacos, pizzas, Thai dishes, burgers, dim sum and more over eight independent outlets. *(olddairyselfoss.com; 11.30am-9pm)*

Rauðhólar — 12km —  Vífilsfell — 4km — Kristnitökuhraun Lavafield

Scenery gets more mountainous in this stretch; enjoy the views.

EXPERIENCE ★

Soak in the Healing Blue Lagoon

This otherworldly blue pool, surrounded by the drama of frozen black lava, is Iceland's most-visited attraction for a reason. It's here that you can experience socialising the Icelandic way – in a warm, steaming body of water. Take this detour from the airport before getting onto the Ring Road, or after completing it before you fly out.

HOW TO

Nearest stop: The closest place on this leg is Reykjavík, but Keflavík airport is closer to the north, so it's a good stop after arriving or before departing from Iceland.

Getting here: Follow Rtes 43 and 41 from the Ring Road. The Blue Lagoon has a large car park.

When to go: Open daily from 8am to 10pm, and between 7am and midnight in peak season (1 June to 20 August).

Cost: From 11,490kr per adult. Children 13 and under visit for free. See *bluelagoon.com*.

Mineral-Rich Waters

The milky waters of the **Blue Lagoon**, rich with silica and mineral algae, attract more than a million visitors a year. Expect steam to be billowing from the lagoon – 70% seawater, 30% freshwater – which hovers at 38°C year-round, no matter if it's sunny or snowing. Its huge appeal means large changing areas, full spa experiences, numerous eating options and even a hotel to stay in overnight.

Vast Lagoon

The 8700-sq-metre pool is not just for bathing – it's a full-on water attraction to explore. Tickets include entry to a swim-up steam or sauna cave, with adjacent cold showers and a basin of ice for cooling off. There are nooks and crannies to find around the volcanic pool, from a quiet zone and cold plunge, to a waterfall for skin dunking. Rehydrate at one of the many in-water drinking fountains or get a juice, smoothie, beer or wine (one drink is included in your ticket) at the swim-up bar. Don't miss a visit to the Mask Bar, where you can apply collagen-rich algae masks or cleansing silica mud masks to your face for their rejuvenating benefits (one mask is likewise included in the ticket).

Added Extras

In-water massages *(30min from 20,900kr)* or float therapies *(25,900kr)* take it one step further, as do the VIP wellness experiences in the Retreat Spa. With these you get private changing rooms for two guests, plus five-hour spa access and a Blue Lagoon

TOP TIPS

Book in advance: tickets go quickly. Keep heads, mouths and eyes out of the water (it's not meant to be consumed). Load up on conditioner, as the water can dry out hair. Bring your own swimwear, but don't fret if you forget – swimwear can be rented at the entrance desk. Don't take jewellery into the water, as the minerals may damage it (and it will get hot!). Phones are fine to take in, but many end up at the bottom of the lagoon; bring a waterproof case. Don't splash around; this is not a swimming pool. Feel free to ask staff to take a picture; they are used to it – and good at it.

Ritual, which involves cleansing the body in silica and donning an algae mask *(from 89,000kr)*. For ultimate luxury, there's yet another add-on – the Lava Cove *(269,000kr for up to 2 people)* is a private spa within the spa, in its own secluded section of Blue Lagoon. You and a companion can lounge around next to a fire, on heated chaise lounges under blankets – ideal for winter visits – while sipping on drinks and nibbling fruit. Hungry? There's a cafe and restaurant on-site, plus the Michelin-starred Moss Restaurant for something more fancy, in the next-door Blue Lagoon Retreat Hotel.

BEST PLACES TO SLEEP

Frost and Fire Hotel, Hveragerði €€€
Sits on a bubbling stream, beneath fizzing geothermal features. Rooms are Scandi-sleek. Relax in the sauna and simmering hot pots fed by a natural borehole. *(frostogfuni.is)*

Inni Boutique Apartments, Hveragerði €
Cosy, simple apartment-style guesthouse that's wonderful for a pit stop and use of the free outdoor spa area with two hot tubs and steam bath. *(inniapartments.is)*

Icelandic Cottages, near Selfoss €€€
Just north of the Ring Road on Rte 30, these cool modern cottages dot the lavafields. They're very well stocked, come with mini kitchens plus barbecues, and sleep up to six. *(icelandiccottages.is)*

continued from p53
was revenge by the Norse gods Þór (Thor), Óðinn and Freyr. The area is still rich with geothermal activity. Explore on horseback with Far and Ride *(farandride.com; prices & stays vary)*.

The Geothermal Exhibition

To really grasp the natural power of the area, visit the terrific **Geothermal Exhibition** *(on.is; adult/child 2500/1300kr)*, at **Hellisheiði Geothermal Power Plant**. Iceland's largest geothermal power plant, operated by ON Power, provides roughly 30% of Iceland's electricity and hot water for the capital region. A multimedia exhibition and tour lay out the details of creating renewable energy and harnessing the earth's hot-water power. Visitors can feel the energy in the engine room, learn about Iceland's rocks and minerals, see geothermal ingenuity in action, and experience the sights, sounds and smells of Mother Nature. It's a great stop to refuel too, in all the ways – refill your water bottle, charge your electric car, grab a bite and a drink at the on-site cafe and pick up gifts at the souvenir shop showcasing Icelandic products.

Hveradalir Geothermal Area

The geothermal activity continues 5km east down the Ring Road, at **Hveradalir Geothermal Area** *(free)*. Also known as the Valley of the Hot Springs, this is one of Iceland's largest geothermal areas, cradled by the orange Kerlingarfjöll range and rhyolite mountains formed from cooled lava. The Hveradalir area has bubbling mud pools and fumaroles, numerous hiking trails, plus rushing glacial rivers and the **Kerlingarfjöll Hot Springs**, which you can bathe in. Tours of the area can be booked with **Arctic Adventures** *(adventures.is; adult/child from 25,000/18,800kr)*.

Hveragerði

Home to fewer than 3000 people, **Hveragerði** (pronounced *kvrr-ah-ger-thhi*) is known as the 'town of hot springs'. Inside its **Geothermal Park** *(visithveragerdi.is; adult/child 400kr/free)* visitors can see mudpots and steaming vents, and dip their feet (only their feet) into naturally hot pools. A small visitor centre on-site offers the chance to boil

Kristnitökuhraun Lavafield — 8km — **The Geothermal Exhibition** — 2km — **Hveradalir Geothermal Area**

The valley of hot springs', with orange rhyolite mountains.

Descend into a Volcano

Þríhnúkagígur volcano might just be the only place on Earth where you can descend 120m below the Earth's surface to explore a volcano's lava chamber.

HOW TO

Nearest stop: Off the Ring Road on the way to Hveragerði; take Rte 417 12km south (15 minutes).

How it works: You must visit on a tour with **Inside the Volcano** (insidethevolcano.com); this is a strictly guided experience.

When to go: Tours generally only operate in the milder months from mid-May to mid-October.

Cost per adult: 49,000kr; 25,000kr per child eight to 12 years old.

The journey to **Þríhnúkagígur** begins with a scenic 3km hike (around 45 minutes) across lavafields covered in moss, surrounded by rugged peaks and sweeping views. En route, your guides will point out lava tubes and guide you across tectonic plates, which move roughly 2cm per year. The final part of the hike climbs to the crater's rim.

Everyone is fitted with a harness and helmet before reaching the opening of the volcano. You'll board an open cable lift, similar to a window-cleaning lift, that slowly descends 120m into into a chamber large enough to fit the Statue of Liberty. Walls are a kaleidoscope of reds, yellows, purples and greys, formed by mineral deposits from past eruptions.

Inside the chamber it's eerily silent, aside from the occasional drip of water, which echoes through the cave. This dormant volcano last erupted over 4000 years ago, and visitors get the rare opportunity to stand where molten rock was churned and magma pushed through to the Earth's surface. Equipped with a head torch, visitors are free to explore the chamber.

Right: inside the magma chamber

an egg in the geothermally heated water, taste bread baked by steam and watch a geyser erupt around every 20 minutes.

Want to really immerse yourself? The town's **Rehabilitation and Health Clinic** *(also known as Heilsugæslustöðin í Hveragerði; heilsustofnun.is; weekly stays from 170,800kr)* has week-long stays with baths (hot mud, herbal and steam), pools, hot tubs, massages, hypnosis and organic dining.

Along with geothermal activity, this area has suffered from the effects of shifting tectonic plates. In 2008, a 6.3 Richter earthquake struck. Its epicentre was located around 2km southeast of the town, but the quake was felt as far away as the Westfjords. Houses in Hveragerði were damaged or destroyed by the quake. Stop by the tourist information centre for a free exhibition on the natural disaster and see an original earthquake crack in the Earth, thought to be around 5000 years old, which is illuminated for visitors. Visitors can also step inside an earthquake simulator to feel the power of the ground move, and learn about the seismic activity in the region.

DETOUR: Sundlaugin Laugaskarð & the Reykjadalur Valley

If you have a little extra time to spend in nature, activities both relaxing and thrilling can be found just north of town.

Do as Hveragerði's locals do and visit **Sundlaugin Laugaskarð** *(laugaskard.is; adult/child/under 5 1220/420kr/free)*, the public open-air geothermal swimming pool beside the Varmá river. Once the largest swimming pool in the country, it has a 50m-long, 12m-wide outdoor pool heated with geothermal steam, plus a massaging hot pot and a steam room built directly over a natural hot spring. You can even rent swimwear and towels if you've forgotten your kit.

Go upstream to the **Reykjadalur Valley** (bring a swimsuit and a towel, free to visit but

Along the Way We Met...

VIKTOR JARL PALMASON I was born and raised in Reykjavík, in the capital. I now live in Spain, but travelling home after living away makes me so interested in what makes us Icelandic. We are very connected to the Norwegians and Danish, but the mysticism of Iceland is ours, we wrote our own books and found our own methods. I also love travelling and hearing people finding connections in different villages. People will say 'My grandfather comes from this area', and chances are you will know someone. Our last names are very connecting in Iceland.

Viktor Jarl Palmason is a programmer living in Spain.

Hveradalir Geothermal Area

Ring Road bends and curves through mountainous terrain.

12km

Hveragerði

Route 35 Adventure

The punchy Rte 35 detour to the north of the Ring Road has a cave, views and plenty of spots for relaxing strolls.

HOW TO

Nearest stop: It's 13km west of Selfoss and 11km east of Hveragerði.

Getting here: If travelling towards Selfoss, Rte 35 is a left turn, heading north off the Ring Road.

When to go: Summer is the best season to visit, when road conditions will be most favourable, followed by autumn and spring.

Top tip: The section of road here is suitable for all vehicles, but if continuing on the road (which is 237km long) further into Iceland's interior, it eventually turns into an F road. Make sure you use a high-clearance vehicle or 4WD for gravel roads, and check weather forecasts and road conditions on *road.is* in advance.

A 15km detour off the Ring Road offers a little jaunt on a side road filled with attractions. Around 1km north on Rte 35 (the first part is named Biskupstungnabraut), there's a little pull-off on the right, where a round-trip walking track (approximately 1km) leads to the supposedly haunted **Stóri-Hellir Cave**, in Hellisskógur forest. Between one and three million years old, this basalt cave is said to be home to a ghost that wears a blue scarf.

Continue north along Rte 35, past large mesas to the east and open plains to the west, until you reach the **Ölfusá Overlook**, offering panoramic views and the rushing river below. It's a great spot for birdwatching. Cross the river to find the glass-walled cabins of **Golden Circle Domes** (*goldencircledomes.is*), ideal for Northern Lights–spotting in winter, and the 18-hole Ondverdarnes golf course, which comes into its own in summer.

Further along the road on the left is **Snæfoksstaðir**, a relaxing park for picnics and nature walks on well-maintained paths. Rugged terrain, rolling hills and expansive views make for dramatic photos.

EXPERIENCE

Snæfoksstaðir

Old Dairy Food Hall

parking fees apply) to have a full bathing experience in a geothermal heated river. It's a roughly 3km hike to the river (around one to two hours' walk) on a fairly easy, flat trail through a deep green valley and canyons, glimpsing Icelandic birdlife and waterfalls, including the 40m-high Djúpagilsfoss. The valley is mesmerising, with white steam rising from the earth throughout.

For some high-octane thrills, the nearby **Mega Zipline** *(megazipline.is; adult/child 9490/6900kr)* is Iceland's longest zipline, soaring at up to 100km/hr for a whole kilometre from the Kambar plateau, with views over the Svartagljúfur gorge and the town. To get active on two wheels, **Ice Bike Adventures** *(icebikeadventures.com; tours from 12,500kr)* has trips of all kinds, from mountain biking on Hveragerði's geo trails right up to heli biking – a once-in-a-lifetime experience starting from the top of a dormant volcano. Or rent your own bike for a custom adventure.

Ölfusá River

Leaving Hveragerði, the scenery turns rural again, almost immediately. Drivers will spot the elevated landscape around the moun-

Hveragerði

17km

Ölfusá River

Cross a suspension bridge over the river, once Iceland's largest.

tain of Bjarnarfell (595m) and green rocky tuffs around Ingolfsfjall (551m) on the left, before reaching Selfoss, where a suspension bridge runs over the mighty **Ölfusá River**, flowing for 25km right through the town and into the Atlantic Ocean. The river is popular with fishers for its excellent salmon, which can be found here from mid-June until around September, and are caught by both sport anglers and nets in the estuaries. Sometimes it's possible for visitors to spot seals swimming upriver in search of fish. Large trout can also be caught here in spring.

Food fans can try the local fish seasonally in some terrific local Icelandic restaurants. Tryggvaskáli (p53), set in a historic house, serves salmon with barley pesto, veggies and chilli nuts, with a side of river views. **MAR Seafood** *(mar-seafood.is)*, set in a relaxed nautical dining room inspired by the sea and local waterways, is another great option. All their fish is überfresh – try Arctic wolffish, char, haddock, cod, halibut and more.

Old Dairy Food Hall

Just across the bridge on the way into Selfoss is the **Old Dairy Food Hall**, a must-visit stop set inside a beautiful former factory building with a lime-green roof. The hall houses eight independent restaurants serving everything from Thai and pizza to dim sum. There's also an exhibition showcasing the history of Icelandic *skyr*, yoghurt-like dessert and the nation's superfood, which has evolved from a Viking staple to a globally renowned health food. Peer inside a miniature turf house and read displays of stories about how the dairy industry has shaped the country.

Selfoss

Don't be deceived by the name of South Iceland's largest residential area. **Selfoss** may translate to 'seal waterfall', but there are no waterfalls near here. Instead, the town of 10,000 residents is set on the flat banks of the Ölfusá River. The area is mentioned in the Icelandic Sagas dating to 873–74, but today is decidedly modern. Its **New Old Town**, expected to be completed by 2028, will be the first environmentally certified town centre in the world. There are already numerous colourful, chalet-style buildings to admire in the pedestrian-friendly area, plus jewellery, clothing and gift shops to peruse.

Chess fans should make a beeline for the **Bobby Fischer Center** *(Fischersetur; fischersetur.is; adult/child 1700kr/free)* dedicated to one of Selfoss' claims to fame – chess champion Bobby Fischer, who is buried 2km northeast in Laugardælirkirkja's cemetery. Displays detail his rise to chess glory, when he defeated Soviet grandmaster and reigning World Champion Boris Spassky in Reykjavík in 1972 in the midst of the Cold War. There are also occasional chess classes and tournaments to get involved in (check the museum website ahead of your visit).

To unwind, jump into the public pool **Sundhöll Selfoss** *(arborg.is; adult/child 1750/350kr)*, with an 18m indoor children's pool, a 25m outdoor pool, three water slides, a steam bath, sauna and hot pots. Visit the town in early August for the **Sumar á Selfossi** *(sumaraselfossi.is)* festival, when residents decorate their gardens in their 'neighbourhood colour' and celebrate with live music and a summer fête.

Roll through the tree-lined streets of South Iceland's largest town.

Detour: Golden Circle

Venturing off your Ring Road journey onto the 300km Golden Circle route brings you to three knockout sights: Iceland's ancient parliament site, Þingvellir, located upon the rending tectonic plates; Geysir, where water erupts over 100 times a day; and roaring waterfall Gullfoss. Most people drive the Golden Circle clockwise from Þingvellir to Gullfoss, heading northeast out of Reykjavík through Mosfellsbær and rejoining the Ring Road at Selfoss, but the route can be driven in either direction. Whether it's an introduction to Iceland's natural marvels or a final hurrah after your Ring Road circumnavigation, this is a detour seriously worth considering.

Alexis Averbuck

Brúarfoss (p70)
ALEKPODREZ/SHUTTERSTOCK

209 KM
3 HOURS' DRIVE

THIS LEG:

- Gljúfrasteinn Laxness Museum
- Þingvellir National Park
- Laugarvatn
- Brúarfoss
- Geysir
- Gullfoss
- Brúarhlöð
- Hvítá River
- Flúðir
- Laugarás Lagoon
- Skálholt
- Sólheimar
- Kerið

Driving Notes

The Golden Circle is easy to self-drive, which allows you to visit outside peak season. In winter, road conditions are only a concern if there's heavy snowfall. Download the Parka app *(parka.app)* to avoid queuing to pay at car parks. No public buses serve the main sights, but countless tours do. Driving the route anticlockwise, finishing with Þingvellir, avoids the tour-bus route.

Breaking Your Journey

You can complete the circuit in a day, or stay at one of the many (relatively pricey) options – but book well ahead. Laugarvatn has good services, and guesthouses dot the valleys south of the three main Golden Circle sights. Otherwise, camp at Þingvellir National Park or each town's campsites – you don't need reservations for those.

Alexis' Tips

BEST MEAL Farm-grown fare at Ylja (p76) in the Laugarás Lagoon.

FAVOURITE VIEW The historic Almannagjá rift (p68) between the tectonic plates with Þingvallavatn alongside.

ESSENTIAL STOP Sample ice cream in the dairy barn at Efstidalur II (p70), then work it off on their trampoline.

ROAD-TRIP TIP In summer, take advantage of the midnight sun and visit late, avoiding tour-bus crowds.

Feel the Roar at Gullfoss, p72
Mesmerising 'golden falls' with trails topping the edges of its massive canyon.

Experience Historic Þingvellir, p68
Continental plates part dramatically at this historic parliamentary site.

Gljúfrasteinn Laxness Museum, p66
Nobel Prize winner's home.

Mosfellsbær

Reykjavík

START

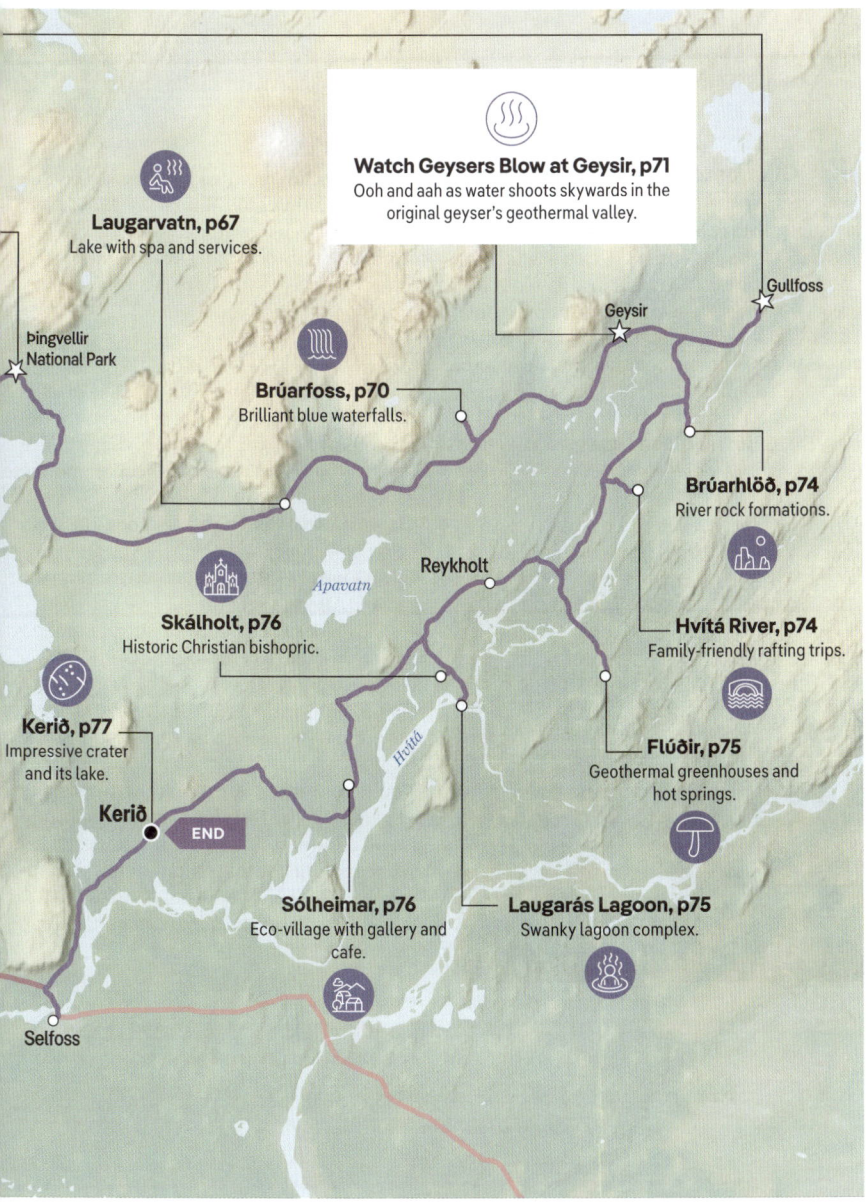

PREVIOUS STOP If you're driving clockwise, Mosfellsbær is about 20 minutes northeast of Reykjavík (p36); anticlockwise, from Selfoss (p61), Kerið is 15 minutes north on Rte 35.

Gljúfrasteinn Laxness Museum

Barely 15 minutes' drive north of Reykjavík city centre, **Mosfellsbær** can seem like just part of the city sprawl. There wouldn't be much to interest travellers in this town if it wasn't for Nobel Prize–winning author Halldór Laxness (1902–98), who lived in Mosfellsbær all his life. As you turn off the Ring Road onto the road to Þingvellir (Rte 36), you'll know you've reached his riverside home, which is now the **Gljúfrasteinn Laxness Museum** (*gljufrasteinn.is; adult/child 1500kr/free*), when you see his beloved white Jaguar parked out the front. The author built this classy, 1950s-style house, and it remains intact with original furniture, a writing room and Laxness' fine-art collection (the needlework is by his wife, Auður). An audio tour leads you around.

The Road Through Þingvellir

Continue along Rte 36 as it climbs into a valley edged by rolling hills, a particularly thrilling sight in winter when they're blanketed in snow. Then you'll curve into the grand Þingvellir National Park (p68), with **Þingvallavatn** lake glinting along the east. You'll likely stop for photo ops as you approach **Hakið Visitor Centre**, which perches atop the dramatic **Almannagjá** rift, the valley stretching into the distance. This was the site of Iceland's ancient parliament, a gathering of settlers from all over Iceland. Plan for a few hours (at least), walking between waterfalls, pools and chasms, plus around the remaining ruins and historic buildings.

You'll continue your drive north, passing the park's **Leirar Service Centre** and campgrounds. The next 19km drive begins by tracing the edge of the foothills along Þingvallavatn lake. You'll start on Rte 36, but turn east on Rte 365 to cut south of the dramatic mountains and emerge at Laugarvatn.

Þingvellir National Park (p68)

FROM LEFT: LEONID ANDRONOV/SHUTTERSTOCK, MARCIA CHAMBERS/ALAMY

Ride horses at local outfits near Þingvellir, like folks of yore.

Dish at Lindin

Laugarvatn

Laugarvatn (Hot Springs Lake) is fed not only by streams running from the misty fells behind it, but also by the hot spring **Vígðalaug**, famous since medieval times. A village, also called Laugarvatn, sits on the lake's western shore in the lap of the foothills. It's one of the better places to take a break on the Golden Circle, with hotels like Héraðsskólinn (p77) and Björk Guesthouse (p77). Unwind at **Laugarvatn Fontana** *(fontana.is)*, a swanky lakeside soaking spot. You can relax inside a cedar-lined steam room that's fed by a naturally occurring

continues p70

BEST PLACES TO EAT

Silfra Restaurant, South of Þingvellir €€€
Beautifully presented meals featuring locally sourced, seasonal ingredients at Ion Adventure Hotel. *(ioniceland.is; noon-2pm & 6-10pm)*

Lindin, Laugarvatn €€€
Cosy restaurant facing the lake serves high-concept Icelandic fare featuring local or wild-caught ingredients. Book ahead for dinner in high season. *(laugarvatn.is; hours vary)*

Friðheimar, Reykholt €€
Book ahead to dine in a Reykholt tomato greenhouse. Rarities include tomato beer and tomato ice cream. *(fridheimar.is; 11.30am-4pm)*

Flúðasveppir Farmers Bistro, Flúðir €€
Run by Iceland's only mushroom farm. Try mushroom soup or mushroom ice cream. *(farmersbistro.is; noon-5pm)*

Þingvellir National Park — Look out for arts-and-crafts shops, great for souvenirs. — 19km — Laugarvatn

Experience Historic Þingvellir

The UNESCO World Heritage Site of Þingvellir National Park is Iceland's most important historical spot. Settlers established the world's first democratic parliament, the Alþingi, here in 930 CE. See where meetings were conducted in this immense valley, surrounded rivers and waterfalls.

Nearest stop: Laugarvatn

Getting here: There are several car parks. Pay parking fees (from 1000kr) with the Parka app or at machines in the visitor centres. No public bus.

When to go: Open 24 hours. Avoid crowds by visiting early or late in the day.

Cost: No fee to enter the site.

Visitor information: thingvellir.is. Hakið Visitor Centre in the south has an exhibition. Leirar Service Centre on the north side of the lake handles camping and fishing licences. Year-round Nyrðri-Leirar campsite is adjacent to Leirar Service Centre. Syðri-Leirar and Vatnskot campsites open June to August.

Behold Tectonic Plates

Þingvellir *(thing-vet-lir)* sits on the tectonic-plate boundary where North America and Europe are tearing apart at 1mm–18mm per year. The world's oldest parliament, Alþingi *(al-thingk-ee)* took place here. From 930 to 1798, meetings were held in this natural amphitheatre. The plain is scarred by dramatic fissures, ponds and rivers, including the great rift **Almannagjá**. Descend on the path into the fault from the clifftop visitor centre's viewing platform. **Öxarárfoss** cascades down the cliffs' edge.

Ancient Ruins & Historic Buildings

The path emerges at **Lögberg** (Law Rock), where the Alþingi met annually, and the *lögsögumaður* (law speaker) recited existing laws. Straddling the Öxará river are ruins of temporary camps called *búðir* (booths). These foundations were covered during sessions and acted like market stalls. **Þingvallabær**, the rift farmhouse, was built for the 1000th anniversary of the Alþingi in 1930 by state architect Guðjón Samúelsson. It's now the park warden's office and prime minister's summer house. **Þingvallakirkja** was one of Iceland's first churches.

Dive Silfra Fissure

Diving at **Silfra** tops many bucket lists. This water-filled crack between the tectonic plates is the only place in the world to swim between continents. Crystal-clear water flows 60km from the **Langjökull** glacier, winding through porous lava rock for decades

EXHIBITIONS & TOURS

Year-round, the Hakið Visitor Centre has a **multimedia exhibition** (adult/child 1200kr/free) on the site's geology and history. Free one-hour guided tours in English run most days from June to August. They're usually at 10am and 2pm, but check ahead online for the schedule and start point. No booking is necessary.

Icelanders have been crossing this area on horseback for generations. You can too, with **Parliament Horses** (facebook.com/parliamenthorses) north of the park, or **Laxnes** (laxnes.is) in the valley on the Rte 36 approach from Reykjavík.

From top: Þingvallakirkja; Silfra fissure

before emerging here. Marine life is limited to bright green algae. This glacial water maintains a consistent temperature of 2–3°C. You can only dive or snorkel on a guided tour – reserve with **Dive.is** (dive.is), **Arctic Adventures** (adventure.is) or **Troll** (troll.is). Park in car park No 5 for trails with views of the fissure.

Quick Break

There's a basic cafe in Leirar Service Centre and a snack bar at Hakið Visitor Centre. Ion Adventure Hotel (p77) has high-end Silfra Restaurant (p67).

Clear winter nights here make for ideal aurora borealis viewing.

> **NATURE'S OVEN**
>
> Icelanders have used hot springs to bake rye bread for generations. *Hverabrauð* (hot-spring bread) is steam-cooked underground for 24 hours in the heat of the geothermal springs. Bakers bury stainless-steel pots of flour, sugar, baking powder, salt and milk, digging up the pots of bread the next day. The Icelandic rye that emerges is cakey with just a hint of sweetness, and goes perfectly with creamy Icelandic butter. Sample it at **Laugarvatn Fontana** (p67) and geothermal park **Hveragerði** (p56).

continued from p67

vent below, and lounge in outdoor mineral baths, then have a cold lake swim. Time your visit around daily **geothermal bakery tours** *(adult/child 3350/1650kr)* to watch fresh pots of bread emerge from hot black sand. Or, if you're on a budget, hop into the municipal **geothermal pool** *(facebook.com/ithrottahusLaugarvatn)* next door.

The restaurant Lindin (p67) is one of the best in the region and has both a casual bistro and a fine-dining lake-view wing in a sweet little silver house. **Vinastræti Veitingahús** *(vinastraeti.is)* is a more casual spot right on the roadside.

 Brúarfoss

As you leave Laugarvatn to the north along scenic Rte 37, you'll wind away from the hills into increasingly open agricultural plains. Keep your eyes open for **Efstidalur II** *(efstidalur.is)* farm, 12km northeast of town, where you can stop for a homemade ice cream while looking through viewing windows into the dairy barn.

The brilliant blue waterfall called **Brúarfoss** originates at the Langjökull glacier, and it's that glacial meltwater flowing into the rivers Brúará and Hvítá that gives this waterfall its bright blue colour. The falls plunge 3m into an azure pool punctuated by white rapids. Pay to park in the main car park *(750kr)*, a few minutes' walk from the falls – or take the scenic route by parking for free in the southern Brúará Trail car park and enjoying a 7km round-trip hike to the waterfall, passing **Hlauptungufoss** and **Miðfoss** along the way. There's usually a snack truck in the main car park from June to August.

Geysir to Gullfoss

Continue along Rte 37 from Brúarfoss until it joins up with Rte 35, which you'll take into Geysir – it's about 15km in all. You'll know you're approaching Geysir when you first glimpse a geothermal outlet venting steam. This merges into the ochre-seared **Haukadalur** geothermal area around the geysers, a bubbling landscape criss-crossed by walking trails. You won't miss seeing the large service centre across the street, where you'll park before walking into the sprawling site.

From Geysir, it's a speedy 10km east to Gullfoss (p72), at the end of Rte 35, before it transforms into the Kjölur route (mountain road F35) and ascends into the highlands. At Gullfoss, you'll park on the east side of the road and walk to the viewing platform and trails around the roaring falls.

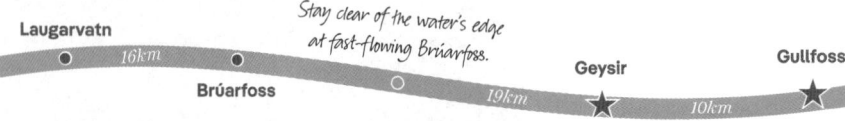

Watch Geysers Blow at Geysir

Geysir (*gay-zeer;* literally 'gusher') is the original hot-water spout after which all other geysers are named. Active for around 800 years, the Great Geysir is now relatively dormant – its neighbour Strokkur steals the show with steady eruptions.

HOW TO

Nearest stop: Laugarvatn

Cost: Admission to the site is currently free. Parking is 1000kr.

There she blows: Stand downwind only if you want a shower. You can grab arresting photos from up the valley, looking back at the volcanic hills and erupting geyser.

Eat & shop: Geysir Center (*hotelgeysir.is*) across from the geysers has an enormous shop, petrol station and many eateries. Hótel Geysir serves a daily buffet.

You'll see smoke rising on the horizon as you approach colourful geothermal valley Haukadalur. Vibrant shades of yellow (sulphur), green (copper) and red (iron) colour the ground. You'll also find mud pools, hot springs and fumaroles – vents in the earth that emit volcanic gas. Geysir once gushed water up to 80m into the air, but nowadays eruptions are rare. Luckily for visitors, the very reliable **Strokkur** sits alongside.

You rarely have to wait more than 10 to 15 minutes for the hot spring to shoot an impressive 15m to 30m plume before vanishing back into the earth.

The area's walking paths connect Geysir to **Blesi**, a beautiful hot spring with steam rising off blue and turquoise water. You can also hike in nearby **Haukadalur forest** or hit the nine-hole **Geysir Golf Course**. **Geysir Hestar** (*geysirhestar.com*) offers horse riding and lodging, while adjacent to it, **Skjol** (*skjolcenter.is*) has ATVs and e-bikes, a handicraft shop and a campground – plus its cafe serves pizzas, salads and snacks.

Strokkur

Feel the Roar at Gullfoss

Iceland's most famous waterfall, Gullfoss is a dramatic 32m double cascade, kicking up magnificent walls of spray before thundering down a rocky ravine carved by the Hvítá river. On sunny days, the mist creates shimmering rainbows, while in winter the falls glitter with ice.

HOW TO

Nearest stop: Geysir

Getting here: There's no public bus. Use your own wheels or come on a tour.

When to go: The falls are free, and open 24 hours, but cafe/shop hours vary – check online.

More info: *gullfoss.is*

Eat & stay: The tourist centre has a shop and cafe (lamb soup, salads, sandwiches, cakes and coffee). Nearby **Hótel Gullfoss** *(hotelgullfoss.is)* offers en-suite rooms (get one facing the valley), hot tubs and a restaurant.

Feel the Power of the Waterfall

Dropping into the rugged canyon of the Hvítá river, Gullfoss has two cascades: the first drop is 11m and the second is 21m. In summer, Gullfoss is at its fullest, and around 38 million tonnes of water charge through daily. Light prisms through the mist into rainbows rising over carpets of bright green moss. But don't let winter weather deter a visit – this waterfall is spectacular when it freezes in places, with enormous icicles shimmering.

Maximise Views & Photo Ops

There are around 3.2km of walking paths, but don't step over the barriers – they're there to protect you and the fragile environment. A tarmac path leads from the main car park and visitor centre to a grand lookout over the falls. Stairs continue down to the level of the falls. For wheelchair-accessible parking, drive in on the spur below the tourist centre at falls-level. A path continues down the valley towards the thundering falls for the most captivating video shots. There's also a less-visited viewing spot on the eastern clifftop.

If you'd like to approach the falls on horseback, book in with **Geysir Hestar** *(geysirhestar.com)*, which offers horse riding for all skill levels and has one route along the river canyon to the falls.

FROM TOP: ROB CRANDALL/SHUTTERSTOCK, VOVA SHEVCHUK/SHUTTERSTOCK

SAVING THE FALLS

Gullfoss is one of Iceland's best-known tourist attractions, but in 1907, it almost became a hydroelectric dam. Sigríður Tómasdóttir (1871–1957) and her sisters made the first stairs to the falls, guiding people through formerly impassable terrain. When foreign investors wanted to dam the river, Sigríður walked barefoot to Reykjavik to protest. Ultimately, the falls escaped destruction, and were donated to the nation. Since 1979 it's been a nature reserve. Sigríður's lawyer, Sveinn Björnsson, was later elected the first president of Iceland. Look for the memorial to Sigríður near the foot of the stairs from the visitors centre.

On grey days, mist can obscure the second drop, making Gullfoss slightly less spectacular.

Touch the Edge of the Kjölur Route

Gullfoss is the final stop on traditional Golden Circle tours. You can continue along magnificent Rte F35 beyond the falls (the highland Kjölur route) for 14.8km while it's paved; after that you need a 4WD, preparation and rental-company permission.

Along the Way We Met...

GÍSLI MATT AUÐUNSSON The region around Laugarás is rich, with amazing farmers and producers growing some of the best food in the country. At our new restaurant at the Laugarás Lagoon, we focus on working with local growers to create food with a story, with a connection to the land, the place and the people. I love making experiences, not just beautifully prepared food. Our menu will continue to evolve along with the people and produce. We harness the geothermal heat to use cooking techniques that are in harmony with the special spot where the lagoon is located, and we also focus on zero waste, hopefully making our restaurant a place that is a value to the community, the farmers and the environment.

Chef and food activist Gísli Matt (gislimatt.is) creates inventive, hyper-local Icelandic cuisine at his restaurants Slippurinn, Næs, Skál, and, most recently Ylja at Laugarás Lagoon.

GISLÍ MATT'S TIP: Visit Sólheimar (p76). It's a special eco-village and a wonderful community growing its own vegetables, roasting coffee and making arts and crafts.

Brúarhlöð

As you circle south from Gullfoss, seek out the canyon **Brúarhlöð** *(parking 1000kr)*, at a sharp bend in Rte 30. It's an overlooked spot where the voluminous Hvítá river cuts through extraordinary breccia rock formations. Sharp cliffs rise from glacial water running through this narrow gorge, showing off hints of blue and green as it flows. The best views of this canyon are from above – and they don't require an arduous hike. The trail is under 1.5km (about 15 to 20 minutes) each way, with an elevation gain of just 9m. Expect to be tempted by the peaceful picnic spots you'll pass on the way.

River-Rafting on the Hvítá River

You're now in the Hvítá river valley, and what better thrill than booking a chance to ride the **Hvítá river** through a majestic canyon just south of thundering Gullfoss. With giant rock walls rising out of the jade-coloured glacial waters, it may be one of the most picturesque rafting locations in the world. The river's name means 'white river', a reflection of its white caps,

| Gullfoss | 13km | Brúarhlöð | 12km | | Hvítá river | 16km |

Book ahead for river trips or stays.

and the rapids (Class II) are suitable for first-time rafters – expect waves, splashes and at least a little thrill. It's only warm enough to raft between May and September.

Tour companies provide life jackets, helmets and wetsuits, but rafters must be at least 11 years old and know how to swim. The remote base camp at **Drumboddsstaðir** offers showers, saunas, changing rooms, a restaurant and a bar. Book ahead with **Arctic Adventures** *(adventures.is)*, or **Arctic Rafting** *(arcticrafting.com)*, a local company that's been leading river-rafting and kayaking tours here since 1985.

Foodie Flúðir

As you travel south on Rte 30 through the fields along the eastern bank of the Hvítá, little agrarian **Flúðir** emerges. This region is known throughout Iceland for its geothermal greenhouses that grow the majority of the country's mushrooms, and it's also a popular weekend getaway for Reykjavikers with private cottages.

To sample the local produce, stop in at Flúðasveppir Farmers Bistro (p67) about 3km northwest of town. Or get picnic supplies at **Sólskinsbúðin** *(solskinsbudin.is)* farmers market. You can also veer northwest off Rte 30 to try the restaurants around Reykholt, like Friðheimar (p67) and its sister wine bar, **Vínstofa Friðheima**, plus overnight in the cheerful Blue Hotel Fagrilundur (p77).

Flúðir's Hot Springs

Flúðir is also a super stop for its beautifully refurbished hot springs, **Gamla Laugin** *(Secret Lagoon; secretlagoon.is)*. Take a few

Vínstofa Friðheima

hours to soak in this broad, calm geothermal pool that traces its history to 1891, the mist rising and ringed by natural rocks. The walking trail along the edge passes the Litla-Laxá river and a series of sizzling vents and geysers. It also has a cafe.

Just outside the town, you'll find the hot spring **Hrunalaug** *(hrunalaug.is)*. It is so far off the beaten path that you just might get it all to yourself. This tiny hot spring has three small pools, and in 2025 bathrooms and a new changing room (the old one was a sheep barn) were being built.

Laugarás Lagoon

Driving south out of Flúðir, the terrain becomes dramatic, with interesting rock buttes rising from rolling green plains. You can zigzag

Flúðir — 23km — Laugarás Lagoon

There's a zoo for the kids in Laugarás.

to Rte 31 and the riverfront hamlet **Laugarás**, where the hottest entry in the Golden Circle soaking game is beautifully designed **Laugarás Lagoon** (laugaraslagoon.is; children 8-plus only), which opened in 2025. The soft arches of its building are planted with native grasses to blend with the exquisite location on the banks of the Hvítá. Immerse yourself in a vast array of pools, taking in river views and relaxing under the waterfall feature. A bespoke skincare line developed with a preeminent herbalist adds to the charms, though perhaps the top perk is **Ylja restaurant**, run by Gísli Matt Auðunsson (p74). Stay over nearby at Brekkugerdi Guesthouse (p77).

Skálholt

Just north up Rte 36, look west across the green fields for the white church at **Skálholt** (skalholt.is). This site was the backdrop to about 700 years of Icelandic history, a time when the country's early political, spiritual and cultural identity was formed. A church was first built on this site in 1056 at a time when religious disputes were common – Christianity was gaining ground on an island where pagan belief systems were the norm. This is also where the last Catholic bishop of Iceland, Jón Arason, was killed in 1550. The great cathedral that once stood here was destroyed by a major earthquake in the 18th century, but you can visit the complex's huge Evangelical Lutheran **Skálholtsdómkirkja**, built from 1956–63. There's also a **museum** (admission 500kr) and a summer concert series.

If you're peckish during your visit, stop for dinner or lunch at **Hvönn** restaurant, part of the Skálholt complex.

Skálholtsdómkirkja

Sólheimar

As you rejoin Rte 35 to glide the last 36.5km back to the Ring Road, it's worth looping onto Rte 354 to **Sólheimar Eco-Village** (solheimar.is), a collection of homes and greenhouses using ecologically sound practices to create a sustainable community. Day visitors should go to the **Græna Kannan Cafe**, where soups and a small lunch buffet are made from ingredients grown on the farm. Don't miss the **art gallery** there, which has summer exhibitions of the residents' fantastic artwork. If you want to buy a piece but can't wait for the exhibition to close to collect it, don't worry – many immediate gratification options are available in the eclectic shop.

If you feel like staying longer, there are also two guesthouses.

Laugarás Lagoon — 3km — Skálholt — 16km — Sólheimar — 17km — Kerið

Check out the art gallery and taste their coffee.

Kerið

Just as Rte 35 approaches the northern edge of Selfoss and the Ring Road (16km northeast of town), you'll come across one of Iceland's best-known volcanic craters, **Kerið** *(kerid.is)*. The site is a 6500-year-old magma chamber that collapsed, leaving vivid red and sienna earth surrounding an ethereal green lake. Much of Kerið is made of rich, red volcanic rock, but its least-steep slope is a bed of mossy green during summer. Hints of yellow are a reflection of the land's sulphur content.

You can walk around the lake – Björk once performed a concert from a raft in the middle of it – in about 30 minutes, or walk from the viewing platform down to the lake in about 15 minutes, before motoring the 14km back to Selfoss, on the Ring Road.

BEST PLACES TO SLEEP

Ion Adventure Hotel, south of Þingvellir €€€
Chic, with sustainable practices. Has a geothermal pool, spa and restaurant. *(ioniceland.is)*

Héraðsskólinn, Laugarvatn €
Historic lakeside boutique hostel built in 1928 by Guðjón Samúelsson. Some private rooms with shared bathrooms. *(heradsskolinn.is)*

Björk Guesthouse, Laugarvatn €€
Central with spacious, clean rooms and helpful owners. *(bjorkguesthouse.is)*

Brekkugerdi Guesthouse, Laugarás €
Welcoming, comfortable guesthouse with en-suite bathrooms in some rooms. Tucked into the trees. *(brekkugerdi.is)*

Blue Hotel Fagrilundur, Reykjolt €€
Log cabin exterior encloses a modern hotel with generous breakfast. *(bluevacations.is)*

Ion Adventure Hotel

Selfoss

This is the gateway to 'waterfall land', home to some of Iceland's most impressive cascades, which thunder down cliffs right off the Ring Road. It's also the entry point to Þórsmörk, the dramatic valley named after Norse god Þór (Thor), and a verdant protected paradise for hikers, with snowcapped mountain ridges and wildflower-filled valleys. On this stretch of asphalt, you'll get a glimpse of the Sólheimajökull outlet glacier, plus a black sandy beach, a plane wreck and the charming community of Vík, with its basalt beach and puffin cliffs.

Jade Bremner

Vík (p91)
SUMMIT ART CREATIONS/SHUTTERSTOCK

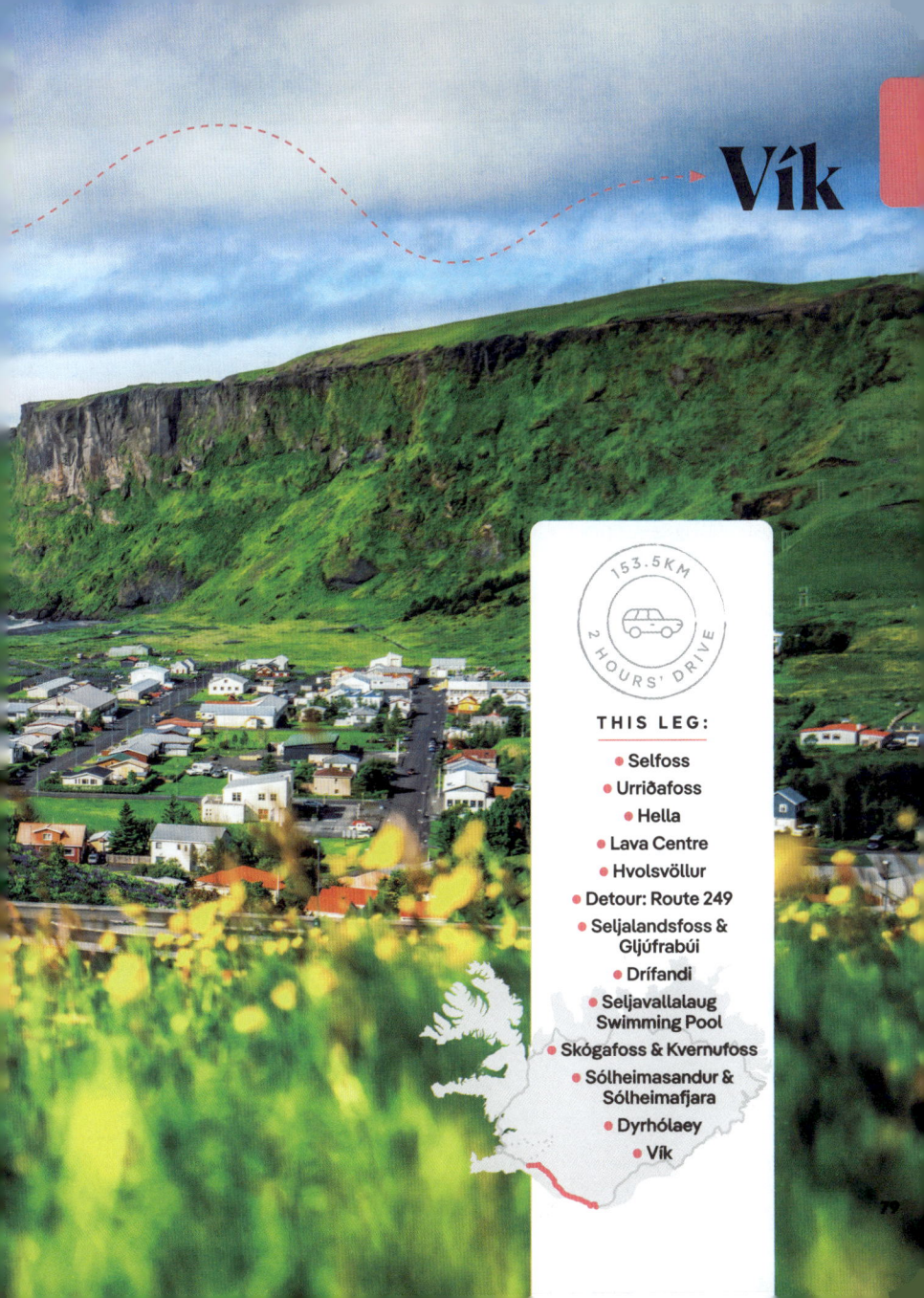

Vík

153.5 KM
2 HOURS' DRIVE

THIS LEG:

- Selfoss
- Urriðafoss
- Hella
- Lava Centre
- Hvolsvöllur
- Detour: Route 249
- Seljalandsfoss & Gljúfrabúi
- Drífandi
- Seljavallalaug Swimming Pool
- Skógafoss & Kvernufoss
- Sólheimasandur & Sólheimafjara
- Dyrhólaey
- Vík

Driving Notes

Things are about to get really impressive and pretty on the Ring Road – which has wild, open views and minimal traffic on this leg. Plan plenty of time at each stop, as there is so much to see and do here. Consider travelling in the long days of June and July, so you can continue sightseeing until the wee hours of the morning.

Breaking Your Journey

There's plenty of opportunity to stretch your legs – the towns of Hella, Hvolsvöllur, Skógar and Vík allow for refuelling, toilet breaks and the chance to get snacks or a meal. The bigger natural sights also have toilets nearby, but be prepared to pay for parking, which will require a credit or debit card and the internet for QR codes and apps.

Jade's Tips

BEST MEAL Warm up with a steaming bread bowls of chilli or vegetable soup at the Soup Company (p83) in Vík.

FAVOURITE VIEW Climb Skógafoss (p87) for views over a 60m cascade to the green hills of the south coast.

ESSENTIAL STOP Get sprayed as you walk behind Seljalandsfoss (p86).

ROAD-TRIP TIP Natural sights are crowded; visit late at night (in summer) to have them to yourself.

Hella, p82 — Believed to be where the first settlers lived.

START — Selfoss

Urriðafoss, p82 — The most voluminous waterfall in the country.

Ægissíðufoss

Lava Centre, p83 — All about seismic life in Iceland.

Route 249, p85 — For off-route waterfalls.

Seljalandsfoss & Gljúfrabúi, p86 — Walk behind the spray at these falls.

ATLANTIC OCEAN

PREVIOUS STOP This route begins at Selfoss (p61), the south's largest town and full of supplies for your onward journey.

Urriðafoss

Just beyond Selfoss off the Ring Road is **Urriðafoss**, the most voluminous waterfall in the country and the second most voluminous in Europe, after the Rheinfall in Switzerland. On the Þjórsá river, it has such a fast flow that 360 cu metres of water goes over the falls per second. Stand and watch its power and energy in action. There are proposals for a power plant to be built here to harness this energy – it would produce approximately 930GWh per year, which is estimated to be enough to power 700,000 homes.

Caves of Hella

Hella

The first town on this leg is a significant one. Some of the first settlers of Iceland – not Vikings but Irish monks – are believed to have used the caves in **Hella** to shelter, as the area has an abundance of fresh water and salmon. Now the town of around 1000 people is a shelter for tourists circling the Ring Road, with many guesthouses serving as a base for South Iceland and Golden Circle (p62) adventures. Visitors can tour five of the 12 human-made **caves** *(cavesofhella.is; adult/child/under 5 6490/2650kr/free)*, where there are archaeological remains such as ancient crosses, wall carvings, a paved floor and carved seats. For years the caves were used as dwellings and to house livestock, but after WWII, as concrete became more available, the caves were no longer used. For an extravagant experience, the caves can be booked out for private Viking-style feasts, with chefs from nearby **Hotel Rangá** creating a three-course candlelight meal *(cavesofhella.is/vikingfeast; book at least 1 week ahead)* in the historic setting. For more leg stretches, a nice hiking trail leads a few kilometres south from the town along the Ytri-Rangá river to **Ægissíðufoss**, a low but rushing waterfall. When driving out of town, look north – on clear days you can see the volcano Hekla in the distance.

For a bite while you're in town, try Restaurant Árhús or the quirky American School Bus Cafe, while nearby Glass Cottages (p86) is an accommodation option big on views.

Selfoss — 20km — **Urriðafoss** — 19km

Drive through wide green (or snowy) plains.

Urriðafoss

🌋 Lava Centre

From Hella, it's only a 10-minute drive to the next town, past flat fields. The **Lava Centre** (*lavacentre.is; adult/child 5200/2600kr*) sits on the outskirts of Hvolsvöllur, and is a full multimedia exhibition on seismic life in Iceland. Visitors can experience a Richter scale 4 earthquake inside a simulator, check live volcano monitoring systems and watch high-definition films of recent eruptions, such as the Fagradalsfjall eruption. Once you've finished exploring, soak in panoramic views of nearby volcanoes, such as Eyjafjallajökull, Katla and Hekla, from a rooftop viewing platform.

BEST PLACES TO EAT

Restaurant Árhús, Hella €€€
One of the oldest restaurants in south Iceland, on the river Rangá. Serving tasty pasta, meat and fish dishes. Gorgeous terrace, too. (*arhusrestaurant.is; 11am-10pm*)

American School Bus Cafe, Hella €
Right next to the historic caves, this retro bus serves up sandwiches, pastries and coffees at mini booths. (*8am-7pm*)

Black Crust Pizzeria, Vík €€
Black dough or sourdough pizzas with classic toppings, plus a few creative pies, such as Icelandic langoustine. Wash it down with a craft beer. (*blackcrustpizzeria.com; noon-9pm*)

Soup Company, Vík €€
Family-run soup shop, serving bread bowls of steaming concoctions, beef goulash and lamb stew. (*thesoup.company; 10.30am-10pm*)

Hella — 12km — *A long, straight stretch, with little but grass.* — Lava Centre

Encounter Þórsmörk

Named after the Norse god of thunder, Þór (Thor), Þórsmörk is a protected reserve so dazzling it looks plucked from a fantasy epic. Hikers can roam pleated valleys dotted with wildflowers, follow curling gorges and cross rushing rivers.

HOW TO

Nearest stop: Hella

Getting here: Due to its rivers, Þórsmörk can't be reached by regular cars. Walk in, get an all-terrain bus from Hveragerði, Selfoss or Hella, or go on a tour. Operators include **Reykjavík Excursions** (re.is; from 12,499kr), **Trex** (trex.is; from 12,900kr) and **Southcoast Adventure** (southadventure.is; from 9000kr).

When to go: June to September. River bridges may be closed and buses stop running outside this period.

The detour of all detours in Iceland, Þórsmörk is one of the most spectacular places on Earth. Due to its remoteness and inaccessibility, it remains untouched. It has only a few places to stay overnight and seemingly endless hiking opportunities between three glaciers: Eyjafjallajökull, Mýrdalsjökull and Tindfjallajökull. Those who make the effort to get here are rewarded with snow-capped mountain ridges, moss-cloaked volcanic slopes and silvery birch forests. The glaciers act as a barrier to the region's harsher weather; its microclimate is often warmer and drier than other parts of Iceland.

An network of marked trails ranges from short family-friendly walks to multiday treks. Short circuits include the Valahnúkur hike (4.6km), with panoramic views of glaciers and valleys, and the Stakkholtsgjá canyon hike (5.4km) with a hidden waterfall. The multiday Laugavegur Trail (55km) is often described as Iceland's most beautiful hike. Many choose to hike into Þórsmörk from Skógar via the Fimmvörðuháls Pass (about 27km), on a challenging, all-day trek that leads past 26 waterfalls, over volcanic craters between glaciers and down a green valley.

Laugavegur Trail

Hvolsvöllur

Set against sweeping views of Eyjafjallajökull glacier and the surrounding farmlands, **Hvolsvöllur** features in *Njál's Saga*, one of Iceland's most famous medieval sagas. Today, with its low-rise buildings and wide streets, it's a practical rural stop on the Ring Road for refuelling and grabbing supplies. It's also become an adventure base camp for those heading into the remote Þórsmörk valley to the northeast, with tonnes of tour operators. The local bus service (with monster-truck wheels for crossing rivers) also departs from here.

Don't leave town without trying an ice cream from **Ísbúðin Valdís Hvolsvelli** *(valdis.is; scoops from 950kr)* with inventive flavours, from liquorice to beer rye bread and lavender – or our favourite, coconut and chilli. Then pop into **Una Local Products** *(@unalocalproduct)*, set inside a large hangar on the Ring Road with all manner of handmade Icelandic crafts, from hand-knitted sweaters and fish-skin purses to jewellery and leather goods. Slightly west off the Ring Road, on Rte 264, the medieval turf-roofed farm at **Keldur** is worth a slight detour – the historic settlement once belonged to Ingjaldur Höskuldsson, a character in *Njál's Saga*.

DETOUR: Route 249

Take this side road off the Ring Road, going 10km north (around a 15-minute drive) to reach an almost secret waterfall away from the Ring Road crowds. **Nauthúsafoss** feels lost in time, falling down a narrow green hidden gorge. It takes roughly 30 to 45 minutes to reach the falls from the car park, and getting here requires a bit of an adventurous traverse of some boulders, climbing a 2m rock face with a chain, and negotiating stones in the river (bring waterproof shoes if you don't trust your balance). In spring, water levels may be too high to reach the falls, but in the colder months you may see icicles hanging from the cliff edges. On the way back to the Ring Road, the red-and-white **Eyvindarholt DC-3 aeroplane wreck** (off gravel Rte 248) is worth a look. It was used by the US Navy

---

CAVE HOUSES & TURF SHEDS

When driving along the Ring Road from Seljalandsfoss to Skógar, keep your eye out for unusual dwellings and shelters, which have been built with natural rocks right off the Ring Road. **Sauðhúsvöllur Kofinn** is the first. Built by a farmer in the 1940s, this turf-covered shed was used to store milk cans. Further down the route, the **Rutshellir Cave** is said to be the largest human-made cave in Iceland. Carved into the bottom of a big boulder, it's around 5m wide and 20m long inside, with a skylight and window. It's believed to have been an ancient dwelling before becoming a store place for hay and stockfish in more recent times. Just before the village of Skógar are **Drangurinn í** and **Drangshlíð 2**. These picturesque turf houses are set below a big rock face that forms part of the Eyjafjöll mountains, with a structure built below the rock itself. They were once used as cowsheds for hay – though local legend also claims that a man once married an elf-woman, and they lived inside Drangurinn rock.

BEST PLACES TO SLEEP

Seljalandsfoss Horizons, near Drífandi €€
Just off the Ring Road, these cosy and reasonably priced cabins have gorgeous views, lovely design and kitchenettes. Convenient access with an entry code.

Glass Cottages, near Hella €€€
Glass-walled cottages dotted around a lavafield, designed for Northern Lights-spotting or simply soaking up the scenery. *(glasscottages.com)*

Volcano Hotel, near Vík €€€
With only seven modern rooms, 11km west of Vík, with a good restaurant and gorgeous mountain views. *(volcanohotel.is)*

Hótel Skógafoss, Skógar €€
In the shadow of Skógafoss (some rooms have waterfall views) with a good bistro on-site. *(hotelskogafoss.is)*

and wrecked after strong winds during landing caused it to veer off the runway. The plane was damaged beyond repair, but no one was hurt. It was moved here in 2023 and has become a photo op for visitors.

Seljalandsfoss & Gljúfrabúi

Pouring over an emerald cliff right off the Ring Road, the 60m **Seljalandsfoss** waterfall drops from the Seljalands river into a deep pool. A slippery path allows visitors behind-the-scenes access to this postcard-perfect chute. You can walk behind the waterfall and feel the spray in certain winds (wear sturdy shoes and a waterproof coat, unless you don't mind getting wet). The waterfall has been featured on screen many times, including in the movie *CKY2K* with music from Björk, and in the music video for Justin Bieber's track 'I'll Show You'. Don't miss the nearby **Gljúfrabúi** waterfall, a quieter cascade north of Seljalandsfoss, where hikers can enter a mossy canyon and see the falls drop into a waterfall chamber.

Drífandi

Not to be confused with another waterfall with the same name (which is much further south in Smiðjuvík), the 70m-high **Drífandi** cascade is a soft slide of water tumbling down a steep cliff off the Ring Road. It's a thinner sheet of water, which peacefully glides down the rock face and occasionally freezes in winter, forming beautiful textures and giant icicles. Take a long-lens camera or binoculars to admire them up close.

Nearby Seljalandsfoss Horizons offers cosy cabins.

Seljavallalaug Swimming Pool

Around 25km south of Seljalandsfoss, moments up the Rte 242 side road just off the Ring Road, is the stunning (and completely free) **Seljavallalaug Swimming Pool**, surrounded by mountains. In the 1920s this 10m by 25m swimming pool was the largest pool in Iceland, and was used to teach school children how to swim. It's a warm spot for a dip – but it's not as hot as other Icelandic pools, hovering at around

Skógafoss

20°C to 30°C. Note that while the setting is spectacular, visitors are required to keep the area clean (and sometimes they do not). The small changing room area is often left messy, and the pool may have natural algae growing in it at certain times of the year. It's a 10-minute walk to reach the pool from the car park.

Skógafoss & Kvernufoss

One of the most photogenic spots on the south coast, **Skógafoss** is a colossal 25m-wide waterfall with a 60m drop into a big pool below. Legend has it that the Viking Þrasi Þórólfsson hid his loot in a cave behind the falls. Climb the 527 steps to the right of the falls for dramatic views down the falls and across the landscape – all the way to the Atlantic Ocean on clear days. This is also the start of the superb Fimmvörðuháls Trail (p88), one of Iceland's most beautiful hikes. It covers 26km of jaw-dropping scenery: 26 waterfalls, volcanic terrain, snowcapped peaks and dramatic valleys as you drop into Þórsmörk (p84). The town next to Skógafoss, **Skógar**, has many accommodation and eating options for hikers to enjoy before embarking on their adventure.

Skógafoss' less-visited neighbour hides behind a cliff wall to the east of Skógar. At the end of a glorious moss-covered canyon, **Kvernufoss** pounds 30m down the cliff into a pool below. To reach

continues p90

Clouds often touch the emerald mountains on the left.

21.5km

Seljavallalaug Swimming Pool

11km

After Rte 242 enjoy Atlantic views on the right.

Skógafoss & Kvernufoss

Hike the Fimmvörðuháls

Traversing up to four different worlds in one day hike – waterfalls, volcanoes, snow and ice, and rich pleated valley – the 26km Fimmvörðuháls trail is about as diverse as hikes get.

HOW TO

Nearest stop: Skógafoss

Getting here: Park overnight at the campground below Skógafoss (from 2200kr overnight).

When to go: The trail is officially open June to September, but can be hiked in earlier or later depending on the weather. Check *safetravel.is* for weather info.

Safety: Download the 112 Iceland app *(112.is/en)* and check in at various points on the trail (the app has a one-touch emergency button, too, in case you need it). While it's a manageable walk in good weather (if you're reasonably fit), there are two treacherous passes – go with a guide if in doubt.

Waterfall Way

Named after the pass between two brooding glaciers, the Fimmvörðuháls starts at the base of the mighty Skógafoss, in the town of Skógar (p87). The first section, from Skógafoss to a bridge, leads through the awesome Waterfall Way (around 8km, two- to three-hour hike), past dozens of fast-flowing voluminous cascades tumbling down striking rock formations. After the initial climb up the staircase at the side of Skógafoss, with 527 stairs to the top of the 60m drop, the path is relatively easy. Elevation increases gradually, and there are plenty of waterfalls of all shapes and sizes to spot through the gorgeous valley. Don't forget to turn around for the spectacular views to the south over the Atlantic.

The Volcano

From the bridge, the landscape drastically changes. The ground becomes lava underfoot, and you might see steam rising over the volcano. In spring and early summer this area will likely be covered in snow and requires proper winter gear (waterproof trousers and crampons) as you climb between two glaciers, **Eyjafjallajökull** and **Mýrdalsjökull**, along icy sheets with white as far as the eye can see. The weather can be variable here, even if you've checked ahead of time.

In summer, it feels more like a giant ashtray, with grey terrain. The two youngest craters in Iceland, **Modi** and **Magni**, were created during Eyjafjallajökull's 2010 volcanic eruption.

FROM TOP: KRISTYNA HENKEOVA/SHUTTERSTOCK, PEDRO CARRILHO/SHUTTERSTOCK

HIKING TIPS

Start early The full hike takes eight to 12 hours. June has the most daylight and the chance to take the hike slowly.

Pack wisely Good hiking boots and layers (including winter gear) are required. Postpone in bad weather. Carry GPS points and an offline app.

Overnight No camping is allowed. Stay overnight on the trail at **Fimmvörðuháls Hut** (utivist.is) or **Baldvinsskáli** (fi.is). Book in advance.

Transport This is not a loop trail. A mega jeep or bus (southadventure.is; from 9000kr) must be booked out of Þórsmörk; regular cars cannot cross the rivers.

From top: Modi and Magni; one of the hike's many waterfalls

Goðaland

After two thrilling passes – one requires holding onto a chain and the other is thin with steep drops on either side, which can be fatal in bad weather – volcanic terrain turns to **Goðaland** or the 'Land of the Gods'. Lush green valleys with Arctic flowers unfold, with glacial rivers and sweeping views of snowcapped peaks, as stone cathedrals emerge in the distance and the path steeply descends into stunning Þórsmörk (p84).

continued from p87

it, park near the Skógakirkja church, climb the stile over the fence and follow the walking path through the field (roughly 15 minutes) towards the cliff. It's possible to scale the (often muddy) banks and feel the energy of Kvernufoss up close.

To overnight at the falls, Hótel Skógafoss (p86) is about as close as you can get.

Sólheimasandur & Sólheimafjara

A 10-minute (11km) drive east on the Ring Road, past the road to **Sólheimajökull** glacier (on the left), leads to the **Sólheimasandur Plane Wreck Trail** (4km each way, roughly three hours). The walk over the sand is pretty uneventful and flat – unless it's windy or raining (you will certainly want waterproof and windproof gear). The trail arrives at the wreckage of a militarised Douglas DC-3 on a black-sand beach. On 21 November 1973, a US Navy aeroplane was forced to crash-land at Sólheimasandur while en route from Höfn to Keflavík. It's thought that severe ice cover caused both engines to fail. Visitors can peer into the weather-worn shell, which has been stripped of its interiors. Some choose to continue walking down the vast, wild, black-sand **Sólheimafjara Beach**, which is virtually untouched.

Dyrhólaey

Around 12km outside the town of Vík, Rte 218 juts off the Ring Road to **Dyrhólaey**'s towering black cliffs and sweeping views, plus

Along the Way We Met...

LÚÐVÍK KARLSSON I'm very interested in ancient art and old stories, from the time that people were making art to sacrifice or to call their spirits in nature, the spirits that grew in the water, the fire, the sky, the sun and so on; it was a way to contact them. In Viking times, we also had fairy tales about trolls, elves, dwarves and monsters, plus our religion and the gods Óðinn, Þór, Loki, Freyja and Freyr. Lots of people travelling to Iceland feel them. We keep the stories going; I told my kids these fairy tales and they've passed them on to their kids. As you get older, these tales have more significance, as you are more in touch with nature, you are drawn to the mountains again and again because they are calling you. On the beaches, we're aware that the ocean is living, the waves are moving, we see the big animals moving in the sky, there are always new pictures and symbols, you will see it everywhere you go in Iceland.

Lúðvík Karlsson, or Liston, is a folk artist. @ludvik.karlsson

Skógafoss & Kvernufoss — 12.5km — Sólheimasandur & Sólheimafjara — *Head south on Rte 218 for five minutes to dramatic shores.* — 15km the striking 120m-high Dyrhólaey stone sea arch, carved by the pounding Atlantic. Atop the cliffs, guiding ships along this treacherous shore, stands **Dyrhólaey Lighthouse**, first built in 1910 and replaced by the current white concrete structure in 1927.

Thousands of Atlantic puffins nest in the grassy cliff edges, usually from early May until late August. They dig burrows into the soft turf where they lay a single egg, taking turns to incubate it. Birders can see them resting on the cliff edges (bring binoculars) and even diving for small fish such as sand eels. Look for the small **Loftsalahellir** cave near here, which was used for council meetings in Saga times.

Vík

Iceland's southernmost village, the charming fishing settlement of **Vík**, sits right on the Ring Road, with many guesthouses and surprisingly good eating options. One of its biggest draws is **Reynisdrangar**, an incredible stack of basalt columns on the town's **Reynisfjara** beach. With dozens of hexagonal stacks, this striking formation looks like a *Lord of the Rings* castle, but these vertical shapes were created when basalt lava cooled and contracted. Local legends claim that these sea stacks are trolls turned to stone by the sun after trying to drag their boats out to sea and getting caught in the dawn light. Don't leave without strolling the dark volcanic sands offset by the frothy white waves of the Atlantic (be aware of the tides and swell, which have been known to pull people out to sea).

Around town, other sights of note include the striking red **Vík í Myrdal Church** high up on the hill against the deep green cliffs. See it all from above on a thrilling zipline ride with

Reynisdrangar

True Adventure *(trueadventure.is; adult/child 11,900/7900kr; Apr-Oct)* over a mossy canyon and mountains, with views of nearby glaciers. Be sure to stop at the **Lava Show** *(lavashow.com/vik; adult/child 6590/3590kr)*, the only place in the world where you can see a recreation of a volcanic eruption indoors. Real, flowing molten lava is recreated at temperatures of up to 1100°C (2000°F), hissing, crackling, warming and illuminating the dark space during this educational and dramatic experience that showcases the power of nature in complete safety.

If you're hungry at the end of your drive, try Black Crust Pizzeria (p83) or the Soup Company (p83).

Dyrhólaey — 18km — Vík

Climb into Iceland's southernmost town (often through clouds).

Walk on Sólheimajökull

With crampons and ice picks, step directly onto the crisp outlet of the mighty Mýrdalsjökull ice cap. As it melts each year, it constantly shape-shifts and changes colour, from ethereal blue to crystal clear.

HOW TO

Nearest stop: Vík

Getting here: At 32km (around 45 minutes) before Vík, off the Ring Road, park in the small car park at the foot of the glacier. It's not possible to walk on the glacier without a guide, so book with adventure outfits.

Cost: Various companies run guided tours on the glacier, including **Mountain Guides** *(mountainguides.is; 3hr tours from 16,999kr)*, **Tröll Expeditions** *(troll.is; 3hr tours from 13,666kr)* and **Arctic Adventures** *(adventures.is; 3hr tours from adult/child 13,990/11,200kr).*

Glacier Walking Experience

Suitable for beginners and adventurers alike, participants get around 90 minutes on the actual ice during a mesmerising glacier walking experience (after a safety briefing and being kitted out with crampons, ice axe, harness and helmet). **Sólheimajökull** is one of Iceland's most accessible glaciers – it's a short but scenic 10-minute walk across the pitch-black volcanic ash, rock and sands between the car park and the glacier. At the foot of the glacier, you will lace up your crampons and step onto the glacial tongue, which is roughly 8km long and 1km to 2km wide (though it is rapidly retreating due to climate change).

The glacier originates at **Mýrdalsjökull**, which is famously also home to the volcano Katla, one of Iceland's most powerful and active volcanoes, which influences the glacier's landscape. Walking on the icy sheet is a serene and majestic experience and the chance to see panoramic scenes of Sólheimajökull and South Iceland in the distance, plus huge scenic crevasses, caused by the movement of different ice blocks. Ice climbing can be added on to the experience with some tour agencies (inquire ahead). Some of the ice is dotted or carpeted in ash and sand, a reminder of how close the **Eyjafjallajökull** stratovolcano is. This is the debris resulting from the 2010 eruption – giving the glacier a dramatic, marbled look.

Sólheimajökull's glacial features, from its moulins (glacial tunnels and sinkholes)

TOP TIPS

Glacier walking on Sólheimajökull is open all year round, but views are better when skies are clear. Sunglasses are a must in bright weather, as is sunscreen, as the glacier reflects light. For walking, bring sturdy boots with ankle support (hiking boots) and warm clothing as a first layer, waterproof clothing as a second layer, plus hat and gloves. Lastly, don't forget a camera to capture your adventure on the ice.

From top: Sólheimajökull; a group glacier walking

to its crevasses, are constantly changing due to global warming. It is believed that the glacier will have completely melted within the next few decades. It's easy to see meltwater draining through the ice, which materialises as streams and even waterfalls, but most strikingly in the glacial lagoon at the bottom of the outlet. Formed as the ice melts, this growing lagoon often has floating icebergs. Hikers may hear a crashing sound as new icebergs detach from the glacier. No two visits to this living, moving structure are the same – and it will never be as big as it is right now.

Ásbyrgi (p178)
IMAGEBROKER.COM/ALAMY

INSIGHT

Iceland's Storied Landscapes

Traces of the past are often visible in Iceland's landscapes, from bumps in fields that mark abandoned settlements to the cairns of ancient routes across lavafields. A drive along the Ring Road is a journey into an epic past of chieftains and farmers, trolls and elves, told by the land itself.

WORDS BY **EMILY LETHBRIDGE**
Emily is an Associate Research Professor at the Árni Magnússon Institute for Icelandic Studies, Reykjavík.

ICELAND WAS UNDISCOVERED for thousands of years, while elsewhere in the world civilisations rose and fell. It was only in the late 9th century CE that the first settlers arrived from Scandinavia and the British Isles. These early Icelanders worshipped gods such as Óðinn (Odin), Þór (Thor) and Freyja. Archaeology and place names give us insights into the society that these people established, their beliefs and settlement patterns, and the famous *Sagas of Icelanders (Íslendingasögur)* give vivid detail about life on this remote Atlantic island.

Sagas and Settlement

The *Sagas of Icelanders* tell of men and women who were passionate and poetic, greedy and generous, wise and foolish, heroic and often hell-bent on protecting the honour of their family. When Iceland's first settlers discovered the uninhabited island, they chose sites for their homes and established a new society that had no king. The early settlers gave their farms names that are still in use today, and many other landmarks around the country are named in the sagas. Almost every part of Iceland is referenced in a saga, and hundreds of saga-sites are just by the Ring Road.

The sagas were written down in the 13th and 14th centuries by descendants of the early settlers, who drew on a rich body of oral traditions. These narratives are now ranked among other classics of world literature, and Icelanders still read and draw inspiration from them today. A saga like *Njál's Saga* is the cultural equivalent of Shakespeare's *Hamlet,* and the medieval Icelandic in which it was written is to modern Icelandic as Shakespeare's English is to modern English. From the 18th century, translations of these stirring stories made them accessible to readers around the world. By the 19th century, they drew many early travellers to Iceland – along with the country's natural marvels (fire, ice, erupting hot springs). Among them were figures such as designer William Morris, novelist Anthony Trollope, and Mary Millais (daughter of Pre-Raphaelite painter John Everett Millais).

Place Names and the Gods

Sometimes, the sagas explain how places got their names. *Egil's Saga Skallagrímssonar* relates how the first settlers in Borgarfjörður, in West Iceland, explored the region, claiming or being given land parcels and naming them after themselves. Þorbjörn *krumr* ('bent' or 'curved') gave his name to the farm Krumshólar ('Þorbjörn krumr's hills') near Borgarnes (p226), and the nearby Krumskelda bog, where Skallagrímur Kveldúlfsson is said to have hidden a valuable hoard of silver to prevent his son Egill from getting hold of it.

A saga called *Kjalnesinga Saga,* set north of Reykjavík around Kjalarnes and on the mountain Esja (p226), describes how a powerful settler, Þorgrímur *goði* ('chieftain') was an ardent worshipper of the old gods. After establishing a farm, he built a great temple there and the farm became known as Hof ('temple'); according to the saga, the temple was dedicated to the god Þór. It tells of a holy fire on a pedestal inside that was never allowed to go out, animal sacrifices that were feasted on and human sacrifices thrown into nearby Blótkelda ('sacrifice bog'). Antiquarians and archaeologists have looked for evidence to support the saga's account, but nothing convincing has come to light.

Place names that seem to be associated with Þór (such as Þórsnes and Þórshöfn) are found all around Iceland. Other gods also appear here and there in the place-name record. However, scholars have been puzzled by the apparent lack of places in Iceland linked to the worship of Óðinn. The spectacular hoofprint-shaped gorge Ásbyrgi ('Fortress of the Æsir'; p178), however, is said to have been created when Óðinn's eight-legged horse Sleipnir put one hoof down on the ground as Óðinn rode in the heavens above. It's uncertain how old this tradition really is: the oldest written source is a 19th-century poem.

As well as being entertaining, many of these folktales served social functions: regulating people's interaction with dangerous spots, or reminding them how to behave.

Þingvellir: Iceland's Parliament

The dramatic rift valley of Þingvellir ('Assembly plains'; p68) is immensely symbolic in both the sagas and Icelandic history. The sagas describe the annual summer meeting of the national parliament (the Alþingi) here, a two-week period that was the highpoint of the Icelandic political, legal and social calendar. Alongside law-making, it allowed people from all parts of the country to exchange news, trade goods, broker marriage alliances and make merry.

One of the most momentous decisions taken at Þingvellir during the Icelandic 'Republic' (which lasted until 1262) was the country's rejection of the old gods and conversion to Christianity in 999 or 1000. According to tradition, the law-speaker Þorgeir Ljósvetningagoði ('chieftain of the Ljósvetnings') considered the matter for a day and a night as he lay silently under his cloak. He decided that the best way of preserving peace was having one law and one religion; for a time, though, old traditions were permitted to be observed in private. A modern stained-glass window in the church in Akureyri (p194) shows Þorgeir clutching a carving of Óðinn, with the waterfall Goðafoss ('Waterfall of the Gods', p189) behind him. Folk tradition says he threw the pagan statues into the churning water after returning from the meeting.

The Hidden Folk

Vibrant folklore traditions lived alongside Christian belief in Iceland over the centuries. Prominent landforms such as rocks or cliffs will likely have a story associated with them, perhaps featuring trolls, ghosts, *huldufólk* (hidden people or elves) or other supernatural beings. Encounters between otherworldly beings and humans sometimes ended well, and sometimes badly. At Nes in Hornafjörður (east of Höfn) a young woman called Guðrún was alone at home one Christmas. After she'd cleaned the house, a troop of *huldufólk* came in and held an all-night party. Guðrún went to bed and read. The same thing happened the next night, when two elves gave Guðrún a silver belt. On the third night, one young elf-man asked Guðrún for her hand in marriage: she agreed and left with him. When Guðrún's mother came home, she found a purse full of silver and a letter explaining what had happened.

Folktales and Modern Iceland

In the bay of Skagafjörður in North Iceland (a short drive from Varmahlíð, p206), the island of Drangey rises sheer out of the water. Drangey is famous for being the last stronghold of the saga-outlaw Grettir, but a folktale tells of how once, two enormous night-trolls led their cow across the bay to mate with a bull on the other side. When daybreak came, the trolls (and their cow) were still in the middle of the fjord and they were turned to stone. The cow became the island, and the trolls turned into two rock stacks: Kerlingin ('the old woman') is still there, but Karlinn ('the old man') crumbled into the sea in 1755 during an earthquake.

As well as being entertaining, many of these folktales served social functions: regulating people's interaction with dangerous spots, or reminding them how to behave. Before printed maps became widely available, knowledge of stories about places helped people to develop mental maps that made navigation easier. Today, digital maps make travelling around Iceland's Ring Road straightforward – but knowing some of the stories of the places along the way adds another dimension to these stunning landscapes.

Goðafoss (p189)

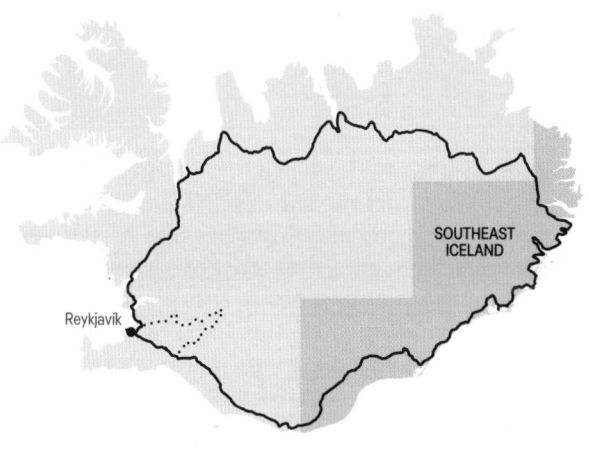

SOUTHEAST ICELAND

Here, the Ring Road enters one of its most spectacular stretches. The road rises and falls gently between a wall of cliffs and glaciers that plunge down off the Vatnajökull ice cap (Europe's largest): Fjaðrárgljúfur, Skaftafell and Jökulsárlón are big-ticket highlights among many. Further east, glacier country recedes behind you and the road winds past deep bays tucked between towering mountains; these once-isolated Eastfjords communities are full of hidden treasures – an invitation to slow down and soak in the wild land around you.

Vatnajökull (p115)
SUMOS/GETTY IMAGES

Vík

If you're coming from the west, this is where the Ring Road really starts to soar. If you're coming from the east, it's like a dramatic crescendo to a remarkable symphony. This glorious stretch of road crosses vast glacial outwash plains, draws near to waterfalls and glaciers, and, at Skaftafell, combines exuberant natural drama with a network of hiking trails just waiting to be explored. Not surprisingly, it's where many first-time visitors irretrievably fall for this miraculous country.

Anthony Ham

Skaftafell (p111)
MORENO01/SHUTTERSTOCK

Skaftafell

142KM — 2 HOURS' DRIVE

THIS LEG:
- Vík
- Hjörleifshöfði
- Blautakvísl
- Mýrdalssandur
- Skaftáreldahraun
- Skaftárstofa Visitor Centre
- Kirkjubæjarklaustur
- Dverghamrar
- Hverfisfljót
- Km99 Picnic Area
- Núpsvötn
- Skaftafell

Driving Notes

There's an old Icelandic saying that the country has three weather conditions (rain, cold and wind), and if just one of these is missing, it's beautiful weather. Count your blessings if you get 'beautiful weather' along this section. Otherwise, drive carefully as roads can be slippery when wet, icy when cold and a challenge when windy.

Breaking Your Journey
With only two hours from start to end if you drive without stopping, there's not much need for a pit stop. Just as well: the only place to get fuel and food is Kirkjubæjarklaustur, which has a handful of places to sleep and eat, and a small supermarket. Otherwise, stock up on supplies in Vík or Höfn.

Anthony's Tips

BEST MEAL Any picnic spot, or the Icelandic lamb at Kjarr in Kirkjubæjarklaustur (p109).

FAVOURITE VIEW The top viewing platform at Fjaðrárgljúfur (p108).

ESSENTIAL STOP It has to be Skaftafell (p111) with everything it offers.

ROAD-TRIP TIP Toilet breaks needn't be an issue: there's a public toilet at the turn-off to Hrífunes, 40km northeast of Vík.

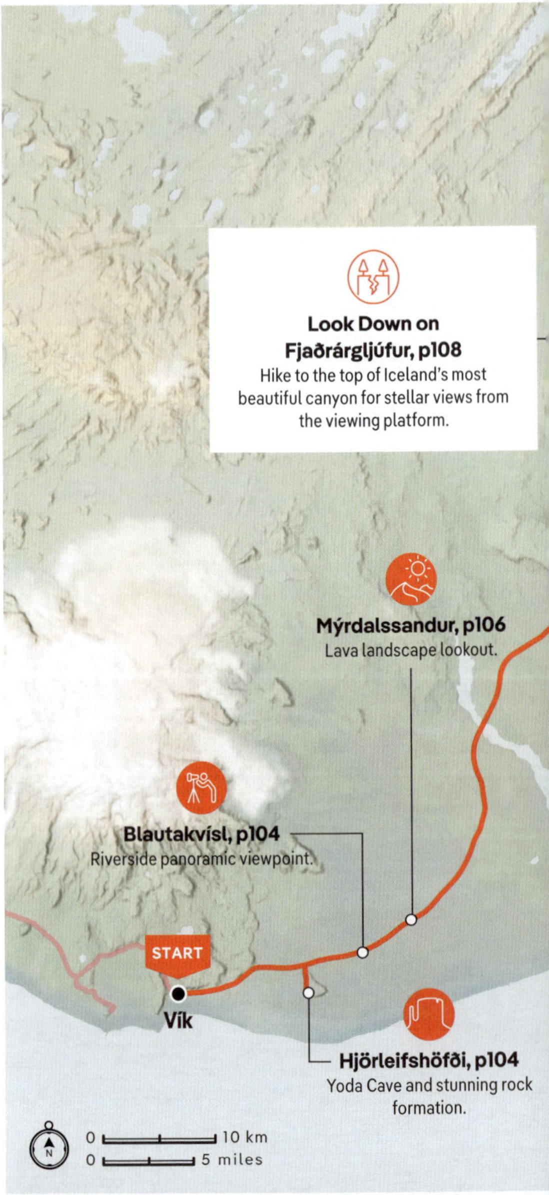

Look Down on Fjaðrárgljúfur, p108
Hike to the top of Iceland's most beautiful canyon for stellar views from the viewing platform.

Mýrdalssandur, p106
Lava landscape lookout.

Blautakvísl, p104
Riverside panoramic viewpoint.

START
Vík

Hjörleifshöfði, p104
Yoda Cave and stunning rock formation.

0 — 10 km
0 — 5 miles

PREVIOUS STOP This route begins at Vík (p91), close to the southernmost tip of mainland Iceland.

Hjörleifshöfði

Long before you reach the turn-off to **Hjörleifshöfði**, which is 13km northwest of Vík, this large and spectacular monolith south off the Ring Road looms superbly on the horizon. Far longer than it is high (221m), it was once an island. Thankfully, it's now accessible by land and still offers fine views all along the coast and to the panoramic sweep of highlands to the north. A rough gravel road – which may be OK for 2WD vehicles in summer – leads south along the western flank of the mountain. This is privately owned land and goes by the name of **Viking Park** (vikingpark.is; per car 750kr). Drive the full 2km to P2, then walk 100m to **Gígjagjá**, or **Yoda Cave** – from the inside, it bears a remarkable resemblance to the *Star Wars* character, Yoda!

Various trails (including from the P1 parking area signposted off the route to Gígjagjá) climb to the high plateau atop Hjörleifshöfði where, at its highest point, the remains of a grave mark the final resting place of Hjörleifur Hróðmarsson, a Viking and brother-in-law of Iceland's first Norse settler, Ingólfur Arnarson. Local legend has it that he was killed by his Irish slaves.

In summer, you can also circumnavigate Hjörleifshöfði on foot; around the rarely visited eastern side, beneath the cliffs, there are moments when you'll feel like the only person on the planet. Allow at least a couple of hours for the full hike, plus another if you climb up and back.

Blautakvísl

As you leave Hjörleifshöfði behind, the landscape opens up; one of those spare and beautiful Icelandic landscapes that feels somehow eternal. South of the road, plains – green as green in summer, or snowbound in winter – unfurl with perspective-altering flatness to the ocean, which is visible from the road. North of the road, broad gravel plains cross an empty landscape all the way to the highlands.

Gígjagjá

Vík — 13km — Hjörleifshöfði — 5km

The road in is rough – stick to 30km/h.

Skaftáreldahraun (p107)

Driving this stretch feels like a road movie set against a backdrop of unrelenting beauty. Roll down the window and feel the wind in your hair.

It's easy to miss this stop, but around 5km beyond the Hjörleifshöfði turn-off a small bridge crosses the river **Blautakvísl**. A blue sign announces the river's name, but it can be difficult to see until you stop; look for the white sign that says 'Skaftárhreppur'. There's enough room for a couple of cars to pull over on the western side of the bridge.

Check that no vehicles are coming, then cross to the north side of the road for spellbinding views. Blautakvísl comes down off the ice cap crowned by the Mýrdalsjökull glacier, one of

VOLCANIC POWER

In 1783, around 135 craters on Laki shot molten rock 1km into the air for eight months, creating the lavafield Skaftáreldahraun (p107). The hundreds of millions of tonnes of ash and sulphuric acid that poured from the fissures blotted out the sun, two-thirds of Iceland's livestock perished from starvation and poisoning, and some 9000 people – a fifth of the country's population – were killed; the survivors faced the *Móðuharðindin* ('Hardship of the Mist'), a terrible famine. Across the northern hemisphere, especially in mainland Europe, clouds of ash blocked the sun. Temperatures dropped and acid rain fell, causing devastating crop failures.

Avoid taking photos from the bridge itself (dangerous when vehicles pass).

Blautakvísl — 5km — Mýrdalssandur

Along the Way We Met...

MONIKA DOMŻALSKA Iceland is a wonderful place to find peace and healing. I love the Yoda Cave – it's a very spiritual place. Or the lavafields – they look very flat, but when you go deeper, it is very beautiful. They believe in elves and trolls here, and there is something about this place – when I am out in nature, I never feel like I am alone. And the glaciers at Skaftafell are next-level – volcanoes are one thing, but glaciers and the ice hold the memory of this land.

Monika is a traveller and photographer from Poland who plans to become a glacier guide.

MONIKA'S TIP: *Shops are very far from places and they don't open for long, so always make sure you have enough food.*

---

the loveliest in Iceland. The river eddies and flows over gravel islands, making scenes of elemental blacks and whites or blues and greens, depending on the season.

Mýrdalssandur

A further 5km up the road, 23km from Vík, a sign points north off the road to a picnic site; however, the sign announcing 'Toilet 17km' is easier to spot. Picnic by all means, but it's a landscape worth contemplating.

What you're crossing to reach this point, and what you can see extending in all directions, are the black-lava sand flats of **Mýrdalssandur**. They were formed by everything – gravel, silt, sand – that was washed out over the years by flowing lava from beneath Mýrdalsjökull, including when the volcano Katla last erupted on a grand scale in 1918. Covering 700 sq km, the landscape is both desolate and eerily beautiful, a hallucinatory void that is utterly compelling; see it at twilight and you'll understand why local legends claim it to be haunted.

One such tale attaches to Katla herself, whom many believed was a witch who lived at a monastery high in the mountains. When she found out that the monastery's abbot had borrowed her magical breeches, which allowed her to run forever without getting tired, she killed him. With the murder about to be discovered, she put on her breeches and was never seen again. But the legend doesn't end there – Katla's eruptions and floods are thought to be the witch venting her fury.

As you think about this, sit quietly by the crystal-blue stream and watch for Arctic foxes on the hunt and seabirds wheeling and screeching overhead.

Skaftáreldahraun

Some landscapes are compelling because of their beauty, others because of their profound strangeness. **Skaftáreldahraun** definitely falls into the latter category.

Coming from the west, you will cross part of the 600-sq-km lavafield from the 1783–84 Laki eruption before reaching the Skaftáreldahraun turn-off. Less obvious and unusual when covered with snow, this lavafield takes on a green tinge when exposed thanks to the moss that has colonised the lava remains; it's an extraordinary sight most of the time, but especially spectacular immediately after rain.

The turn-off leads to a small car park (which, unusually for South Iceland, is free!), where a 50m track between the boulders brings you to an elevated viewing platform that rises above this otherworldly terrain.

Alongside the path and car park, you can see the moss up close; in places it grows 50cm deep.

Skaftárstofa Visitor Centre

Just after passing the turn-off to Fjaðrárgljúfur (p108) and Laki, and on the cusp of arriving in Kirkjubæjarklaustur, turn north to the excellent **Skaftárstofa Visitor Centre** (8.30am-5.30pm mid-May–mid-Sep, 9am-5pm rest of year). It was built to celebrate Vatnajökull National Park's inscription on UNESCO's World Heritage List in 2019. The first thing you notice is the daring design – the sharp, jutting angles mimic the ice cap's jagged shapes, and the turf roof honours traditional turf houses (p216).

Inside, there's an airy cafe, an information desk that can help with advice on hiking and exploring the park, and a small gift shop. But the

Mýrdalssandur

Look Down on Fjaðrárgljúfur

A prime candidate for the coveted title of Iceland's most beautiful canyon, Fjaðrárgljúfur is a natural gem that lies hidden from the Ring Road in its own magical world.

HOW TO

Nearest stop: Kirkjubæjarklaustur is 5km east of the Fjaðrárgljúfur turn-off.

Getting here: The easiest way to reach the site is by car; otherwise it's a 2km uphill climb from the turn-off.

Parking: The main parking area leaves you with a 2km uphill hike that takes you past three viewpoints. The much smaller top car park (follow the signs to Laki) is 500m from the top of the canyon. Both cost 1040kr per vehicle *(parka.is)*.

When to go: The site is usually open year-round but gets incredibly busy in July and August. Visit under the midnight sun and have it all to yourself.

Anyone of reasonable fitness can make the climb to Fjaðrárgljúfur from the lower (main) car park, and everyone who can, should: it's simply the best way to experience this natural marvel.

The path is steady rather than steep, and passes between a grassy hillside on your right, and glimpses of the lower part of the canyon on your left. In no time at all, you reach the first viewpoint (which has a small rock window).

There are better views higher up, but this is a chance to catch your breath and see the canyon's distinctive form with the river Fjaðrá at the bottom, and jutting cliff outcrops crowding in above.

All the way up, you'll catch photo-worthy glimpses, with the tall, textured mountain wall behind it as backdrop. But the best views are from the metal viewing platform – the waterfall, with emerald-green hues offset by the black cliffs that seem to interweave above the waters.

And yes, it's true – Justin Bieber did film the clip for 'I'll Show You' here.

MARTIN VALIGURSKY/SHUTTERSTOCK

star of the show is the interactive exhibition 'Life with Nature', covering the ecology and geology of the park. It's only small, but allow an hour to do it justice.

There are a couple of good sleeping options not far away, including Maddis (p112) and Hótel Hrífunes by Ourhotels (p112).

Kirkjubæjarklaustur

The only 'town' of any size along the entire route (albeit with a population of fewer than 200 people), **Kirkjubæjarklaustur** is an important way station. Part of its value is practical – it has a handful of restaurants, a small supermarket and a couple of petrol stations.

But it's also worth a quick explore for its own sake. Start with the basalt columns of **Kirkjugólf** (Church Floor), 400m northwest of the N1 petrol station along Rte 203. Although entirely natural in origin, the formations were once thought to be the ruins of a church – an easy mistake to make. Just west of the supermarket, the A-frame stone-and-wood village church, **Steingrímsson Memorial Chapel**, dates back to 1974 and honours Jón Steingrímsson's famous 'Eldmessa' (Fire Sermon), which 'saved' the town from lava on 20 July 1783.

Keep going west through town to the pretty double waterfall, **Systrafoss**. Apart from the falls themselves, walks lead through a copse of Iceland's tallest trees. Take the steps that lead up above the falls to see lake **Systravatn**, which, according to local legend, was once a suitably secluded bathing place for nuns and now offers all-encompassing views.

Kirkjubæjarklaustur has easily the best range of eating options between Vík and Skaftafell – try Kjarr or Systrakaffi.

BEST PLACES TO EAT

Kjarr, Kirkjubæjarklaustur $$
Excellent contemporary bistro near the base of Systrafoss, signposted throughout town; the seasonal menu includes locally caught Arctic char. *(kjarrrestaurant.is; noon-10pm)*

Systrakaffi, Kirkjubæjarklaustur $$
Charming cafe with an outdoor terrace. This place does terrific Icelandic lamb and local trout in a deliberately non-wi-fi setting. It gets super-busy in summer. *(systrakaffi.is; noon-9.30pm)*

Glacier Goodies, Skaftafell $
This food truck near the visitor centre is wildly and deservedly popular at lunchtime for its lobster soup, fish and chips and baby back ribs. *(11.30am-7.30pm mid-May–Sep)*

Dverghamrar

Around 11km east of Kirkjubæjarklaustur, on the south side of the road, a sign indicates a small car park. From here, a short walking path leads down off the bluff to **Dverghamrar** ('Dwarf Rocks'), two low but striking cliffs of basalt columns. Formed some two million years ago by cooling, contracting lava, the cliffs aren't visible until near the end of the path – the whole site seems very low-key until they suddenly emerge like an apparition. Local legend holds that the cliffs are inhabited by Iceland's 'hidden people'...

Hverfisfljót

A few clicks past Dverghamrar, the road swings around to the north, and a vast coastal floodplain opens up. You're about to enter another of the more spectacular sections of the route. Just before the bridge that crosses the river **Hverfisfljót**, a parking and picnic area eases down off the Ring Road to a pretty spot just above the riverbank.

This is one of our favourite pull-overs anywhere along the route, with everything that's good about South Iceland on display. To the north and northwest, the Siðujökull and Skeiðarárjökull glaciers wash down off the looming Vatnajökull ice cap; these giant rivers of ice are two of the largest in this part of the country. Looking east, the cliffs that form the backdrop to the delta floodplain take on the most dramatic of shapes. And the river itself, which carried lava and debris down off the heights during the 1783 Laki eruption (p105), is one of the country's wonderfully textured waterways, with gravel islands, grassy riverbanks and gushing waters.

Dverghamrar (p109)

Km99 Picnic Area

There is so much magnificence in Iceland that even unheralded picnic spots can prompt one to stop and stare in wonder. Around 99km from Vík, or 38km from the Skaftafell turn-off, an unnamed **picnic area** on the north side of the road is one of our favourite roadside viewpoints in all Iceland.

The picnic area faces a gorgeous river canyon coming down out of the mountains from the north. The combination of rushing water, low, jagged cliffs, and superb backdrop of the ice cap makes this a really special sight, although it's a little concealed from the picnic tables. It's so beautiful that, this being Iceland, we're not sure why someone hasn't built a larger car park and started charging for the privilege of enjoying the view.

Núpsvötn

Another quite spectacular picnic area by a river near **Núpsvötn** offers the opportunity to look in awe upon the **Skeiðarársandur**.

At 1300 sq km, it's the largest sandur (sand delta) in the world, and it's still growing, eating away at the margins and continuing its centuries-long consumption of farmland. It all began with the 1362 eruption of the volcano beneath Öræfajökull (at the time known as Knappafellsjökull) and the subsequent *jökulhlaup* (flooding caused by volcanic eruption beneath ice) wiped out the entire district.

After 1362, the area became known as Öræfi (Wasteland).

The stretch of Ring Road that crosses Skeiðarársandur was not completed until 1974; before then, to reach Reykjavík from Höfn, locals had to travel via Akureyri. It's still susceptible to the vagaries of high-country volcanoes: in late 1996 three Ring Road bridges were washed away by the massive *jökulhlaup* released by the Grímsvötn (or Gjálp) eruption.

Skaftafell

One of the most remarkable and accessible natural wonders in Iceland, **Skaftafell** *(parking per vehicle 1040kr)* is worth as much time as you can give it. The hikes here are among the finest along the south coast, and it's a terrific opportunity to enjoy all of Iceland's greatest hits – glaciers (p113), waterfalls, mountains, hiking (p114) – in one place, and in one day.

> **SHIFTING SANDS & SAGAS**
>
> Skaftafell may now be an integral part of **Vatnajökull National Park**, but it was formerly private land. A homestead once lay at the base of the mountains, west of the current campsite. Over the centuries, floods and shifting glacial sands consumed the fields until Skaftafell became known as Hérað Milli Sanda (Land Between the Sands). All hope of farming here came to an end after several volcanic eruptions in 1362. Although the glacier nearly swallowed it in the 17th century, the farm survived over at Svínafell – it is the setting for one of Iceland's best-loved tales, *Njál's Saga*.

Skeiðarársandur

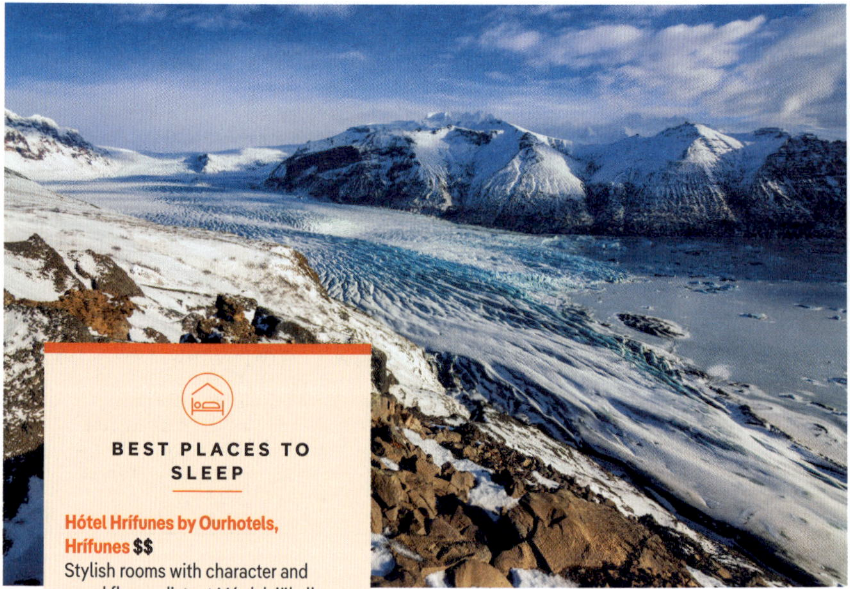

FROM LEFT: JULEN ARABAOLAZA/GETTY IMAGES, NATALLIA YAUMENENKA/SHUTTERSTOCK, ROMAN SHATKHIN/SHUTTERSTOCK

Skaftafellsjökull

BEST PLACES TO SLEEP

Hótel Hrífunes by Ourhotels, Hrífunes $$
Stylish rooms with character and wood floors, distant Mýrdalsjökull views from the property and good breakfasts. It's 7km off the Ring Road. *(ourhotels.is)*

Fosshotel Glacier Lagoon, near Skaftafell $$$
One of few full-service hotels in the area, this four-star place has sleek Nordic design and a good restaurant. *(islandshotel.is)*

Maddis, Fjaðrárgljúfur $$$
Slick Nordic cabins in light timber hues and lots of glass make this the pick of the places close to Fjaðrárgljúfur canyon. You're so close (2km), you could even walk.

But Skaftafell is also an important place to meet other needs, especially along this stretch of road that has only one town and very few other facilities. Staff at the small visitor centre can help you choose which hikes best suit your interests, and there's a food van and a cafe, public toilets and a couple of adventure tour operators. You could easily spend an hour absorbing the fascinating information panels and photos.

For a meal, the cafe is good, but the street food van Glacier Goodies (p109) is our pick. To stay nearby overnight, consider Fosshotel Glacier Lagoon.

Núpsvötn

35km

Plan on spending five to six hours at Skaftafell.

Skaftafell

Walk to Skaftafellsjökull

On a short walk from the visitor centre at Skaftafell, you can get so close to the glacier you can almost reach out and touch it.

HOW TO

Nearest stop: The walk starts at Skaftafell visitor centre.

Getting here: There's a large car park here *(parka.is; 1040kr per vehicle)*. Reykjavík–Höfn buses stop at the visitor centre, and there's a summer bus shuttle between Skaftafell and Jökulsárlón.

When to go: The walking track is usually open year-round, but winds can be icy and rain always possible.

Most glaciers aren't this easy to reach; certainly not on foot. Most of the track to Skaftafellsjökull (path S1; 3.7km return) passes in the shadow of the steep hillside and is flat and easy: you'll walk among bluebells in summer and see tiny waterfalls dripping down off the heights. The visitor centre estimates that the walk should take 30 minutes one-way, although it's certainly possible to do it in less time than that. Skaftafellsjökull is a relatively small glacier by Iceland's standards, although it's mighty impressive up close. The path takes you to an overlook, from which steps lead down onto the black volcanic sands that surround a large glacier lagoon, with a handful of floating icebergs usually bobbing on the waters. Paths also lead around to the narrow gap between glacier and mountain, and this is where you get *really* close. Although the ice this low down is more black than white, it's still riven with white fissures, and it's here that you'll be spellbound by the bumps and groans of the ice.

From left: Bluebells; Skaftafell glacier lagoon

Beyond the Crowds

Too often in Iceland, the best trails are accessible only to those on major, multiday expeditions. Skaftafell's gift is to open up landscapes just as beautiful to everyone. The only question is how far you're willing to go.

Nearest stop: Like the glacier walk (p113), these hikes begin at Skaftafell Visitor Centre. Only this time, head west, instead of east.

Getting here by car: Park at the large multi-section car park *(parka.is; 1040kr per vehicle)*; get here as early in the day as you can in summer as spaces fill up fast.

Getting here by public transport: Buses between Reykjavík and Höfn pass by the visitor centre, or take the summer-only bus between Jökulsárlón and Skaftafell.

When to go: Most tracks are year-round, but ask at the visitor centre. Early morning or late evening make for quieter trails.

The Svartifoss Hike Up

Svartifoss (Black Falls) occupies a special place in the pantheon of Icelandic waterfalls. And even if you think you've seen enough waterfalls for a lifetime, don't miss this one.

The walk up here begins at the visitor centre and climbs gently through the forest for 1.8km to a spot where, previously hidden from view, Svartifoss appears in all its brooding glory. Far from the highest of Iceland's cascades, it wins plaudits for the vertical basalt columns, some seemingly suspended in mid-air, that surround the falls. It's hard to look away, and easy to imagine trolls lurking in the shadows.

A Different Way Back

In summer, this is one of Iceland's most popular hikes. To make sure that the trail doesn't get overrun, the park authorities encourage hikers to return via a different route. Instead of returning down the hill, continue west up the track to **Sjónarsker**, where a view disc identifies all the landmarks you can see. From here, Skeiðarársandur (p110)

seems to stretch for a dizzying eternity. On your way back down to the base of the mountains (coming out near the campsite), you'll pass the turf-roofed farmhouse known as **Sel**.

All told, the trek (path S2) covers 5.3km and should take around two hours.

Going into the Backcountry

If you were to hike beyond Svartifoss, you'd lose perhaps 98% of the crowds. The landscape up here is like a highland plateau, haired with heath and feeling like a soulful escape high above the world and its noise.

ANNA GORIN/GETTY IMAGES

THE LARGEST ICE CAP

Vatnajökull is the world's largest ice cap outside the poles. At 7800 sq km, it's more than three times the size of Luxembourg, with an average thickness of 400m to 600m (and a maximum of 950m, or nearly a kilometre!). Beneath this enormous blanket of ice lie countless peaks and valleys, including live volcanoes and subglacial lakes, plus Iceland's highest point – the 2110m mountain Hvannadalshnúkur. Around 30 outlet glaciers flow down from the centre of Vatnajökull to the lowlands along Iceland's south coast.

Svartifoss

One such option (path S5/S6) extends east from Svartifoss, across the heathlands to a lookout called **Sjónarnípa** – the views from here out over Skaftafellsjökull are superb. By the time you get back down to the visitor centre, you'll have walked 7.4km, probably in around three hours in total.

Also possible is the five- to six-hour traverse (path S3; 16.7km) of Skaftafellsheiði (Skaftafell Heath) to a point where you can look down into the lost, rarely seen world of **Morsárjökull** and its iceberg-filled lagoon.

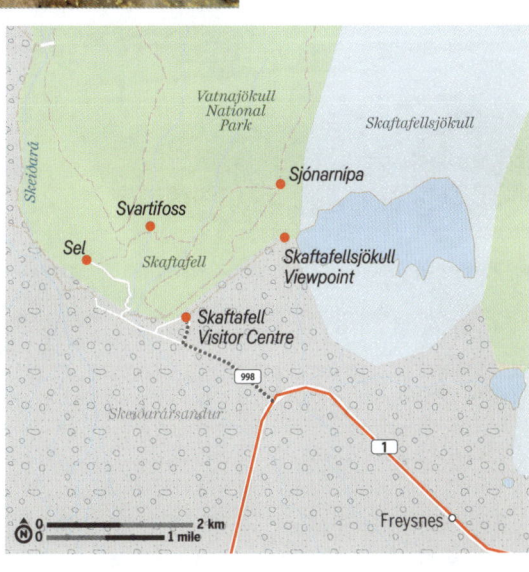

Skaftafell

When people imagine Iceland, there's a good chance many of them are dreaming of Jökulsárlón – its looming glaciers, or lagoons and black-sand beaches scattered with icebergs. Having arrived at one of Iceland's premier attractions, you'll discover glacier upon glacier, with just a few lonely settlements in between. At journey's end, Höfn combines superb location and glacier views with a growing reputation as the best place to eat in southern Iceland.

Jökulsárlón glacier lagoon (p128)
NORTHSKY FILMS/SHUTTERSTOCK

Anthony Ham

Höfn

141.5 KM
2 HOURS' DRIVE

THIS LEG:

- Skaftafell
- Svínafellsjökull
- Glacier Horses
- Sandfell
- Litla Hof
- Kvíárjökull
- Fjallsárlón
- Nýgræðuöldur
- Jökulsárlón
- Fellsfjara
- Heinabergsjökull
- Hoffellsjökull
- Höfn

Driving Notes

Everyone who visits Iceland visits Jökulsárlón, which means long processions of vehicles and full car parks in summer. Give space to cars in front – drivers tend to stop suddenly in the middle of this stretch of road for a photo, or to decipher a road sign! More than anywhere else in Iceland, arriving early at Jökulsárlón (or later in the evening) is strongly advised.

Breaking Your Journey

There are no towns along this route; only Höfn, at journey's end, has supermarkets, petrol stations and proper restaurants. Thankfully, Jökulsárlón has a basic cafe and three excellent food trucks right next to the main car park, where there's also a handful of charging stations for EVs.

Anthony's Tips

BEST MEAL A tie between the lobster baguette at Hafnarbúðin (p131) or anything at Pakkhús (p131).

FAVOURITE VIEW Into the maw of Jökulsárlón on a boat tour (p128).

ESSENTIAL STOP Yes, it's a cliché, but it's popular for good reason – Jökulsárlón (p128).

ROAD-TRIP TIP Pay for parking at Jökulsárlón (and elsewhere in Iceland) on the Parka app or at *parka.is*.

Fjallsárlón, p123 Take a Zodiac to the edge of the ice.

Svínafellsjökull, p120 Hike to this quiet glacier.

Sandfell, p121 Relive an ancient story.

Kvíárjökull, p122 A beautiful lagoon and glacier.

START Skaftafell

Glacier Horses, p120 Ride an Icelandic horse.

Litla Hof, p122 Visit a turf-roofed church.

Ingólfshöfði Hut

Ingólfshöfði

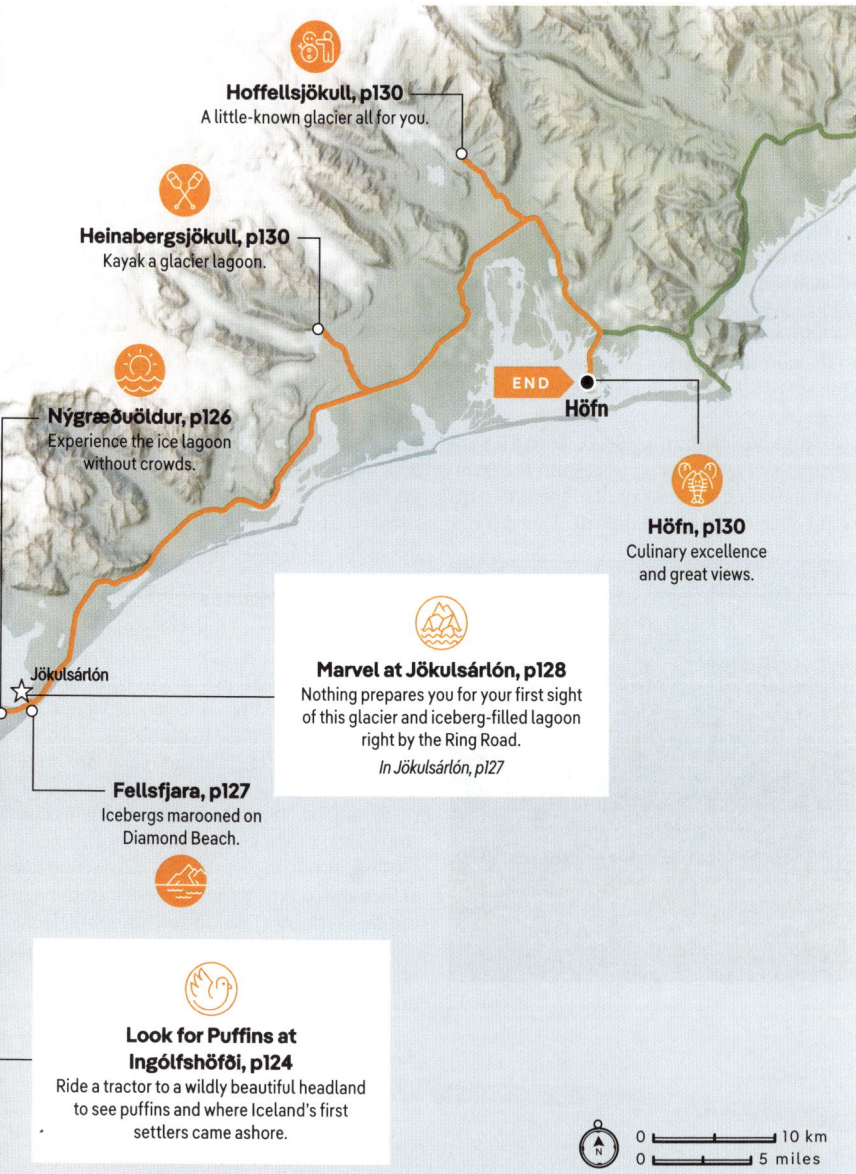

PREVIOUS STOP This leg starts at Skaftafell (p111), around halfway between Vík and Höfn.

Svínafellsjökull

Across the outwash plain east of Skaftafell, two tiny farm settlements, Svínafell and Freysnes, provide an antidote to the popularity of Skaftafell. They lie just off the Ring Road and they're bypassed by almost everyone as people rush from one big-ticket attraction (Skaftafell) to the next (Jökulsárlón). There's no reason to stop at Freysnes, but Svínafell is another matter altogether.

Around 2km off the Ring Road, down a rough-hewn gravel track that goes beyond the farm, you can walk from a car park to the very edge of the glacier **Svínafellsjökull**. There aren't many places you can get this close to the glacier snout (which threatened to engulf the farm in the 17th century but is now retreating). Don't even think about climbing up onto the glacier without a guide and the necessary equipment. Some tour companies run glacier tours here as well as trips to ice caves in winter.

Another option (which you can also begin just east of the visitor centre at Skaftafell) is the **Jöklaleið** or **Ölduslóð** (Glacier Trail; J3) – a hike or cycle (if you have your own bike) between Svínafell and Skaftafell, from one glacier to the next and across the quiet moraine and plains in between. The 8km walk should take around two hours one-way, with fabulous views all the way.

Glacier Horses

Close to Svínafell, the small operator **Glacier Horses** (*glacierhorses.is; per person 14,500-18,000kr*) allows you to combine two of our favourite things in Iceland: glaciers and Icelandic horses. Unlike many outfits, this place specialises in short (75-minute and two-hour) trail rides, meaning that you can enjoy the experience and fold it neatly into a day rich in other stops. Most riding levels are catered for, and on the longer trail, they promise to take you to one of their own secret glacier viewpoints (although the views are breathtaking on both trails).

They open at 9am and remain open until 6pm, offering rides from May to mid-November. Book in advance.

Svínafell

FROM LEFT: HEMIS/ALAMY, SERGOD/GETTY IMAGES

Skaftafell — 6km — Svínafellsjökull — 6km —

The road here is unpaved but fine for 2WDs.

Svínafellsjökull

Sandfell

There's something about **Sandfell**... This quiet spot on the lower slopes of a steep hillside a few hundred metres off the Ring Road tells a haunting tale.

The site was settled during the first wave of Viking arrivals to Iceland. It was owned by a widow, Þogerður, whose husband died at sea en route to Iceland; she was the only female settler to own land in Iceland at the time. Local custom held that women could own land 'no larger than the area a two-year-old heifer could be led between sunrise and sunset on a spring

SAGAS IN SVÍNAFELL

Njál's Saga is one of the most popular and best-known of all Icelandic sagas – bookshops and souvenir shops across the country sell a Penguin edition of the epic tale, which begins around 960 CE and runs through to 1020. The farm here at Svínafell was the home of one of the lead characters, Flosi Þórðarson, who burned Njál and his family to death in *Njál's Saga*. It was also at the Svínafell site that the two families were finally reconciled, ending one of the bloodiest feuds in Icelandic history.

Glacier Horses — 4km — *For horse riding in North Iceland, see p176.* — **Sandfell**

> **BEST PLACES TO SLEEP**
>
> **Guesthouse Skálafell, near Heinabergsjökull $$**
> Stay on this working farm, with rooms in the farmhouse and motel-style units and cottages. *(skalafell.net)*
>
> **Milk Factory, Höfn $$**
> There's no better place to stay in Höfn than this renovated dairy factory with 17 modern, hotel-standard rooms. *(milkfactory.is)*
>
> **REY Stays, Höfn $$**
> Cute cabin rooms that face onto the mountains just off the Ring Road 5km from Höfn. There's also a two-bedroom apartment nearby.
>
> **Hótel Jökulsárlón, Ring Road $$$**
> One of the closest full-service hotels to Jökulsárlón, this stylish spot swathed in Scandi pine has big-sky views.

day'. Undeterred, Þogerður walked her cow all through the Ingólfshöfði district, between the rivers Kviá and Jökulsá. It was, in the end, one of the largest farms in the area, and she built her main farm buildings here at Sandfell. After catastrophic flooding and volcanic eruptions through the centuries, the farm was abandoned in the 1940s.

This reminder of the difficulty of surviving Iceland's brutal natural disasters is now a forlorn site – the cemetery survives, but the church and all the farm buildings were long ago dismantled. The two shady areas contain a few traces of the settlement, and they're beautiful spots to look out towards the distant sea and wonder what might have been.

Litla Hof

As you travel around Iceland, you'll see plenty of turf-roofed homes. But only a handful of turf-roofed churches remain, and there's none prettier than **Hofskirkja** at **Litla Hof**, a tiny hamlet just off the Ring Road. Looking for all the world like a hobbit dwelling, the cute yellow facade opens onto a brightly coloured interior (perhaps to compensate for the lack of windows on three sides) with rock walls.

Entering, you will immediately notice how well the traditional design muffles all outside noise and keeps the warmth within – the effect is particularly obvious on a cold winter's day. Still a functioning church, it's the venue for small Sunday services.

Kvíárjökull

Kvíárjökull is another of Southeast Iceland's glaciers that is easily seen from a Ring Road car park; reaching the actual ice would require quite a hike, as the glacier retreats further with each passing year. Park in the small car park and follow the path into the scenic valley.

Kvíárjökull's specs are pretty impressive – it's 11km long and starts its descent high on the crater rim of Öræfajökull, dropping steeply for nearly 2km in altitude. For its final descent, it pushes through a narrow (700m-wide) gap in the mountains that the glacier itself created – a reminder of the sheer weight and unstoppable earth-shaping force of so much ice.

Sandfell — 8km — Litla Hof — 14km — Kvíárjökull — 14km — Fjallsárlón

For Kvíárjökull, look for the sign for 'Kvíármýrarkambur'.

The glacier once reached much closer to the road and car park, but its retreat has left behind a vast, 100m-deep amphitheatre, now filled by a glacial lagoon. It is believed that the glacier itself filled the amphitheatre until as recently as 1890, and blocks of ice once tumbled down to what is now the Ring Road. The melting of the ice and the glacier's retreat has accelerated since the early 2000s. The view is worth the climb.

Fjallsárlón

If it weren't for Jökulsárlón, **Fjallsárlón** would be world-famous. Here, the superb glacier Fjallsjökull forges down off the Vatnajökull ice cap. At its base, huge blocks of ice calve off into a lagoon, where the newly formed icebergs look for an outlet to the sea. It's not quite as visually arresting as Jökulsárlón – you don't tend to get the really blue icebergs here, and they're not visible from the road. But nonetheless, don't miss it – it's a spectacular spot. The lagoon here is smaller and more concentrated, and Fjallsárlón is a whole lot quieter than its better-known neighbour, which lies 10km to the east.

Apart from walking to the viewing platform and setting out around the lagoon's shoreline, the best way to see Fjallsárlón is with **Fjallsárlón Glacial Lagoon Boat Tours** *(fjallsarlon.is; adult/child 10,500/5500kr)*, which have a ticket office in the car park. From April to October, it runs 45-minute Zodiac trips among lagoon icebergs and close to the glacier's snout.

Also in summer, from mid-June to mid-August at 3pm daily, park rangers lead a free guided walk (45 minutes) around the lagoon, explaining the region's natural and human history.

If you're here in winter, the same outfit runs 3½-hour excursions to a stunning **ice cave** *(adult/child 24,500/18,375kr)* at the **Breiðamerkurjökull** glacier tongue, a four-hour **glacier hike** *(per person 14 years & over 19,800kr)*, and longer overnight expeditions.

Hofskirkja, Litla Hof

Look for Puffins at Ingólfshöfði

Ingólfshöfði is like something out of a hallucinatory dream. The headland landscape with its unimaginable sweep of black sand is one thing, but the animating presence of puffins and the fun tractor ride to get there mean no-one forgets a visit.

HOW TO

Nearest stop: Sits between the stops of Litla Hof and Kvíárjökull.

Getting here: The only way to visit is on a tour, which you need to organise through **From Coast to Mountains** *(fromcoasttomountains.is)*; the company is run by Einar, one of Iceland's most experienced guides.

When to go: May to late August.

Tip: Don't just turn up and expect to go – bookings must be made in advance and online.

A First Look
At the turn-off along the Ring Road to **Ingólfshöfði** (pronounced *in-golvs-huv-thi*), the coastal plain sweeps down towards the glittering sea, and it can be difficult to tell where land ends and the ocean begins. On a clear day, you might be able to make out Ingólfshöfði, a magical 76m-high tableland promontory that rises from the flatlands like an apparition so beautiful you wonder if it isn't a mirage.

Open to visitors only in spring and summer, this superb, isolated nature reserve with its seabird colonies can only be visited on a tour through **From Coast to Mountains** *(fromcoasttomountains.com; adult/child 11,500/5750kr)*. And just to really cement this place in the affections of Icelanders, it's named after the first (9th-century) settler to land on Icelandic shores.

The Approach
To reach the reserve, everyone piles into a tractor-drawn wagon! It's an odd but strangely enjoyable way to travel, and there is a reason for it – it harks back to the first tours ever offered here by the owner-farmer of the land. It has become such a part of the experience that we can't imagine it any other way.

The tractor takes you towards Ingólfshöfði for 30 minutes (6km) across a tidal lagoon – views on the final approach are stunning.

The Headland
Once you arrive at the site – a deeply strange desolation of

FIRST LANDINGS

Credit for the first intentional permanent settlement on Iceland, according to the 12th-century *Íslendingabók*, or Book of Settlement, goes to Ingólfur Arnarson, who fled Norway with his blood brother Hjörleifur. He landed at Ingólfshöfði (Southeast Iceland) in 871, then continued around the coast and set up house in 874 at a place he called Reykjavík (Smoky Bay), named after the steam from thermal springs there. Hjörleifur settled near the present town of Vík, but was murdered by his slaves shortly after.

From top: Ingólfshöfði headland; puffin in flight

black sand that feels like the surface of the moon – you climb steeply to the headland, followed by a 1½-hour guided walk around the headland. Every year from sometime in May until they leave Iceland around mid-August, nesting puffins, skuas and other seabirds in their tens of thousands take over Ingólfshöfði. The emphasis may be on birdwatching, but with stunning mountain backdrops to marvel over on clear days, you don't have to be a birder to fall in love with the experience. And anyway, doesn't everyone just *love* puffins?

Nýgræðuöldur

Around 2km west of the Jökulsárlón bridge, a small car park on the north side of the road marks an excellent way to begin your Jökulsárlón experience.

Known as **Nýgræðuöldur**, this is where a 2km trail begins – although you can't see it from the car park, just beyond the low hill is the western end of the Jökulsárlón glacial lagoon, and the trail hugs the shoreline. At the information boards in the car park, there should be a brochure (although supplies sometimes run low) – take one along for the hike and you'll find information for the seven marked posts along the trail, explaining various aspects of the region's natural history. And before setting out, the information board itself has a map showing the worrying retreat of the main Breiðamerkurjökull glacier.

The trail itself is an easy, spectacular walk, with views across the water to the glacier and floating icebergs. Fewer icebergs head out this far west, as they're drawn to the sea via the eastern outlet, but the trail goes around and under a bridge and down to a black-sand beach.

And there's one big advantage to stopping here – Nýgræðuöldur sees only a fraction of the crowds with whom you'll share Jökulsárlón.

Along the Way We Met...

SÚSANNA RUTH MAGNÚSDÓTTIR, MARCELA SLOBODANIUC & JOSH PERSELLO, VATNAJÖKULL NATIONAL PARK RANGERS

Favourite season? Winter (Súsanna, Josh), summer (Marcela)
Why? The glaciers are more blue, and it's ice-cave season (Súsanna). The icebergs, too are really blue, and it all has a dusting of snow, and if we're lucky, we can see the polar stratospheric clouds (Josh).
Do you ever tire of this place? The weather is always changing, so there's always something new going on (Josh).
Favourite way to experience Jökulsárlón? Zodiac boats, because they take you all the way to the glacier on the lagoon (Súsanna). Ice caves – they are super beautiful and the ice is changing all the time (Marcela). I've been an accredited glacier guide for eight years, so glacier hiking for me (Josh).
How to escape the crowds? Going on a small-group tour is everything (Marcela). Nýgræðuöldur and Fjallsárlón (Súsanna). Everyone says their favourite glacier is Fjallsjökull (Josh).

Fjallsárlón — 7km — **Nýgræðuöldur** — 2km

You can't (in theory) cross the bridge to Jökulsárlón on foot.

Fellsfjara (Diamond Beach)

Jökulsárlón

Welcome to miraculous **Jökulsárlón**. Yes, it's one of Iceland's busiest sites, and yes, the number of visitors can be a little overwhelming at times. But on no account miss this glorious place.

Even at the height of summer, there are moments when, if you plan well, there will be far fewer people around. We have arrived at 8am in late July, for example, and easily found a spot in the main car park, which didn't fill until around 10am. Conversely, we've also arrived at midday in winter and struggled to find room in the overflow car park. And we're always surprised how few people come to see Jökulsárlón bathed in June's or July's midnight sun.

There is no visitor centre here, but there is a ranger station for Vatnajökull National Park. Every day at 11am from the start of June until the middle of September, rangers lead a free one-hour **guided walk** along the shore of the lagoon. The meeting point is at the food trucks next to the main car park. The nearest hotel is Hótel Jökulsárlón (p122).

Fellsfjara (Diamond Beach)

When you're done with Jökulsárlón and the lagoon, follow the icebergs as they accelerate down under the bridge and out to the mouth of the Jökulsá river and into the sea. Only some

continues p130

Icebergs at Jökulsárlón can spend five years floating in the lagoon.

Marvel at Jökulsárlón

It's a name you'll hear whispered all over the south – Jökulsárlón is a national treasure. There is something elemental about this special place – an epic glacier snakes down off Europe's largest ice cap, and icebergs an ethereal shade of blue float in the lagoon. Take to the water and see what all the fuss is about.

HOW TO

Nearest stop: Jökulsárlón is a stop in itself, and there are entrances to its car parks on both sides of the Ring Road.

Getting here: Parking *(parka.is)* costs 1040kr per vehicle; pay online through the website or app, or at one of the on-site pay stations. Buses between Reykjavík and Höfn stop at the visitor centre, or take the summer bus shuttle between Jökulsárlón and Skaftafell.

When to go: The site is open year-round and is always busy; early morning or evening are best.

Tip: Don't miss the free guided walk by the park rangers (p126).

Kayak the Lagoon

Of all the options for getting out on the waters of Jökulsárlón, this is our favourite. After all the clamour of the car park, where tourists wander around looking lost in high-vis overalls, there's something special about taking to the water with the only sound the gentle slap of paddle on water. You'll lose the crowds, move at your own pace, and draw alongside icebergs. **IceGuide** *(iceguide.is; per person 18,400kr)* leads hour-long paddles from May to early October.

Zodiac Boat Tours

They're the opposite of a quiet encounter with the ice, but Zodiac tours get you closer to the glacier than any other kind of boat. **Glacier Lagoon** *(icelagoon.is)* and **Ice Lagoon Adventure Tours** *(icelagoon.com)* offer 75-minute Zodiac tours *(per person 15,900kr)*, with a maximum of 10 passengers per boat. Book ahead online; minimum age between eight and 10 years old, depending on the company.

Amphibious Boats

They're big, they're cumbersome, they don't get very far and they pack you in like sardines, but we can't deny the novelty of the amphibious boats operated by **Glacier Lagoon** *(adult/child 6900/3500kr)*. For 40 minutes, they rumble along the shore, then – in a *Chitty Chitty Bang Bang* moment that always brings squeals of delight – they become a boat and take to the water. On board, taste 1000-year-old ice. Trips run from May to October; book online.

ICE TOURS

From Coast to Mountains
Owner Einar, Iceland's first ice-cave guide, offers climbing, cave and puffin tours. *(fromcoasttomountains.com)*

Local Guide
Family-owned and in the area for generations; first-rate local knowledge, year-round glacier hikes and ice climbs. *(localguide.is)*

Heading North
Small groups make for outstanding glacier and ice-cave tours. *(headingnorth.is)*

Vivid Iceland
Excellent private and small-group glacier tours by a park ranger and qualified glacier guide. *(vividiceland.is)*

From top: Jökulsárlón glacier lagoon; ice caves

Glacier Hikes & Ice Caves

One way to get an entirely different perspective on Jökulsárlón is to organise a glacier hike – most operators can make it happen. Standing atop a groaning, crevassed glacier is a dizzying yet quintessential Iceland experience. Expect to pay at least 17,000kr per person for a half-day glacier hike.

Joining a tour to an ice cave *under* the glacier is also incredibly special, but it's only possible in winter, from November to March. Expect to pay around 25,000kr for a three-hour tour.

continued from p127

of them don't make it that far – most wash up on the black-sand beach of Fellsfjara. Dubbed 'Diamond Beach' online, the name has stuck, and it's easy to see why: ice chunks and sculptures dazzle in the shallows, offset by the black sand. It's an amazing sight.

Only 500m separates Fellsfjara from Jökulsárlón – you only need to park once to see both.

Heinabergsjökull

If your passion for glaciers remains undimmed, east of Jökulsárlón, the glacier tongue of **Heinabergsjökull** offers a radically different experience that is more easy DIY adventure than Instagram moment.

Heinabergsjökull is 8km off the Ring Road down an easy-to-miss gravel road – the sign is just east of Guesthouse Skálafell (p122). Walking trails from the guesthouse include the 7.5km hike to Heinabergslón (the icy lagoon at the foot of Heinabergsjökull). For the full experience, book in advance with **IceGuide** *(iceguide.is; per person 14 years & over 20,900kr)* for a stunning 3½-hour kayaking trip (including two hours on the water) on the lagoon. You might be the only ones there.

Hoffellsjökull

This one's for those with a newly found passion for glaciers and all the time in the world for exploring them.

To reach **Hoffellsjökull**, take the signed, 4km gravel road to Hoffel Guesthouse (recently rebranded as Glacier World Guesthouse); don't set out down this road if there has been recent heavy rain, as it washes out. From the guesthouse it's an easy walk to the glacier tongue, which calves into a small lagoon. And all the way there and back, you'll be dreaming of the guesthouse's open-air hot tubs to soothe tired muscles (or just because you feel like it).

The area between Heinabergsjökull and Hoffellsjökull is in the early stages of opening up for tourists. Check in at the visitor centres in Skaftafell (p111) or Kirkjubæjarklaustur (p109), or the ranger hut at Jökulsárlón, to find out about road conditions, learn if any areas are newly accessible, and buy a map.

Höfn

Strung out along a peninsula that thrusts into the wild North Atlantic Ocean, Höfn is the only town of any size for hundreds of kilometres

---

> **SEALS OF JÖKULSÁRLÓN**
>
> You could pay a lot of money to go looking for seals on a whale-watching trip in Húsavík (p192) or out of Hvammstangi (p212). Or you could just walk along the lagoon shore at Jökulsárlón. Of the two seal species in Iceland's waters, harbour seals and grey seals, you're most likely to see harbour seals here. Harbour seals, with their distinctive spot markings, can weigh 100kg and be up to 2m long. Seal pups are often born in the area around May or June. Cute as they may be, keep in mind that every year seal pups die after tourists get too close and force the mothers to abandon the pups.

Beware of changing speed limits on the road into Höfn.

Fellsfjara (Diamond Beach) — 47km — Heinabergsjökull — 9km — Hoffellsjökull — 24km — Höfn

in any direction. Drive to the southernmost tip of the Ósland promontory, where, about 1km beyond the fishing harbour, there's a windswept **Seamen's Monument** and views across the water to the Vatnajökull ice cap. The views are just as good (and just as windy!) from the cute little rising headland at the southwestern end of Hofðavegur.

Höfn is also known as a brilliant place to eat, thanks to having one of South Iceland's larger fishing fleets. In fact 'Höfn' simply means 'harbour', and to blend in with the locals you need to pronounce it like an unexpected hiccup (just say 'hup' while inhaling). It's especially well known for its *humar* (what everyone translates as lobster, but is actually langoustine).

The best places are Pakkhús, Otto Matur & Drykkur, and cheap and cheerful Hafnarbúðin. To stay, there's REY Stays (p122) and Milk Factory (p122).

BEST PLACES TO EAT

Hafnarbúðin, Höfn $
Tiny old-school diner with a drive-thru window and big breakfasts, fast-food favourites and fine langoustine baguette. *(9am-10pm Sat-Thu, noon-10pm Fri Jun-Aug, shorter hours rest of year)*

Otto Matur & Drykkur, Höfn $$
Inhabiting Höfn's oldest house (1897), this elegant space is high on Nordic style, with delicate dishes like artfully prepared lamb or salmon. *(5.30-9pm)*

Pakkhús, Höfn $$
Boisterous harbourside warehouse with high-level kitchen creativity and great service. Try the lamb, lobster – or sheep-dung-smoked local whisky. Wait for a table in its downstairs bar. *(pakkhus.is; noon-9pm)*

Humar in Höfn

 **PHOTO ESSAY**

Right: Gljúfrabúi (p86)

Elemental Iceland

IN ICELAND, EVERY element – water, ice, rock, fire, snow – comes in its purest and rawest form. My experience in the country was equal parts magical, beautiful and eye-opening. You know you're in a good place when you get bored looking at waterfalls!

My telephoto lens was really helpful. Not just for photographing puffins, but also for reaching distant landscapes. Remember that the best, most dynamic light may be while you're asleep. The summer days are endless, so stay up late or get up early: I visited in June and even at midnight I was able to photograph without a tripod and get a beautiful quality of light.

The quieter counterpart to star attraction Seljalandsfoss (p86), Gljúfrabúi is tucked away down a rocky passage. Travellers who venture into the canyon are rewarded with a pale cascade tumbling down moss-covered cliffs.

PHOTOGRAPHED BY DANIEL DORSA
Daniel is an LA-based photographer whose work explores the relationships between people, the environments they inhabit and the landscapes that connect them.

From left: Southeast Iceland; Fellsfjara (p122)

Below: Puffins in Borgarfjarðarhöfn, near Bakkagerði (p162)

From the Ring Road you'll catch a glimpse of the beautiful high falls at Seljalandsfoss, which tumble over a rocky scarp into a deep, green pool. A (somewhat slippery) path runs around the back of the waterfall that allows you to soak in the spray from its spectacular 60m drop.

Above: Seljalandsfoss (p86); Right: Rauðhólar (p52)

Below: Caves of Hella (p82)

Mystery surrounds the origins of the 12 human-made caves in Hella, on the south coast of Iceland. In more recent centuries they were used as shelters for people and livestock, but ancient crosses and carvings hint at an earlier purpose. Some believe that they pre-date Settlement Era itself.

View from the Ring Road near Hella (p82)

This was shot close to Hella during a really intense wind storm on our first day out on the road. Iceland's weather is all over the map. This was also shot quite late, close to midnight.
– Daniel Dorsa

Below: Fellsfjara (Diamond Beach; p127)

Geothermal energy has shaped a landscape like no other at the Hveradalir Geothermal Area. White steam billows against the shifting colours of the earth, framed by striking rhyolite mountains.

Above: Views from the top of Skógafoss (p87); Right: Hveradalir Geothermal Area (p56)

Höfn

As you exit Höfn, the southern Eastfjords greet you with majestic mountains and deep bays, along which the Ring Road slings. Prepare for awe-inspiring views (and sometimes a thick veil of fog), tumbling waterfalls, colourful cliffs and a myriad of natural treasures hidden in plain sight. Pay attention to parking signs by the road – these usually indicate scenic spots – and strike up a conversation with a local in one of the villages for tips.

Coastal scenery near Fauskasandur (p144)
NO01/SHUTTERSTOCK

Eygló Svala Arnarsdóttir

Stöðvarfjörður

185 KM
2 HOURS' DRIVE

THIS LEG:

- Höfn
- Stokksnes
- Skútafoss
- Fauskasandur
- Djúpivogur
- Nykurhylsfoss
- Blábjörg
- Streitishvarf
- Breiðdalsvík
- Kambaskriður
- Óseyri
- Stöðvarfjörður

Driving Notes

In the east, the Ring Road is often narrow, with only one lane in either direction. The road twists and turns, so drive carefully, especially at blind rises and curves, and when crossing one-lane bridges. Look out for birds on the road, the occasional sheep or even reindeer. Conditions are often foggy (the infamous Austfjarðaþokan, or Eastfjords fog) and, in winter, slippery.

Breaking Your Journey

It's quite possible to cover this leg in one day and thoroughly enjoy it. However, if you want to make time for tours, hikes or other activities, booking accommodation in Djúpivogur or Breiðdalsvík, or in any of the farmstays between the two towns, would be optimal.

Eygló's Tips

BEST MEAL *Ástarpungur* (doughnut balls) and coffee at Hafið Bistro (p145).

FAVOURITE VIEW Kambaskriður (p148) screes on one side of the road and the open ocean on the other.

ESSENTIAL STOP Stokksnes (p144), for iconic Vestrahorn and a Viking village movie set.

ROAD-TRIP TIP Drop by the towns en route, take in the atmosphere and get a treat at a cafe or restaurant (p145).

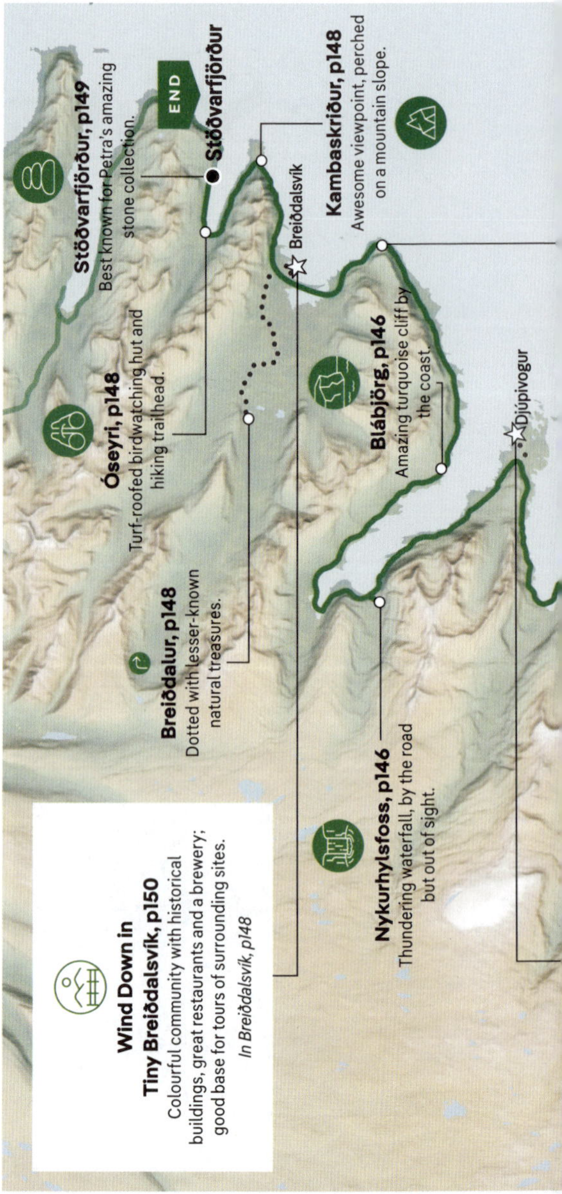

Stöðvarfjörður, p149 — Best known for Petra's amazing stone collection.

END Stöðvarfjörður

Breiðdalsvík

Kambaskriður, p148 — Awesome viewpoint, perched on a mountain slope.

Ósevri, p148 — Turf-roofed birdwatching hut and hiking trailhead.

Blábjörg, p146 — Amazing turquoise cliff by the coast.

Djúpivogur

Breiðdalur, p148 — Dotted with lesser-known natural treasures.

Nykurhylsfoss, p146 — Thundering waterfall, by the road but out of sight.

Wind Down in Tiny Breiðdalsvík, p150

Colourful community with historical buildings, great restaurants and a brewery; good base for tours of surrounding sites.

In Breiðdalsvík, p148

PREVIOUS STOP As you exit Höfn (p130), glacial landscapes give way to a dramatic coastline.

Stokksnes

A short drive from Höfn will take you to the **Vestrahorn** mountain. The reflection of its jagged peaks in the tidal flats is one of Iceland's most iconic images. You can see the mountain from Höfn, but for a closer look, drive for a few minutes on the Ring Road, then turn right on a gravel road, which leads to **Stokksnes**, past colourful screes. You can pay for entrance to the area and viewpoint at **Viking Cafe** *(vikingcafe.is; 1100kr per person over 16)*, where you can also have a light meal or coffee. Take the time to stroll on the black-sand beach – there's a map of different routes in the cafe – and admire the mountain. If the weather is clear, there's a view of Höfn and Vatnajökull glacier to the other side.

Curiously, Stokksnes is also the site of a set designed for an ambitious Viking film, which was never shot. Explore the Viking village, complete with a ship. Climb aboard, or scale a tower, and fancy yourself an explorer or Skaldic warrior.

Skútafoss

Back on the Ring Road, you'll pass through a tunnel. Shortly after you exit it, the road crosses a small river with a sign that reads 'Þorgeirsstaðaá'; after the sign, turn up the gravel road on the left. It leads to a little cave near the road and a gem of a waterfall called **Skútafoss**. Park your car, then take the brief walk to the waterfall. If the cliff isn't too slippery, walk behind it and observe the world through a veil of water. On the opposite side of the Ring Road, look out for a huge red chair, great for pictures.

Fauskasandur

After open vistas, the road leads between towering mountains and cliffs plunging into the sea. Approximately halfway between Höfn and Djúpivogur, after passing the orange **Hvalnes** lighthouse, you'll see a humble parking sign on the right side of the Ring Road. This is **Fauskasandur**, a grey-sand beach where some of the pebbles look like gemstones (admire them

Langabúð

Turn right before the tunnel to reach Vestrahorn.

Vestrahorn and its reflection in the tidal flats

where they are and leave them on the beach). Seagulls nest atop a tall cliff, which looks like a human-made pillar, and in the background loom triangular peaks.

Djúpivogur

As you get closer to **Djúpivogur**, keep an eye out for birds (p147), including flocks of whooper swans, and reindeer, as they often graze in the lowlands around the town. Take a right towards the sea and head for **Langabúð**, a stately red house, the village's oldest building. Dating back to 1790, it hosts a heritage **museum** *(adult/child 500/300kr; 10am-6pm Jun-Aug)*.

BEST PLACES TO EAT

Langabúð Cafe, Djúpivogur €€
Filling soup with homemade bread and traditional Icelandic lunches in the town's oldest house. *(9am-5pm)*

Hafið Bistro, Djúpivogur €€
Cosy family-owned place with a varied menu, ranging from tempting cakes and pastries like *ástarpungur* (doughnut 'love balls'), to pizzas and Polish dumplings. Excellent coffee. *(9am-9pm Mon-Fri, 10am-10pm Sat-Sun)*

Bláfell Restaurant, Breiðdalsvík €€
A great place for dinner; serves local lamb and fish along with other dishes, and locally made ice cream for dessert. Try Beljandi beer, brewed in Breiðdalsvík. *(6-9pm)*

Fauskasandur — 45km — Djúpivogur — *Keep an eye out for reindeer!* — 17km — Nykurhylsfoss

Along the Way We Met...

BORGÞÓR ARNGRÍMSSON When I was growing up in Höfn, the Ring Road hadn't been completed, and the glacial rivers to the west and east of the town were unbridged. The only way in and out by car was across the Lónsheiði mountain pass, which was open for three to four months a year. Now I'm here travelling with a group of old classmates from Bifröst University – we're celebrating our 54th graduation anniversary.

Borgþór is a retired reporter, now living in Reykjavík.

BORGÞÓR'S TIP: *On the eastern end of the tunnel, just after the exit to Stokksnes, take a left up the old road to Almannaskarð, where the view is breathtaking.*

Walk between the artefacts and imagine what life was like here without modern comforts.

Take a walk to the marina and visit the **memorial** to Hans Jónatan (1784–1827), Iceland's first documented black settler. He escaped slavery in Copenhagen and became a respected merchant, farmer and family man in Djúpivogur.

For lunch, head to cosy Hafið Bistro (p145), or try the Langabúð Cafe (p145) for hearty soups, homemade bread, traditional lunches and tempting cakes. To stay in Djúpivogur, we recommend Hótel Framtíð (p149).

Nykurhylsfoss

The road from Djúpivogur leads into the narrow Berufjörður fjord, lined by mountains. A loud surprise in the quiet fjord is thundering waterfall **Nykurhylsfoss**. When you've almost reached the innermost part of the fjord, take a left at the sign reading 'Fjarðaá'. Up the hill is a car park by the falls.

Feel its power and try to spot the *nykur,* a horse-shaped monster that inhabits its basin. The road leads on to the **Fossárdalur** campsite, from where you can set out to explore more waterfalls upstream. Fossárdalur also has a guesthouse in the area (p149).

Blábjörg

Continuing along the coastline of Berufjörður, make sure to stop at **Blábjörg**, a little-known geological phenomenon and natural monument. A parking and information sign indicates the location of the site, right by the Ring Road near the mouth of the fjord.

From the parking lot, descend the stairs to the beach to find turquoise cliffs of the rare Berufjörður acid tuff, only found in this area. The blue-green colour of the cliffs is striking against the black sand and the mountainous landscape.

Wing It Round Djúpivogur

As you enter Djúpivogur, note how townspeople respect their history, heritage and environment, paying special tribute to their feathered friends.

HOW TO

Getting there: Djúpivogur is just off the Ring Road, approximately 75 minutes from Höfn.

When to go: May to August, when the birdlife is the most active.

Getting around: There is no public transport. Drive or walk – everything is within walking distance.

Sleeping: Hótel Framtíð (p149) has cosy rooms, and operates a range of other accommodation.

Take a walk along black-sand beaches or on the paths encircling the ponds on the outskirts of town to enjoy the peaceful landscape and cheerful birdsong – especially lively in spring and early summer when the migrant birds arrive, mate and nest. Different types of waders can be spotted in the area, as well as various duck species, including the common shelduck and the northern shoveler. The rare horned grebe has also nested by the ponds. From birdwatching huts, you can enjoy the birdlife unnoticed.

At the harbour, you'll find *Eggin í Gleðivík*, egg sculptures by Sigurður Guðmundsson, a Djúpivogur local and one of Iceland's most celebrated visual artists. The 34 eggs represent each of the bird species nesting in the area. They rest on concrete pillars, which used to support a landing pipe between the pier and the old herring smelter. The largest egg is that of the red-throated loon, the area's emblem bird.

For more information on the region, visit *east.is*. For tour operators in Djúpivogur, see *adventura.squarespace.com* and *voxeytrips.com*.

From left: Northern shovelers; a horned grebe

Streitishvarf

Shortly before reaching Breiðdalsvík, you'll see a lone white lighthouse by the sea. It's not the main reason for stopping, though. A path leads down to **Streitishvarf**, an ancient composite dyke, which looks like a human-made harbour and hallway, but is actually a spectacular testimony to the forces of nature. Note the varied colouring of the rock. About 30m wide and at least 14km long, the dyke is believed to have formed when rhyolite magma shot in between hot basalt segments.

Walk up to the lighthouse on the way back from viewing the dyke. It was built in 1984 to replace an older lighthouse, which stood on a reef, but was destroyed by wild waves.

Breiðdalsvík

After the lighthouse, the road leads around the mountain and into **Breiðdalsvík** cove, where the eponymous village lies. You're faced with open vistas: the ocean on the right and Breiðdalur valley on the left. Cross a bridge and you'll come to peaceful **Meleyri** beach and its lyme grass–covered dunes. A couple of minutes on, take a right into Breiðdalsvík village, and tune into its quiet, retro atmosphere (p150).

If you want to break your drive up, our favourite is Hótel Breiðdalsvík (p149) – on-site Bláfell Restaurant is a great option for dinner.

DETOUR: Breiðdalur

Until 2017, the Ring Road went through the **Breiðdalur** valley, and it's worth taking a couple of hours off the Ring Road to explore the valley's smattering of hidden gems, among them **Beljandi**, an unusual, hard-to-find waterfall. Turn left off the Ring Road up Rte 95, and double back to stop by the **Heydalir church** on Rte 964, then continue on to Rte 966. Cross two bridges, then turn onto an unmarked gravel road on your right. Park and follow the track for about 20 minutes to reach Beljandi. For another nearby waterfall, **Flögufoss**, continue on Rte 966 to Flaga farm. Follow the path for about 30 minutes and take in the tall, thin waterfall, cascading over layered cliffs.

Rte 966 leads back to Rte 95, looping back to the Ring Road, or cutting over to Egilsstaðir.

Kambaskriður

You're about to enter one of the most awesome (and scariest) stretches of the Ring Road in this region, between Breiðdalsvík and Stöðvarfjörður, where the road has been carved out of a scree slope called **Kambaskriður** (Skriðurnar for short). Be sure to stop at the viewpoint and look out at the open ocean, Breiðdalsvík to the west and Stöðvarfjörður to the right. And then...turn and look up at the almost vertical slope, and feel stunned at how close the mountain is.

Óseyri

Follow the road along the mountains into Stöðvarfjörður fjord. On the beach, in its most sheltered curve, is a turf-roofed birdwatching house belonging to **Óseyri** farm – a great spot for spying on shorebirds.

On the other side of the Ring Road is a gravel road with a sign that says 'Stöðvarskarð', marking the hiking path over to **Fáskrúðsfjörður**. En route, in the Jafnadalur valley, there's a giant boulder called **Einbúi**. The hike to Einbúi and back takes four to five hours. If you don't have time for a hike, continue by car for a few kilometres along the gravel road to **Stöð**, where some of the oldest remains in Iceland have been excavated, predating the official settlement of 874 CE.

Stöðvarfjörður

Enter the sleepy village of **Stöðvarfjörður** and stop at **Petra's Stone Collection** *(adult/child 1500kr/free; 9am-5pm daily May-Oct)*. East Iceland is a rock collector's dream. When the Ice Age glacier tore through the mountains, carving fjords and valleys, various minerals came to light. The region has several rock museums, but this is the largest, a lifelong labour of love for Petra Sveinsdóttir (1922–2012). Her favourite pastime was walking out her front door, up the hills and to the mountains above, keeping an eye out for something unusual and sparkly. Petra's house and garden are lined with colourful minerals, a testimony to her dedication.

BEST PLACES TO SLEEP

Hótel Framtíð, Djúpivogur €€€
Historic hotel by the harbour, originally built as a store in 1905-06. Comfortable rooms and authentic atmosphere. *(hotelframtid.com)*

Fossárdalur, Berufjörður €€
Farmhouse from the 1920s, renovated as a guesthouse. Set in a secluded valley between tall mountains and next to a waterfall trail. *(fossardalur.is)*

Hótel Breiðdalsvík, Breiðdalsvík €€
Beautiful hotel in a tiny, peaceful village with cosy rooms, a hot tub and a sauna. Restaurant serves fresh local food and local beer. *(breiddalsvik.is)*

Kambaskriður

Wind Down in Tiny Breiðdalsvík

Just shy of 150 inhabitants, this is truly one of the tiniest towns in Iceland. Nestling by the sea, and thriving off its bounty, the townspeople here are happy to have visitors. As you enter Breiðdalsvík, remember to slow down – and not just the car. This miniscule town invites you to take a breather, stroll its few streets and absorb the laid-back atmosphere.

HOW TO

Getting here: Breiðdalsvík is just off the Ring Road, 60km from Djúpivogur.

When to go: The hotel is typically closed for two months in winter (January and February). The shoulder season is good for solitude, reindeer in the lowlands, winter adventures and the Northern Lights. In summer, more services are open.

More info: Family-run **Tinna Adventure** (tinna-adventure.is), based in Breiðdalsvík, offers a variety of tours of the surrounding area and the entire eastern region.

Beach Walks & Hot Tubs

Do as the locals do and take a stroll to black-sand beach **Meleyri**, which you drove past on the way into town. On a calm and sunny day, as the waves wash against the shore, it's the perfect place for a picnic – or to practise mindfulness. Check out the yoga tours offered by local company Tinna Adventure.

There's nothing more relaxing than a soak. The town's tiny public pool has hot tubs (open in summer) and **Hótel Breiðdalsvík** (hotelblafell.is) has a hot tub and sauna. In clear winter weather, you can gaze at the stars from the hot tub – and even catch the Northern Lights.

A Taste of Tradition

After your relaxation, drop by **Kaupfjelagið** (facebook.com/kaupfjelagid), a charming vintage store and cafe. It's maintained as a museum but operated as a shop, still carrying products that were sold when it opened over 60 years ago. You can buy fresh, locally caught fish, try a *skyr* (yoghurt) cake or have something more filling.

Enjoy a tasty meal at **Bláfell Restaurant** (p145), where dishes are made with the freshest available seafood and ingredients from nearby farms. Pair it with the local beer, **Beljandi** (facebook.com/beljandibrugghus), which is made in the brewery across the

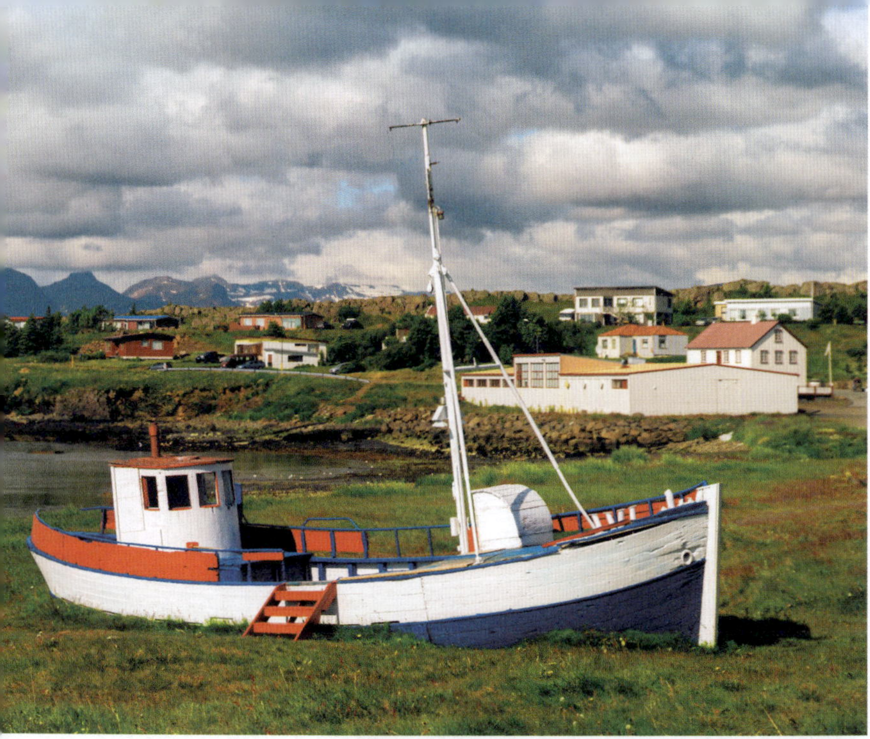

street. The brewery welcomes visitors in summer and by appointment.

Dig into Geology

The area is known for its unique geology. In town, you'll find the **Breiðdalur Geology Centre** and the **Drill Core Library (DCL)** of the Icelandic Institute of Natural History, with an impressive collection of kilometres worth of drill cores. Admission is free, but email *mariahg@hi.is* ahead of your visit.

From top: Breiðdalsvík; Meleyri

FROM TOP: VOLKER RAUCH/SHUTTERSTOCK, MAURITIUS IMAGES GMBH/ALAMY

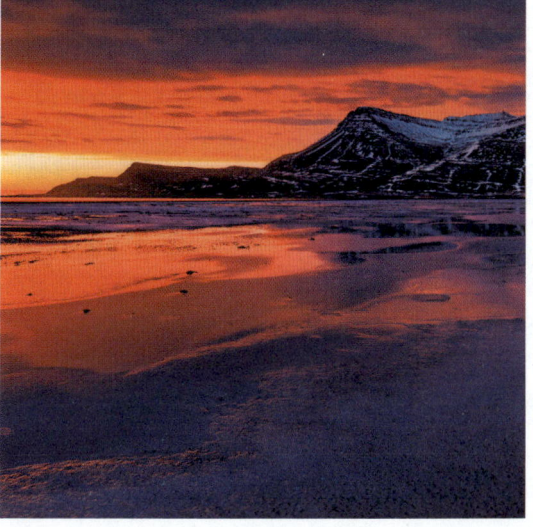

Stöðvarfjörður

The Ring Road winds along the rugged coastline of the Eastfjords, in and out of coves and past imposing mountains. In each of the fjords lies a fishing village, clinging to a steep slope beneath avalanche barriers. Tunnels have now replaced mountain passes and broken the isolation of many of these Eastfjords communities. History buffs will enjoy Fáskrúðsfjörður's French connection, and studying Reyðarfjörður's role in WWII.

Fáskrúðsfjörður (p156)
ILIJA ASCIC/SHUTTERSTOCK

Eygló Svala Arnarsdóttir

Egilsstaðir

84 KM — 1 HOUR'S DRIVE

THIS LEG:

- Stöðvarfjörður
- Saxa Sea Geyser
- Hafnarnesviti Lighthouse
- Fáskrúðsfjörður (Búðir)
- Reyðarfjörður (Búðareyri)
- Búðarárfoss
- Egilsstaðir

Driving Notes

There are many bends on the Ring Road as it follows the fjords, so drive carefully, especially in foggy conditions and during winter. Slow down when you pass through the tunnel between Fáskrúðsfjörður and Reyðarfjörður, as the speed limit drops from 90km/hr to 70km/hr. It's a quick drive between Stöðvarfjörður and Egilsstaðir, but this section is best enjoyed with extended detours.

Breaking Your Journey

Give yourself plenty of time to experience the Eastfjords and Fljótsdalur, especially if you're into extended treks. Base yourself in a fjord or around Egilsstaðir, walk or hike in beautiful landscapes, visit museums, go sightseeing by boat or join a horse-riding tour.

Eygló's Tips

BEST MEAL Icelandic cod with a French twist at L'Abri (p157), Fáskrúðsfjörður.

FAVOURITE VIEW Skrúður island seen from the Hafnarnesviti Lighthouse (p156).

ESSENTIAL STOP Visit Reyðarfjörður (p157) for its bakery, WWII museum and stunning waterfall.

ROAD-TRIP TIP It's a short stretch of road but a huge region. Take your time and plan detours to fully explore it.

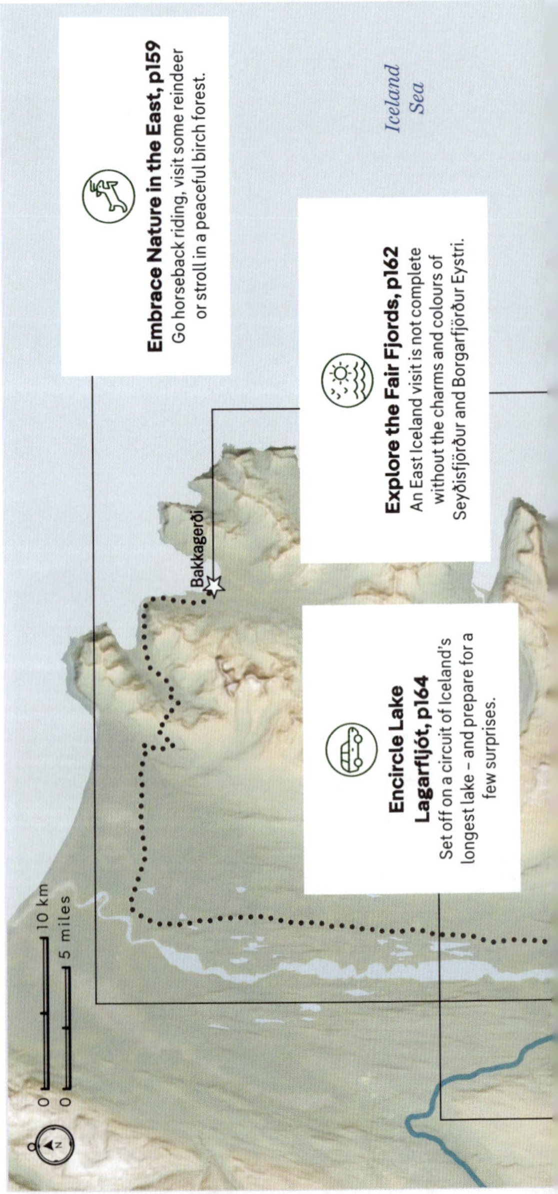

Embrace Nature in the East, p159
Go horseback riding, visit some reindeer or stroll in a peaceful birch forest.

Explore the Fair Fjords, p162
An East Iceland visit is not complete without the charms and colours of Seyðisfjörður and Borgarfjörður Eystri.

Encircle Lake Lagarfljót, p164
Set off on a circuit of Iceland's longest lake – and prepare for a few surprises.

Iceland Sea

Bakkagerði

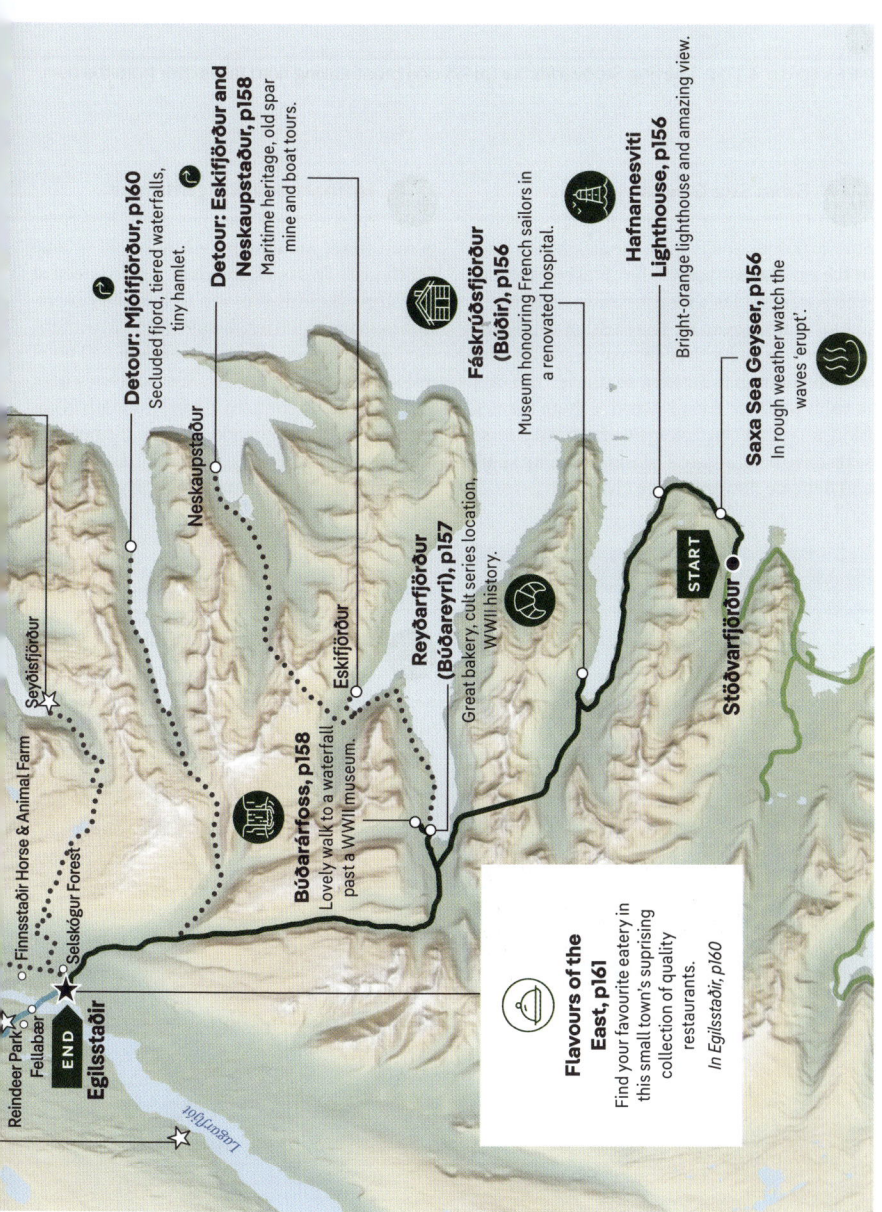

PREVIOUS STOP Leaving Stöðvarfjörður (p149), one breathtaking fjord takes over from the next.

Saxa Sea Geyser

Only after a few minutes after leaving Stöðvarfjörður, you'll find a special phenomenon by the sea. **Saxa** ('the Grinder') is a dyke through which waves splash, tossing seaweed in the air, like an erupting geyser. The weather conditions must be just right, though, with a strong wind blowing in from the east or southeast. But even in calm weather, Saxa is worth a stop, because it's also a spot where colourful ducks and curious seals have been sighted, along with cute snails and delicate flowers – even elves.

Hafnarnesviti Lighthouse

Hafnarnesviti Lighthouse

As you reach the opening of Fáskrúðsfjörður fjord, you'll notice a tiny, bright-orange lighthouse. This is **Hafnarnes**, a place steeped in history. There used to be a fishing village here, with as many as 100 inhabitants. Mid-last century, the French hospital – now a museum and hotel in Fáskrúðsfjörður town – served as a school and apartment complex here. Gradually, Hafnarnes village was abandoned, and the hospital building was moved, too. Now, all that remains are crumbling stone foundations. Nonetheless, it's a peaceful place to stretch your legs. Walk to the lighthouse and take in the view of the fjord and Skrúður island, after which it is named, and imagine what the once-thriving village was like.

Fáskrúðsfjörður (Búðir)

Continue into the innermost part of the narrow fjord, enclosed by rugged mountains, and turn onto Rte 955 to visit the town of **Fáskrúðsfjörður**. Officially known as Búðir, it was one of the main fishing stations for French schooners in Iceland in the late 1800s and early 1900s. Young Frenchmen flooded the village and traded wine and biscuits with the locals for woollen garments.

In 1903 a hospital was built in Búðir to care for ill and injured sailors. Now meticulously renovated, it serves as an atmospheric hotel and museum (open in summer) honouring the town's French history. Lifelike wax figurines provide an insight into the hardship fishers faced onboard

Reyðarfjörður

the schooners, while video artwork *Ocean of Memories* powerfully demonstrates the massive death toll in the fishing industry.

Reyðarfjörður (Búðareyri)

Pass through a tunnel, and you're almost in **Reyðarfjörður**, officially known as Búðareyri. Right after the tunnel, there's a parking spot with a great view of the town – just try not to look at the aluminium smelter.

Take a left on Rte 92 to visit the town, and before you do anything else, fuel up at legendary bakery **Sesam Brauðhús** *(sesam.is)*. The shelves are lined with freshly baked sourdough loaves, and

---

BEST PLACES TO EAT

L'Abri, Fosshotel Eastfjords, Fáskrúðsfjörður €€
In a historic French hospital-turned-hotel, tempting dishes are inspired by French cuisine, with freshly caught cod the star of the menu. *(islandshotel.is; 6-10pm daily)*

Norð Austur Sushi & Bar, Seyðisfjörður €€
Iceland's freshest and most authentic sushi, made according to Japanese tradition with local seafood, along with other Japanese dishes with Icelandic ingredients. *(nordaustur.is; 6-10pm Thu-Sun May-Aug)*

Eldhúsið, Lake Hotel, Egilsstaðir €€€
Varied selection made with local produce; rooted in tradition but with an international twist. Try the three-course farm-to-table menu. *(lakehotel.is; 11.30am-10pm daily)*

19km — **Fáskrúðsfjörður (Búðir)**

20km — **Reyðarfjörður (Búðareyri)** — *Charming town with a fascinating French history.*

BEST PLACES TO SLEEP

Tehúsið Hostel & Guesthouse, Egilsstaðir €€
Easy-going atmosphere and simple comfort. Tune into the chill vibe, enjoy a tea or draught beer – and occasional live music – before heading to your room or dormitory. Shared bathroom and kitchen facilities. *(tehusid.is)*

Hotel 1001 nótt, Egilsstaðir €€€
Lovely family-run luxury hotel in a secluded location on the banks of Lagarfljót. Lakeside hot tubs and excellent restaurant. *(1001nott.is)*

Snæfell – Hotel by Aldan, Seyðisfjörður €€€
Part of a string of hotels and apartments in historical houses in the charming seaside town, 30 minutes from Egilsstaðir. Chic comfort, shared kitchen. *(hotelaldan.is)*

baskets are filled with rolls and savoury treats like *ostaslaufa,* a cheese-filled Icelandic bread. For a more old-fashioned Icelandic experience, try *soðið brauð* (deep-fried bread), *kleinur* (twisted doughnuts) or *ástarpungur* (doughnut balls with raisins). There are plenty of pastries to choose from: Danish, cinnamon rolls, cream buns and more. The coffee is excellent, too. Fans of cult TV show *Fortitude,* which was shot here, may want to drop by black-and-white guesthouse Tærgesen *(taergesen.com),* featured in the series.

Búðarárfoss

Still in Reyðarfjörður, drive up to the Wartime Museum car park for a walk to the majestic **Búðarárfoss** waterfall, which gushes into the river Búðará that flows through the town, past the museum. For an approximately 30-minute walk, choose the path that leads first through a small forest, then up towards the mountain before looping back to the river. Shortly after crossing a footbridge, Búðarárfoss appears downstream, cascading down a steep drop. Follow the river, with several smaller falls, back to the museum.

For a shorter walk, head upstream from the museum instead, or drive almost all the way and park by the water tanks. Be sure to visit the **Wartime Museum** *(stridsarasafn.fjard abyggd.is)* to learn more about the occupation of Iceland during WWII and Reyðarfjörður's role. On 1 July, 1940, British troops set up camp here, outnumbering the local residents tenfold. Some of the barracks they built are still there.

DETOUR: Eskifjörður & Neskaupstaður

A mere 15-minute drive from Reyðarfjörður on Rte 92 lies **Eskifjörður**, another picturesque fishing town. Dive into its maritime heritage in **Randulffssjóhús** *(mjoeyri.is),* a museum-cum-restaurant in a renovated seasonal house for fishers, open in summer. Outside town is **Helgustaðanáma**, an old mine for Iceland spar, a scientifically significant mineral. It's under protection, so leave the spar where it is.

Drive on 20 minutes through a tunnel to reach **Neskaupstaður**, beneath eerie mountains. If you're still in the mood for fish, try the seafood inside an old department store at **Hildibrand**

Embrace Nature in the East

Before you hit the 'big smoke' of Egilsstaðir, take some time to explore the beautiful landscapes that surround it – reserve a couple of hours for horse riding or birch forest strolls.

HOW TO

Getting here: Finnsstaðir Horse & Animal Farm is just a few minutes outside Egilsstaðir off Rte 94. Selskógur Forest is nearby, off Rte 93 on the town's outskirts.

When to go: Finnsstaðir offers tours and stable visits year-round. Selskógur is always open. In winter, tracks are made for cross-country skiers.

More info: finnsstadir.is; east.is

Off Rte 94 lies **Finnsstaðir** (finnsstadir.is), a farm and petting zoo. Meet, ride and learn about the captivating Icelandic horse. Sweet-natured, sure-footed and soft-gaited, these creatures help you experience nature in a whole new way. You'll feel in touch with your surroundings as you ride along riverbanks, cross streams and trot past farms and fields.

Riders of all levels can take one-hour to multiday tours. Small children can ride hand-led horses, and meet the farm's other animals: rabbits, ducks, guinea pigs, sheep, dogs and cats.

Selskógur is a beloved natural birch forest covering 80 hectares. There are several paths to choose from: the longest (3.7km) goes along Eyvindará river, then back through the forest to the viewpoints on Selhæð and Egilsstaðaöxl. Rare flowers bloom here in summer, including harebell and Arctic starflower. The forest has a playground and outdoor BBQ, and benches in scenic spots perfect for picnics. If your timing is right, catch a play or concert.

Reindeer were imported from Norway to Iceland in the late 1700s, but only survived in the East, which is home to several thousand wild reindeer. To experience these animals up close, follow the Ring Road along the banks of Lagarfljót and cross the bridge to **Fellabær**. Its biggest attraction is the **Reindeer Park** (reindeerpark.is), a passion project for Björn Magnússon, who in 2021 adopted two motherless calves found in the wild. Garpur and Mosi have grown along with the park, and other abandoned reindeer have joined them.

Icelandic horses

Along the Way We Met...

PAULA KORN AND JOHANNES LOTT We're taking 14 days to drive the Ring Road, and our favourite thing so far was the glacial hike. It's worth the money (because you have to book a tour), but you need a basic level of fitness. We decided to travel in May, off-season, but the South was still crowded with tourists. The East is more quiet. It's interesting to watch the landscapes change frequently and the wildlife, puffins, seals and reindeer.

Paula and Johannes live in Cologne, Germany.

THEIR TIP: *Slow down, relax, enjoy the ride and make spontaneous stops. It's a relief from the stress of daily life.*

Hotel *(hildibrand.com)*, or something simpler at **Beituskúrinn** *(facebook.com/beituskurinn)*, an old bait shack turned gastropub, open in summer. Look out for events in the loft. **Fjarðaferðir** *(fjardaferdir.com)* offers sightseeing tours by boat.

DETOUR: Mjóifjörður

Pay attention or you might miss the exit! With fewer than 15 inhabitants and an often-impassible gravel road, **Mjóifjörður** locals are happy to have visitors. The 'secret' entrance to this magical fjord is Rte 953, about 20 minutes along the Ring Road from Reyðarfjörður, 10 minutes before reaching Egilsstaðir. Allow for more than an hour one-way to drive to the fjord's tiny hamlet, and check the road conditions before you leave. The narrow fjord with its welcoming community is worth the drive. Locals are proud of their seven-tiered **Klifbrekkufossar** falls, cute church, wondrous views and serene solitude. You can also book a winter adventure on *mjoifjordur.is*, take the ferry from Neskaupstaður (p158) and stay for a few days to fully appreciate the fjord's attractions.

Egilsstaðir

From the turn-off to Reyðarfjörður, it's a 30-minute drive to **Egilsstaðir**, the region's largest town. The road goes through Fagridalur valley, with viewpoints along the way that are good for a picnic. Some double as starting points for hikes (look out for the signs).

Continue into the centre of town and lose yourself in the unassuming design store **Hús handanna** *(10am-6pm Mon-Fri, 10am-4pm Sat & Sun)*. It carries mainly Icelandic and Scandinavian clothing brands, accessories, home decor and toys with an emphasis on quality and sustainability. You'll find a selection of photographs, artwork, crafts and design products by Icelandic designers and artists, highlighting culture and nature. A special platform is given to local creatives. Invest in a special souvenir, such as Saumakassinn, an inventive cross-stitch kit that allows you to recreate Icelandic landscapes yourself, or a piece of handmade chocolate.

Búðarárfoss • — 34km — Culture centre and culinary cradle of the East. — Egilsstaðir •

Flavours of the East

In Egilsstaðir, the region's culinary capital, make the most of local produce: homegrown barley, handpicked berries, local cheeses, free-roaming lamb and wild reindeer, among other delights.

HOW TO

Local eats: At Nielsen Restaurant, the menu usually includes at least one reindeer dish, as wild reindeer only exist in the East.

While you're here: Next door to Tehúsið, in a defunct slaughterhouse, **Sláturhúsið Art Center** *(11am-4pm Mon-Fri, noon-4pm Sat)* offers rotating exhibitions and regular performances.

Tip: Try Tehúsið's version of *hjónabandssæla* ('happy marriage' rhubarb-oat cake) called *Héraðssæla* in honour of the Fljótsdalshérað region.

As you enter the town, you'll drive past **Askur Taproom & Pizzeria** *(askurpizzeria.is/en)*, serving craft beer and great pizzas with interesting toppings.

As you continue into town, notice a grey timber building on the intersection of Rte 1 and Tjarnarbraut. **Nielsen Restaurant** *(cafenielsen.is)* is set in Egilsstaðir's oldest house, built in 1944. Local couple Sólveig and Kári returned from Reykjavík to open a fine-dining restaurant in their hometown that embraces the region's seasonal flavours. The lunch menu is simple: soup or fish of the day. The constantly evolving dinner menu highlights a fusion of local ingredients in creatively composed dishes built on tradition.

Cross over to the artsy part of town, and take a left on Rte 95, then right on Fénaðarklöpp. Hip hangout and hostel **Tehúsið** *(tehusid.is)* is great for an afternoon coffee – or raw cacao drink – and a slice of homemade cake, or filling homemade soup. In the evening, Tehúsið transforms into a lively bar, which visitors and locals seek out to have a chat and a beer, or to listen to live music – there are regular happenings.

On the way out of town, stop by **Eldhúsið** (p157) for creative cuisine on the lake's edge.

EXPERIENCE ★

Wild Icelandic blueberries

Explore the Fair Fjords

Over the mountains and down to the sea, no more than an hour from Egilsstaðir, you'll find picture-perfect seaside towns Seyðisfjörður and Bakkagerði in the Borgarfjörður Eystri fjord. Soak in their colourful landscapes, feast on delicious food and partake in cultural happenings.

HOW TO

Nearest stop: Egilsstaðir

Getting there: Rte 93 goes to Seyðisfjörður and Rte 94 to Borgarfjörður Eystri. The drive takes 30 minutes and one hour, respectively, but as you'll cross mountain passes, allow more time and be careful when it's foggy, snowy or slippery. The roads may close in winter – check on *road.is*.

When to go: Most services, restaurants and tours are available June to August; some can be booked in other seasons. More cultural events are on in summer, when most tourists visit. Spot puffins May to August. Winter brings skiing, Northern Lights, an art festival and snowy landscapes.

More info: Visit Austurland *(east.is)* is the region's tourism office; also check out *visitseydisfjordur.com* and *borgarfjordureystri.is*.

Cradle of Creativity

Trapped between tall mountains, **Seyðisfjörður** is not as isolated as it seems – it's the country's only international ferry port. Artists have long been drawn to this friendly fishing town, transforming it into a colourful cultural hub known for its rainbow street and blue church.

Walk 15 to 20 minutes up a hill to view *Tvísöngur*, a sound sculpture by German artist Lukas Kühne, consisting of five concrete domes. Then, visit **Skaftfell** *(skaftfell.is)*, East Iceland's regional visual art centre, founded in 1998 in honour of Swiss artist Dieter Roth. In addition to exhibitions and cultural events, Skaftfell has an artist residency and a bistro. Pop into artsy **Blóðberg** *(blodberg.com)* for Icelandic design products, or invest in a hand-knitted *lopapeysa* sweater in **Handverksmarkaður**.

In February, **List í ljósi** *(listiljosi.com)* art festival illuminates Seyðisfjörður with glowing artwork, and in summer, musicians perform as part of the **Blue Church Summer Concert Series** *(blaakirkjan.is)*.

Wonders of Nature

The colourful landscapes of Borgarfjörður Eystri inspired painter Jóhannes S Kjarval (1885–1972), who painted the altar for the **Bakkagerði** church, and film director Guðmundur Arnar Guðmundsson, who set his 2016 coming-of-age drama *Heartstone* there.

A paradise for hikers, the area has myriad marked paths, the best-known leading to **Stórurð**, a turquoise pond encircled by massive boulders. For guided exploration of Borgarfjörður Eystri,

WHERE TO EAT

Japanese cuisine meets Icelandic fishing culture in Seyðisfjörður's **Norð Austur Sushi & Bar** (p157), serving the freshest possible seafood.

At **Kaffi Lára – El Grillo Bar** in Seyðisfjörður *(facebook.com/kaffilara; 11.30am-10pm daily)*, the grilled lamb is the star, best enjoyed with the house lager. Listen to live music with the locals.

A day in Borgarfjörður Eystri calls for a delicious dinner at **Frystiklefinn Restaurant** *(blabjorg.is; noon-9pm summer)*. Tuck into local lamb or fish with a beer brewed next door.

From top: Blue Church, Seyðisfjörður; Stórurð

book a walk, hike or bike tour with **Fjord Bikes** *(fjordbikes.com)*.

Nowhere else in Iceland can you get as close to puffins as in Borgarfjörður Eystri. On land-tied islet **Hafnarhólmi**, a few minutes' drive out of town, is a bird-watching house where puffins and other nesting seabirds can be observed. **Puffin Adventures** *(puffin.is)* offers puffin and other wildlife-watching by boat.

On the last weekend in July, visitors crowd the village for the annual **Bræðslan** *(braedslan.is)* music festival, where many of Iceland's leading musicians perform. Tickets must be booked far in advance.

Circle Lake Lagarfljót

Prepare for an adventurous drive around Lagarfljót, Iceland's longest and third-largest lake. Murky and mysterious, it's believed to be the hideout of a malicious giant serpent that pops up a hump occasionally

Nearest stop: Egilsstaðir

Getting there: The drive takes about 1½ hours but allow at least half a day to enjoy the experiences along the way. Take Rte 931, then Rte 933 with optional detours on Rte 934 to the Wilderness Center or Rte 910 to the highlands.

When to go: In spring, the trees are budding and migrant birds arrive; fewer tourists but more unreliable weather. Summer means warmer weather, endless daylight, all services available and everything in bloom. In autumn, the foliage turns vivid colours. Winter offers snow-covered landscapes, cross-country skiing and the Northern Lights.

More info: Visit Austurland *(east.is)* is the region's tourism office.

Head out from Egilsstaðir along the lake's southern bank. After about 20 minutes you'll enter **Hallormsstaðaskógur**, Iceland's largest forest. With 40km of marked paths, you can take short or long walks through the woods, through the arboretum, up to Fálkaklettur cliff for a marvellous view, or down to the lake at Atlavík. Tucked away in the forest is **Hótel Hallormsstaður** *(hotel701.is)* with a range of rooms, two restaurants and a spa, open from mid-May through September.

Drive through the forest on Rte 931, then continue on Rte 933 to **Hrafnkelsstaðir** farm, where a saga hero once lived. Check out the info sign at a viewpoint by the lake before driving around it to **Skriðuklaustur**. This stately country manor was once home to author Gunnar Gunnarsson. Immerse yourself in his stories, and afterwards visit the monastery, which was operated at Skriðuklaustur in the Middle Ages, via virtual reality. Next to the manor is **Snæfellsstofa**, a visitor centre for Vatnajökull National Park. Learn about its flora and fauna in a free exhibition about the East.

Lace up your boots – the hike to **Hengifoss** awaits! The starting point is just five minutes from Skriðuklaustur. Park the car and start the short but relatively steep hike (2.5km each way). Take a breather midway to admire its sister fall, **Litlanesfoss**, framed by columnar basalt. As you reach the top, Hengifoss reveals its 128m glory, tumbling through a layered horseshoe-shaped canyon. Cross the footbridge and, as you make your way down, remember to take in the view of Lagarfljót and the sprawling forest on the other side.

WILDERNESS CENTER

Take Rte 933 from Skriðuklaustur further inland, then continue on Rte 934 to the **Wilderness Center** (wilderness.is), a 15-minute drive in total. It's like a time warp: the farmhouse, where the centre is based, looks exactly like it did in its heyday, in the early 1900s. The centre offers refreshments and accommodation, tours and a fascinating exhibition on life on the edge of the wilderness. Hungry for more adventures? Rte 910 takes you to mountain retreat **Laugarfell** (laugarfell.is; summer only), onwards to Kárahnjúkar hydropower plant, natural wonders and wilderness within an hour's drive from Skriðuklaustur.

If you work up a hunger, head to **Asparhúsið** (modirjord.is; 10am-5pm Tue-Sat Jun-Aug, 11am-5pm Tue-Sat May & Sep), the restaurant of organic farm Móðir jörð, for filling soup, homemade bread and homegrown greens. In a renovated farmhouse on the highlands' borders, the **Wilderness Center** (wilderness.is) serves traditional, hearty meals, and cake at 'coffee time'. Or reap your rewards after your waterfall hike at the **Hengifoss Food Truck** (facebook.com/hengifossfoodtruck; 11am-6pm Jun-Aug). Order lamb or vegetable soup, fresh waffles, ewe's-milk ice cream and other local treats.

The author in a hot spring on the Snæfellsnes Peninsula (p228)
LAUREN BREEDLOVE

 INSIGHT

Slow and Solo on the Ring Road

Lauren Breedlove used to max out her time, packing everything she could into every minute. That changed after a solo summer road trip in Iceland, where she navigated the Ring Road. Iceland's striking beauty, healing hot springs and unpredictable weather helped her slow down and savour the moment.

WORDS BY **LAUREN BREEDLOVE**
Lauren is a New York-based writer and photographer specialising in authentic culinary and cultural experiences.

WHILE I'VE EMBARKED on solo trips all over the world, from road tripping the Faroe Islands to hiking in Peru, the notion of driving the entire way around Iceland alone was initially a little daunting. But there's no better way to explore the country than with the freedom and flexibility that self-driving offers, particularly since I tend to stop every five minutes to take photos. Photography is my passion, and trust me, in Iceland you will fill up your memory cards.

I hit the ground running; no, sprinting. I had prepared a jam-packed itinerary for my 11 days, fuelled by excitement, petrol-station hot dogs and my usual need to see absolutely everything. My carefully curated map of what

I wanted to see and do included all the main attractions, from Skógafoss and Jökulsárlón glacier lagoon in the south to Goðafoss and Mývatn in the north.

Partway through Southwest Iceland, I started to feel as though I was checking off these gorgeous places with each photo, moving onto the next without really absorbing the wonder of what I'd seen. Finally, on a planned visit to Seljavallalaug, Iceland's oldest swimming pool, my fast-paced mindset started to shift. It was close to midnight, and although I still had daylight on my side, I'd had a long, nonstop day, so I allowed myself to linger. I was taking my time, setting up different shots, experimenting with angles and relishing the mountain scenery surrounding the thermal pool, when a fellow photographer arrived. We bonded, trading highlights and tips from our trip so far, and it felt refreshing to just enjoy the place I was in instead of rushing to my next stop.

Slower travel wasn't a simple thing to adopt, but I found myself craving a gentler pace in order to get more out of each location I visited. As it turns out, the old saying 'quality over quantity' is right. Thermal hot springs, in particular, are not places to rush through – traditionally they're places to chat and relax, and a big part of Icelandic culture. I've gained precious insights while soaking in their steaming waters, such as a recommendation to visit Uppspuni, Iceland's first mini wool-processing mill, and its adorable wool boutique, located just off the Ring Road near the village of Hella. Hot springs are also where I learned about the country's national liquor, Brennivín (the traditional accompaniment to fermented shark), and got a hot tip for a spot off the Ring Road in the Eastfjords where puffins abound. When delayed by a sudden storm (a common occurrence in Iceland), I discovered Soup Company in Vík, where I warmed up with the best fish soup I'd ever had.

By the time I made it to the north, I was feeling less frantic, yet still fulfilled with all that I had seen and done. I ventured down a bumpy gravel road to Dettifoss, where I stayed to watch the changing light for a possible afternoon rainbow. As I made my way west, I found time for a trek to Glymur Waterfall, testing my limits as a solo hiker. From the top, the view was spectacular: seabirds diving through the mist of Iceland's second-tallest waterfall. My loop around the Ring Road came to an end in Reykjavík, where I explored the city on foot with no real agenda in mind, discovering a cool flea market, fresh fish and chips and killer coffee that I sipped on a rainy morning while reading a book, with nowhere to be. Slow travel got the best of me, and I was grateful.

While the Ring Road is Iceland's main highway, it's peppered with detour opportunities that feel like an adventure within an adventure. Take the time to check them out and you'll stumble across natural attractions and photo ops that'll blow your mind, such as the lesser-known Kvernufoss, tucked into a cinematic canyon just a short hike down from the ever-popular Skógafoss. Or Hrunalaug, a small natural hot spring that is absolutely worth the half-hour trip from the Ring Road.

Although I still practise fast travel at times, this solo road trip helped me find a balance. Now, I seek out situations where slow travel will leave me with a deeper sense of place. I credit this solo road trip around the Ring Road with forging my deep connection to Iceland, inspiring my seven (and counting) return trips – that and the hot dogs, because they are delicious.

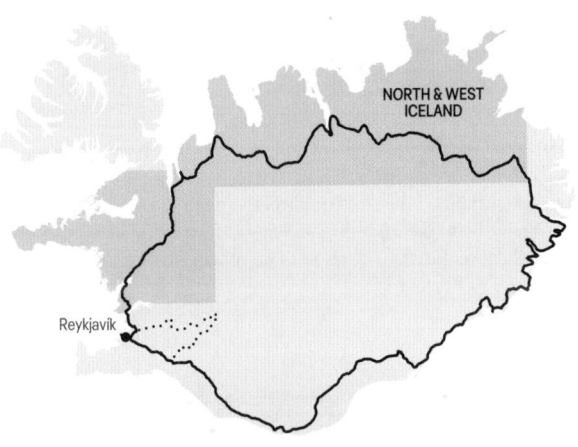

NORTH & WEST ICELAND

Driving across Iceland's north, you'll cross a series of high plateaux and traverse deep valleys that lie between the remote northern coast and the astonishing volcanic highlands of the interior. Detours are many – to Iceland's highest farm at Möðrudalur, the remarkable waterfall-and-canyon combo of Dettifoss and Jökulsárgljúfur, or whale watching off Húsavík. Beautifully sited Akureyri is one of our favourite Icelandic towns, and beyond lie the pristine landscapes of Iceland's wild west, with dramatic falls and ancient volcanic craters.

Snæfellsjökull (p228)
MATHIAS BERLIN/SHUTTERSTOCK

Egilsstaðir

For much of the way until now, the Ring Road has rarely strayed far from the coast. But the route beyond Egilsstaðir cuts across a swathe of Iceland's northern interior, and at times it's like crossing the moon. The route follows river valleys, traverses vast treeless plains, and passes turn-offs to Iceland's highest farm, a waterfall-canyon combo and a climbable volcano that we dare you to resist. The route ends on the shores of Lake Mývatn, in the tiny town of Reykjahlíð.

Anthony Ham

Hverir (p180)
LORENZA62/SHUTTERSTOCK

Reykjahlíð

172.5 KM
2–3 HOURS' DRIVE

THIS LEG:
- Egilsstaðir
- Vök Baths
- Jökuldalur
- Rjúkandafoss
- Km97 Lookout
- Beitarhúsið Café
- Bishop's Cairn Viewpoint
- Hrossaborg
- Hverir
- Mývatn Lookout
- Jarðböðin
- Reykjahlíð

Driving Notes

Road conditions along this stretch are excellent; as ever, approach one-lane bridges with caution. Campervans and caravans seem more prevalent here than elsewhere – overtake with care. If you're heading for Möðrudalur, there are two turn-offs for the F901; we recommend the westernmost one (8km), at Beitarhúsið Café, but the earlier turn-off (31km) has its fans.

Breaking Your Journey

There are no towns between Egilsstaðir and Reykjahlíð. But at the 103km mark, cosy Beitarhúsið Café (p177) is a refuge of hearty meals. And just 8km down the F901, its larger, sister property at Möðrudalur has another cafe and lots of different accommodation. At both properties, you pay 100kr to use the bathroom.

Anthony's Tips

BEST MEAL Pull over for the *kjötsúpa* (Icelandic lamb meat soup) or waffles at Beitarhúsið Café (p175).

FAVOURITE VIEW Anywhere along the Jökuldalur Canyon (p174).

ESSENTIAL STOP Take the side road to Möðrudalur (p176) and organise an adventure that goes further.

ROAD-TRIP TIP Although Rte 901 to Möðrudalur is only 'semi-paved', it is accessible by 2WD in summer.

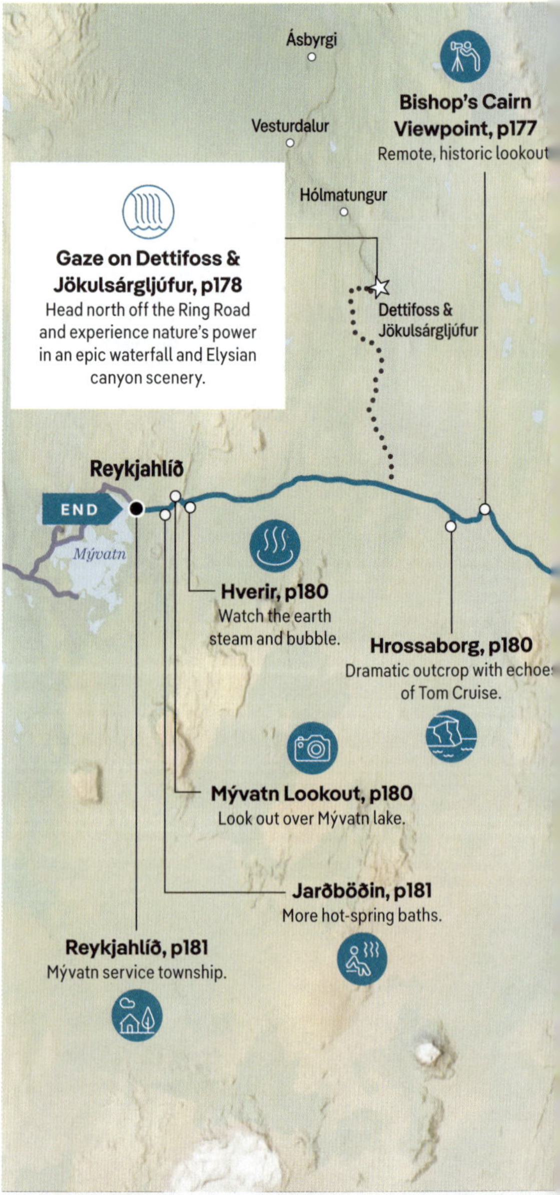

Ásbyrgi

Vesturdalur

Bishop's Cairn Viewpoint, p177
Remote, historic lookout

Hólmatungur

Gaze on Dettifoss & Jökulsárgljúfur, p178
Head north off the Ring Road and experience nature's power in an epic waterfall and Elysian canyon scenery.

Dettifoss & Jökulsárgljúfur

Reykjahlíð
END
Mývatn

Hverir, p180
Watch the earth steam and bubble.

Hrossaborg, p180
Dramatic outcrop with echoes of Tom Cruise.

Mývatn Lookout, p180
Look out over Mývatn lake.

Jarðböðin, p181
More hot-spring baths.

Reykjahlíð, p181
Mývatn service township.

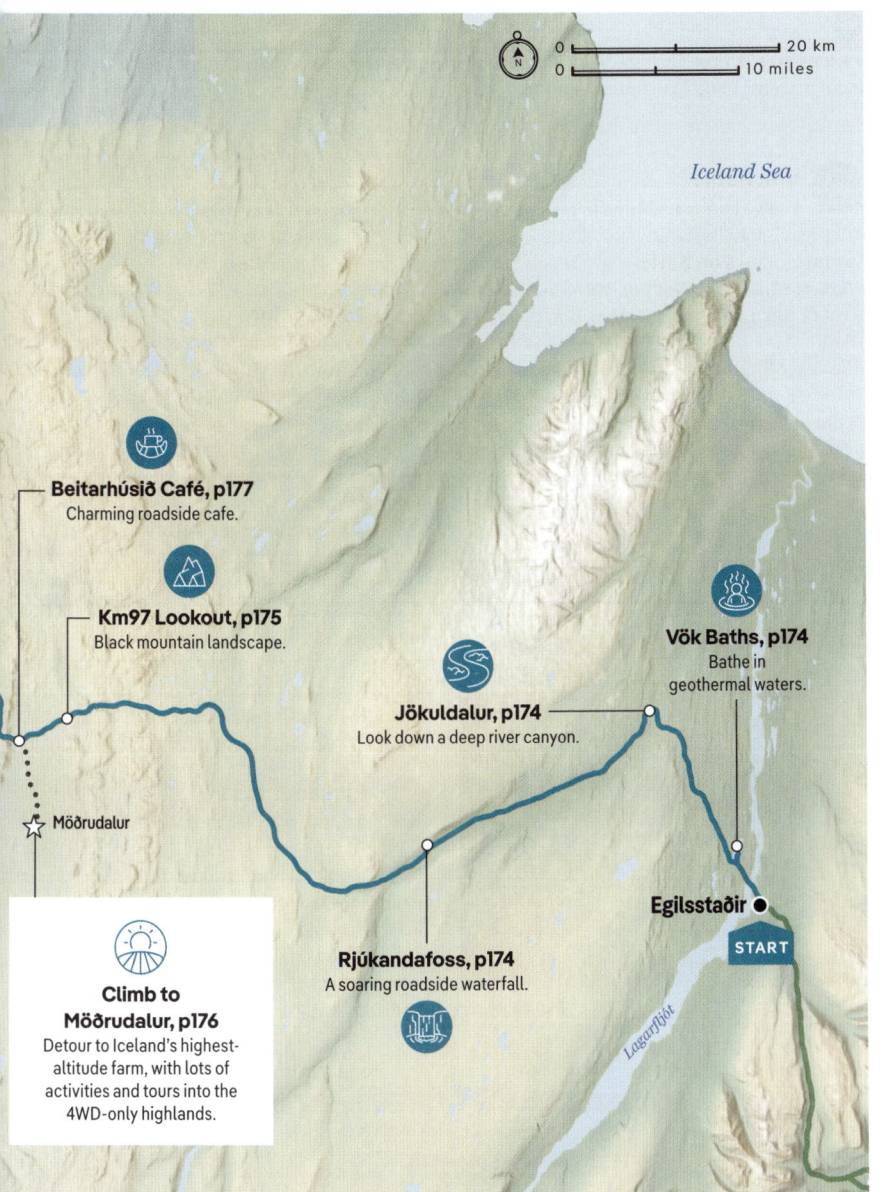

PREVIOUS STOP Egilsstaðir (p160) is the starting point of this leg, which goes all the way from Iceland's east to deep in the inner north.

Vök Baths

You've barely had time to pick up speed after leaving Egilsstaðir when it's time to take the turn-off to **Vök Baths** *(vokbaths.is; adult/student/child 7490/5290/3590kr)*, 5km northwest of town and just a further 1km down the road.

This geothermal bathing spot on lake Urriðavatn has four stunning baths, including two pentagonal pools out on the lake that are a little like infinity pools. You can even jump into the lake to cool off before returning to waters that can usually range between 37°C and 41°C. You can rent swimsuits, bathrobes and towels for an additional cost.

The complex was designed by the same architects that brought you the world-famous Blue Lagoon (p54) near Reykjavík.

Jökuldalur

Around 23km after leaving Egilsstaðir (or 18km from the Vök Baths turn-off), you will round a bend and descend towards a bridge – be ready, because the car park is just before the bridge and easy to overshoot. If you see it too late, cross the bridge and turn around at the turn-off for Rte 917.

The **Jökuldalur river valley** here is a glorious surprise, cutting a straight, frothing path between 50m- to 100m-high cliffs. This is one of Iceland's larger rivers in the northeast of the country, and the road, which swings here to the southwest, will follow the river for another 30km, offering glimpses along the way. But the view from the car park is the best of all, and really sets up the trip for the road ahead.

Rjúkandafoss

As always in Iceland, drive too fast and you'll miss these lovely falls down off the high cliffs. Sure, 139m-high **Rjúkandafoss** isn't going to make the list of Iceland's Top Five Waterfalls. But they would be a main attraction anywhere else, and, personally, we never tire of these quiet natural miracles that animate the Icelandic roadside.

Rjúkandafoss

FROM LEFT: GESTUR GISLASON/SHUTTERSTOCK, SEOL.C/SHUTTERSTOCK

Egilsstaðir — 5.5km — Vök Baths — 18km — Jökuldalur — 26km —

Pull over and enjoy the view in this stretch.

Dishes at Vogafjós Cowshed Cafe, Reykjahlíð

It's a short walk of perhaps 250m up the hill to the base of the waterfall, where you can sign the visitor log. The falls are fed by the river Ysti-Rjúkandi, coming down off Mt Sandfell, and drop down all the way to near the road's edge.

Km97 Lookout

The further from Egilsstaðir and Iceland's east, the more the landscape transforms into a high volcanic plateau, devoid of trees and as black as the River Styx. It's an eerie crossing, until you come over a minor pass at close to the 97km mark and one of northern Iceland's finest **panoramas** explodes into view. Thankfully, there's a spot to pull over and take photos or simply gaze in awe.

BEST PLACES TO EAT

Beitarhúsið Café, Ring Road $$
Waffles, 'love ball' donuts, Icelandic lamb meat soup: the food here is excellent. Keep warm inside or outside in the sun; it opens year-round. *(9am-8pm Jun-Sep, 9am-7pm Mar-May & Oct-Dec, 9am-6pm Jan & Feb)*

Fjallakaffi, Möðrudalur $$
Same owners as Beitarhúsið, same great food, and an equally spectacular setting 8km down the road. *(fjalladyrd.is; 7am-10pm May-Sep, shorter hours rest of year)*

Vogafjós Cowshed Cafe, Reykjahlíð $$
Part of a working dairy farm south of Reykjahlíð. Order smoked lamb, housemade mozzarella, dill-cured Arctic char and geysir bread. *(vogafjosfarmresort.is/en/restaurant; noon-10pm May-Sep, shorter hours rest of year)*

Rjúkandafoss — 50km — Km97 Lookout — 6km — Beitarhúsið Café

The road to Möðrudalur is kept open year-round.

Climb to Möðrudalur

The highest-altitude farm in Iceland – it sits at 469m above sea level – Möðrudalur gives you a taste of the drama-filled highlands of Iceland's epic interior.

Nearest stop: The turn-off to Möðrudalur is at Beitarhúsið Café.

Getting here: The 8km from the cafe to Möðrudalur is unpaved but is kept in excellent condition. Even in winter it's normally cleared daily, but you can check conditions on *umferdin.is/en*. You can drive this section in a 2WD vehicle.

When to go: Year-round.

Tip: Stay overnight at Möðrudalur at Fjalladýrð (p180) and listen to the night silence.

For centuries, Möðrudalur (pronounced *muh-thru-dalur*) was one of Iceland's most isolated farms, the kind of place where the line between survival and famine was razor-thin. If you've ever been here during a winter snowstorm, as we have, you'll understand just how small the human footprint is when confronted by nature's fury.

If you were to come here and go no further, you'd still have a worthwhile detour. But Möðrudalur is all part of one larger, integrated complex that includes an information office, tour/activities operator named **Fjalladýrð** *(fjalladyrd.is)*, cafe and accommodation. Enjoy a hearty soup in the charming Fjallakaffi (p180), watch the fascinating 20-minute film of the 2014 Holuhraun eruption, Iceland's largest in nearly 300 years, in the small on-site information office, and take in the views of **Herðubreið** (1682m), which Icelanders call the 'Queen of the Mountains'. Better still, do all of it and stay overnight for the full immersive experience. Ask at the info office about hiking, horse riding and mountain biking.

If you have the time, consider one of its day or multiday super-jeep tours into the highlands; one tour takes you to the summit of Herðubreið.

From left: Icelandic horse; Cabin at Möðrudalur

Along the Way We Met...

ADAM PLEDZIEWICZ Möðrudalur really is the gateway to the highlands, especially for people who travel around Iceland in a 2WD. The super-jeep tours from here can take you places you simply can't reach otherwise, like Askja, Herðubreið and Kverkfjöll. And I always tell travellers to take the 901 beyond here as a 23km prettier alternative to the Ring Road; it used to be part of the Ring Road until the early 2000s. It's now much quieter, goes over the mountains and is fine in a 2WD.

Adam has worked at Möðrudalur for more than eight years.

ADAM'S TIP: Don't even think of driving down into the highlands along the F905 and F910 in a 2WD because of deep holes and river crossings.

The black lava landscape eases down into a valley with a backdrop of conical mountains scattered near and far. If the sun is shining and white puffs of clouds fill the sky, the photos you'll take home will surely be among your favourites.

Beitarhúsið Café

Right by the roadside, around 6km beyond the viewpoint and down on the valley floor, the charming **Beitarhúsið Café** is both a remote human outpost and oasis-like reprieve from the blackness all around you. Inhabiting two conjoined, gorgeous wood-plank traditional buildings, it's cosy and intimate inside. It's worth stopping regardless of whether you're hungry – for coffee, waffles or a warming soup.

Stop here for its own sake, but also consider taking the detour to the owners' other property at Möðrudalur, only 8km up the road and just as lovely.

Bishop's Cairn Viewpoint

If you thought the landscape to this point was desolate, this small **lookout** just below a black-sand pass can feel like the very gates of hell. It's a brooding setting, facing down through a gap in the hills onto black sands to the far horizon. Known as **Hólsfjöll**, this is one of the least-inhabited parts of the country. There were a handful of farms here in the 10th century, then three more in the 17th century; it is believed that the landscape was covered in vegetation until the 16th century. However, severe wind erosion, desertification as a result of volcanoes up on the Vatnajökull ice cap and devastating flash floods from the Jökulsá á Fjöllum river have since laid waste to the landscape.

The name of the lookout dates back to the 12th century, when it marked the boundary between Iceland's two bishoprics – bishops and their emissaries would meet here to resolve disputes.

continues p180

Gaze on Dettifoss & Jökulsárgljúfur

If you want to get a sense of what the raw power of Icelandic nature can create, don't miss these world-class spots. Dettifoss has the highest volume of any European waterfall, and volcanic floods and flows off the Vatnajökull ice cap have carved a canyon that is one of the country's most dramatic.

HOW TO

Nearest stop: The turn-off is almost equidistant between Hrossaborg and Hverir, although it's a little closer to the latter.

Getting here: There is no public transport to the site. Unless you're on a tour, you'll need your own wheels. The road north of the Ring Road is paved as far as Ásbyrgi.

When to go: The road to Dettifoss and beyond may be closed in winter. When this happens, the only way here is on a tour (through Möðrudalur (p176), for example).

Dettifoss

There are times up here when you just look at the landscape and shake your head in wonder and disbelief. That's partly because there's nothing anywhere in Europe that can match the raw power of Dettifoss. Close to 400 cu metres of water thunder over its edge every second in summer; sometimes the spray is so dense it can be difficult to see which way the water flows.

The falls can be seen from either side of the canyon, but there is no bridge at the site itself, so you have to make a choice when leaving the Ring Road. We prefer the more westerly Rte 862, because it puts you on the right side for other attractions. Access from the west via Rte 862 is also easiest, although check conditions first on *umferdin.is/en* during winter. On both sides of the canyon, you'll need to walk 15 to 20 minutes from the car park to reach the falls.

Dettifoss may be the most impressive, but nearby, smaller **Selfoss** (upstream) and **Hafragilsfoss** (downstream) are part of the same system.

Ásbyrgi & Beyond

The furthest north you can go in Jökulsárgljúfur (and where the paved road ends), Ásbyrgi is a U-shaped canyon encircled by 50m-high cliffs. Hiking here is like entering a lost, almost paradisical world. All hikes begin from Ásbyrgi's **Gljúfrastofa Visitor Centre** *(vjp.is)*, which also has maps and bathrooms.

THE JÖKULSÁRGLJÚFUR CONTEXT

Jökulsárgljúfur (or 'Glacial River Canyon') was formed by glacial melt waters and their accompanying debris. There have been 'super floods' here the volume of four Amazon rivers, and they have scoured and scrubbed the cliffs, buffeting them with giant basalt blocks. And all of that in the mere blink of a geological moment, over just 4000 years. Even today, the river that goes down the canyon discharges the equivalent of one Olympic-sized swimming pool every 13 seconds.

Dettifoss

But there are numerous entry points into the canyon, with its cathedral-like spaces, along the Jökulsá river. One of these is pristine **Vesturdalur**, a valley filled with trolls turned to rock pillars after being caught by the sun's arrival.

South of Vesturdalur is **Hólmatungur**, where the river channel narrows, creating roiling water and whirlpools.

Hljóðaklettar (Echo Rocks) is a good picnic stop between Dettifoss and Ásbyrgi. The area gets its name from an acousitc effect of the rock formations that makes it impossible to determine the direction of the roaring river.

> **BEST PLACES TO SLEEP**
>
> **Helluhraun 13, Reykjahlíð** $$
> Host Ásdis welcomes guests to this small, homely B&B with lava-field views, three rooms, shared bathrooms and bright, spotless everything. *(helluhraun13.blogspot.com)*
>
> **Berjaya Hotel Mývatn, Reykjahlíð** $$
> Sleek guest rooms, some with partial views of the lake across the road, make this one of the better choices on the lakeshore. *(icelandairhotels.com)*
>
> **Fosshotel Mývatn, Reykjahlíð** $$$
> Large, contemporary full-service hotel with elevated lake rooms, all swathed in Scandinavian pine. *(fosshotel.is)*
>
> **Fjalladýrð, Möðrudalur** $$
> At high-altitude Möðrudalur farm, there's something for every budget, from camping to guesthouses, turf-roofed cottages and luxe en-suite rooms, all with views of Herðubreið. Open year-round. *(fjalladyrd.is)*

continued from p177

The viewpoint is not clearly signed, but the turn-off is next to the county sign for 'NorðurÞing' with 'Hólsfjöll' beneath it.

Hrossaborg

There are so many beautiful mountains and volcanic uplifts in these parts that it's easy to miss **Hrossaborg**, which lies south of the Ring Road around 30km beyond Beitarhúsið Café. Setting south off the Ring Road down Rte F88 can feel like casting off into an ocean from a deserted shore. Hrossaborg itself is a 10,000-year-old crater shaped like an amphitheatre, and its main claim to human fame is that it was used as a film set for the Tom Cruise sci-fi flick *Oblivion* (2013).

It's a glorious spot, especially the views from the crater rim, and, if you're lucky, you may even have it to yourself.

Hverir

Just before the final approach to Reykjahlíð, magical, ochre-hued **Hverir** *(parking per vehicle 1000kr)* is an otherworldly collection of mud cauldrons, steaming vents, radiant mineral deposits and piping fumaroles. It really does feel like you're on another planet.

Follow the safe paths, marked by ropes, through these toxic brews and broths – they are there to protect both you from serious injury and this fragile landscape from human misadventures. And avoid any lighter-coloured soil as well.

A walking trail climbs up adjacent **Námafjall** ridge, which perches atop the spreading zone of the Mid-Atlantic Ridge plate boundary. This 30-minute climb provides a grand vista over the steamy surroundings, even if you don't go all the way to the top.

Mývatn Lookout

After Hverir, the Ring Road loops up and over the mountains, before continuing down into Reykjahlíð. Just over the pass, take the turn-off to the car park and viewpoint. This will be your first glimpse of the lake **Mývatn** – on a sunny day, the distant waters can appear somewhere between turquoise and cerulean.

Hverir — 3km — Mývatn Lookout — 2km — Jarðböðin — 18km — Reykjahlíð

The steam here emerges at 200°C.

Also of interest on the slope to the northwest are the steaming geothermal vents known as **Bjarnarflag**; the steam sometimes emerges at close to 200°C, and farming attempts here failed because the potatoes often emerged from the ground already boiled! At the base of the hill is a visually arresting but toxic turquoise pond.

Jarðböðin

Down a side road heading southwest just after the pond, **Jarðböðin**, or **Mývatn Nature Baths** *(myvatnnaturebaths.is; adult/concession/ 13-15-year-old/child 7400/4800/3600kr/free)*, is northern Iceland's answer to Reykjavík's Blue Lagoon (p54); it nicely bookends this leg of the Ring Road between two indulgent bathing experiences. Here you can soak in powder-blue, mineral-rich waters while enjoying the picturesque steam baths or order from the swim-up bar. Arrive early or late in the day to avoid tour groups.

Reykjahlíð

If tiny **Reykjahlíð**, perched on the shores of Mývatn, were anywhere else, you'd probably pass by without noticing. But after arriving here without having seen another town in 168km or more of driving, you'll either welcome the return to 'civilisation' or miss the empty horizon, depending on your perspective. It's a good place to stop to fill up the fuel tank, eat something – check out Vogafjós Cowshed Cafe (p175) – or even stay overnight and plot your next move. For accommodation, try Helluhraun 13, Berjaya Hotel Mývatn or Fosshotel Mývatn . The only attraction of note is the **village church**, which has a miraculous backstory. During the Krafla eruption in 1729, lava destroyed most of the village, but the flow parted, missing the church by only metres. Make of that what you will...

Hrossaborg

Reykjahlíð

This journey across Iceland's north is both a gateway to another world – to the cluster of sites around Mývatn, and the wonderful world of whales off Húsavík – and a picturesque drive in its own right. For the most part, it's a route of quiet pleasures, but the thundering falls of Goðafoss provide more than their fair share of excitement. And at journey's end, Northern Iceland's beautifully situated main town – Akureyri.

Anthony Ham

Pseudocraters near Mývatn (p188)
NEUROBIT/SHUTTERSTOCK

Akureyri

**112 KM
1½ HOURS' DRIVE**

THIS LEG:

- Reykjahlíð
- Mývatn North Lookout
- Sigurgeir's Bird Museum
- Vindbelgjarfjall
- Skútustaðagígar & Southern Mývatn
- Laugar
- Goðafoss
- Ljósavatn
- Eyjafjörður Viewpoint
- Akureyri Lookout
- Akureyri

Driving Notes

This stretch of the Ring Road is busier than most, linking as it does a number of towns and small settlements. There's a choice to be made as you approach Akureyri – take the 7km-long tunnel *(2150kr)* or Rte 84; the latter is free and very scenic, but it does add 16km to your trip. As you might imagine, we've taken the scenic route.

Breaking Your Journey

This leg's hardly long enough to need a pit stop, but Akureyri has dozens of places to eat and stay. If you forgot to fuel up, Laugar, 37km out of Reykjahlíð, has a petrol station and snacks right by the roadside. Otherwise, for most other needs, hold on for Akureyri.

Anthony's Tips

BEST MEAL Right on the harbour, Gamli Baukur (p193) has atmosphere and great food.

FAVOURITE VIEW From the Eyjafjörður Viewpoint (p190), or a breaching humpback whale (p192).

ESSENTIAL STOP It just has to be the waterfalls at Goðafoss (p189).

ROAD-TRIP TIP If you do take the Akureyri tunnel, pay online at *tunnel.is* within 24 hours.

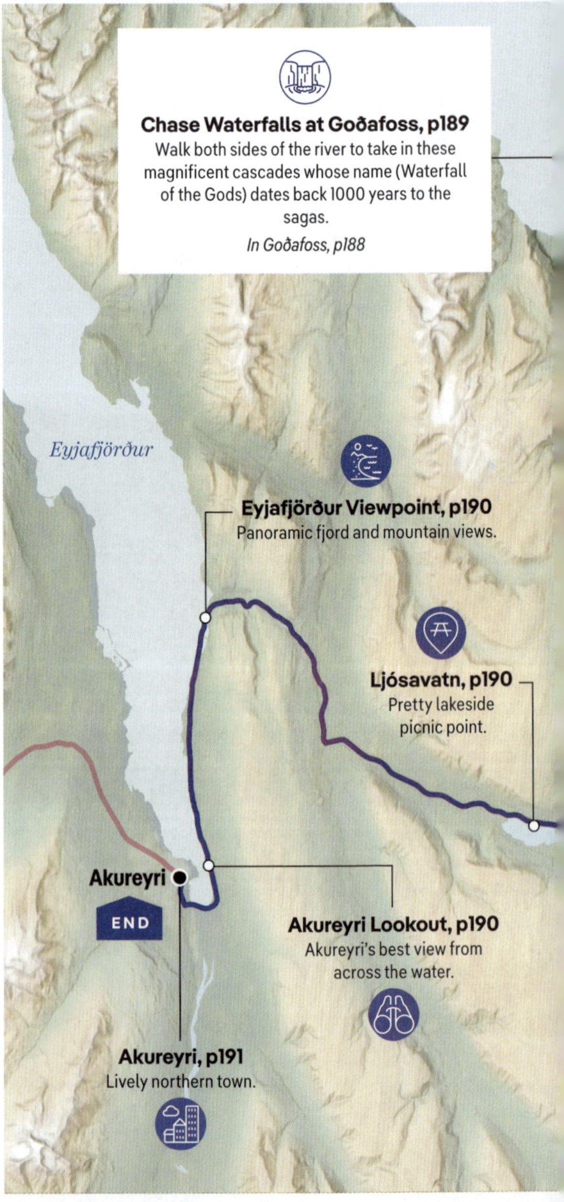

Chase Waterfalls at Goðafoss, p189
Walk both sides of the river to take in these magnificent cascades whose name (Waterfall of the Gods) dates back 1000 years to the sagas.
In Goðafoss, p188

Eyjafjörður

Eyjafjörður Viewpoint, p190
Panoramic fjord and mountain views.

Ljósavatn, p190
Pretty lakeside picnic point.

Akureyri ● END

Akureyri Lookout, p190
Akureyri's best view from across the water.

Akureyri, p191
Lively northern town.

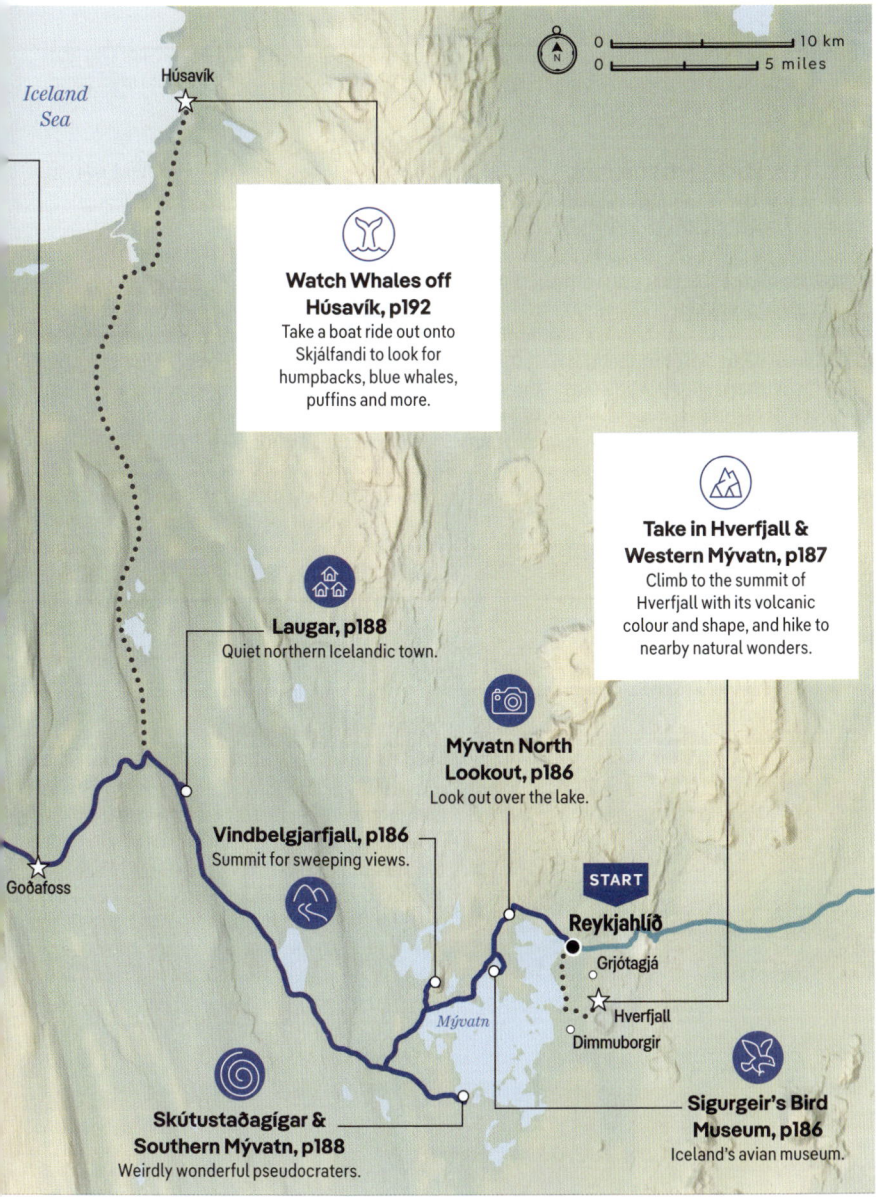

PREVIOUS STOP Begin this leg at Reykjahlíð (p181) near the eastern shore of Mývatn. The first stop, Mývatn North Lookout, is a short distance around the northern shore of the lake from there.

Mývatn North Lookout

A few kilometres northwest of Reykjahlíð – just past the church and opposite the turn-off where Rte 87 heads north to Húsavík – this elevated **lookout** is perhaps Mývatn's best from ground level. From here, you can take in almost the whole lake, and, as such, it's a good place to get your bearings. Vindbelgjarfjall dominates the western shore, while out to the east, the black Hverfjall is impossible to miss. In between, islands lie scattered across waters that can be any shade between turquoise and black, depending on the weather – few lakes have such a variety of hues and moods; the black feels like foreboding and the turquoise is amazing.

Sigurgeir's Bird Museum

If you're into birds and need a real-life primer to familiarise yourself with what you might see out in the wild, **Sigurgeir's Bird Museum** (*fuglasafn.is*) is much better than any field guide. The museum occupies a beautiful lakeside structure in which contemporary lines meet traditional turf house. Inside, all but one of Iceland's bird species (the grey phalarope) have been stuffed by a taxidermist and mounted on display, as well as species from elsewhere around the world. This is not some stuffy old natural history museum basement – think designer lighting, lively, detailed captions and a cool cafe.

To practise what you've learned, rent a high-tech telescope here and head to one of the museum's bird hides.

Vindbelgjarfjall

Although Mývatn is surrounded by eye-catching landforms, none is as close to the shore – or dominates Mývatn views – quite like **Vindbelgjarfjall** (also known as Vindbelgur). For some of the best views anywhere in the area, climb to the 529m-high summit. The hike is steep and steady, but otherwise easy if you follow the trail that starts at a car park south of the peak, near the farm Vagnbrekka; signposts point you in the right direction. From up the top, look

View of Hverfjall over Mývatn

WENLIOU/SHUTTERSTOCK

Reykjahlíð — 4km — Sigurgeir's Bird Museum — 6km — Vindbelgjarfjall

Look for the museum turn-off as soon as you leave the lookout.

Take in Hverfjall & Western Mývatn

Looking like an artist's impression of a volcano, Hverfjall is a major highlight in these parts. Add in nearby Dimmuborgir and Grjótagjá and let Iceland again mess with your mind.

HOW TO

Nearest stop: Hverfjall is 6km from Reykjahlíð (p181), the starting point of this leg.

Getting here: Take Rte 848 (paved) south from Reykjahlíð for 3.5km, then take the gravel road (2.5km) east to the Hverfjall car park. The other sites are nearby.

When to go: Year-round.

Tip: You can visit as part of this route, or the previous leg from Egilsstaðir to Reykjahlíð (p171).

East of Mývatn, lavafields extend to the hills, and rising from their midst is Hverfjall (also called Hverfell). It's a classic version of what they call a tephra ring, which is formed by volcanic material (in this case, mostly ash) expelled during an eruption. This one was created 2500 years ago in a massive eruption and, unusually, its near-symmetrical form perfectly replicates the shape of a volcano. The highest point on the rim is 452m above sea level (although it's just 80m to 180m above the level of the car park) and the crater has a diameter of 1040m.

From the car park *(parking per vehicle 1000kr)*, which has toilets, a steep, 600m-long gravel path (HV1) scales the outer wall to the rim. Having made the effort, consider the challenging 3.2km trail that encircles the rim.

One option is to descend south off the rim to **Dimmuborgir** (literally 'Dark Castles'), a jagged lavafield of striking rock pillars; from mid-June to mid-August, there's a free, one-hour guided ranger walk here, starting at 10am. Another alternative is to hike the nearly 2km to **Grjótagjá**, a gaping fissure with a 45°C water-filled cave made famous by *Game of Thrones*.

Grjótagjá

> ### BEST PLACES TO EAT
>
>
>
> This isn't an area known for its restaurants – there are some to recommend at the start of the journey in Reykjahlíð (p181) and at journey's end in Akureyri (p194), but nothing in between. Where to stop for lunch? Plan ahead by buying food for a picnic and stop by the lakeshore at Mývatn North Lookout (p186), accompanied by an awesome natural soundtrack at Goðafoss (p189) or in likely solitude at Ljósavatn (p190). Of course, the other alternative is to detour to Húsavík (p192), which has a good selection of places near the harbour – try Fish & Chips (p193) or Gamli Baukur (p193).

out across the waters and, along the southern shore, its utterly bizarre pseudocraters.

The walk takes at least a half-hour to reach the base of the mountain, and another half-hour to climb to the summit.

Skútustaðagígar & Southern Mývatn

Mývatn's southern lakeshore is home to some of Iceland's weirdest-looking natural structures – and that's saying something in this country of weird-and-wonderful features. The **Skútustaðagígar** pseudocraters were created when boiling molten lava flowed into Mývatn lake millions of years ago, setting off gas explosions. These dramatic green dimples – they look like a field of mini meteor strikes – then came into being when trapped subsurface water boiled and popped, forming small scoria cones and craters. The easiest ones to reach are along a short path near Skútustaðir. From mid-June to mid-August, join the free, hour-long ranger-guided walk at 2pm.

While you're in the area, stop by **Mývatn Visitor Centre**, which has a fantastic relief map of the area.

Laugar

So empty are many roads in Iceland that it almost comes as a surprise when you see more than a couple of farm buildings huddled together. **Laugar** is one such place, with a service area – petrol station selling hot dogs and the like – up on the Ring Road, and a road heading east for around a kilometre, down into the valley and across to the village. There's nothing much to see, although this quiet place does offer a window on a way of life that's fairly representative of many Icelanders who live outside the larger settlements.

Goðafoss

One of Iceland's most celebrated waterfalls, steeped in saga legend, **Goðafoss** is far and away the most thrilling place to stop between Mývatn and Akureyri. There are two car parks, one on either side of the river, and unusually for Iceland, neither charges a fee! Park in either and walk to the other side via the footbridge. The west side of the river generally has fewer visitors, but the best and most varied views are from the east.

Chase Waterfalls at Goðafoss

Goðafoss could only happen in Iceland. Yes, the waters are dramatic and crash down with frightening natural force. But local legends dating back to the sagas also take centre stage.

HOW TO

Nearest stop: Goðafoss is itself a stop along this route.

Getting here: You could, in theory, take any bus along the Ring Road, but you could end up stranded. The two car parks are either side of a longish one-way bridge.

When to go: Year-round.

Tip: Try to get here early morning or evening to avoid the considerable crowds.

There are bigger, more powerful waterfalls in Iceland than Goðafoss (Waterfall of the Gods), but not many more beautiful. And not that you'd describe its flow as gentle – from whichever vantage point you view them, the waters vault over the rim with astonishing force and volume, cutting a swathe through the Bárðardalur lavafield as they go. There are two main currents, framing a narrower one in between, with a handful of other side falls, all launching down into the churning tumult below. The three main vantage points we recommend are the elevated viewing decks on both sides of the river, and the gravel 'beach' at water level on the east bank of the river.

As told in the Icelandic Sagas, in the year 1000 CE, the Alþingi (National Parliamet) agreed to let the *lögsögumaður* (law speaker), Þorgeir, decide whether Iceland would be Christian or pagan. He chose the former, and, on his way home, he cast his pagan idols to Norse gods into the waterfall, thus bestowing the falls' present name.

View of Goðafoss from above

Along the Way We Met...

CHRISTIAN SCHMIDT Why Húsavík? It's where the whales are! I love being able to go home at the end of the day and know that I've been able to take people who have never seen a whale out onto the water and show them these miraculous creatures. There's so much we don't know about them and there's always something new.

Christian has been a whale-watching guide for over 16 years.

CHRISTIAN'S TIP: *There's no real difference in what you'll see out on the water depending on the time of day, but if you take an evening tour in summer, it's so much quieter, with fewer boats and people.*

Ljósavatn

Just after Rte 85 rejoins the Ring Road from Húsavík, a small turn-off leads down to a picnic area on the shores of the lake **Ljósavatn**, dwarfed by towering mountains along its southern flank. Pray for sunshine and you might be rewarded with a fabulous view of the deeply textured mountain wall. Dozens of long parallel lines plunge down off the heights, carved by spring waterfalls and rivulets – the whole mountain face looks like it has been scoured by a rake.

Few people pull over here, which means that it may, if you're lucky, be yours alone to enjoy.

Eyjafjörður Viewpoint

This **lookout** (more a small pull-over point by the roadside) is situated on Rte 84 – the non-tunnel, longer route of the final approach into Akureyri. If you stayed on the Ring Road for the fast option, you miss out on this one...

After leaving the Ring Road, the road meanders alongside the scenic river Dalsmynni, climbing gently up the west wall of the valley, then rising more steeply up and over a pass to the northwest. After a couple of tight bends on the descent, a longer, straighter section begins running parallel to the eastern shore of Eyjafjörður. The view over the water is pretty enough, but pull into the parking area (room for only a couple of cars at a time) and you get the magical (almost ethereal when the sun is shining) view down the summit-studded valley, with layers of mountains in silhouette, to the southwest.

Akureyri Lookout

Just a few hundred metres beyond the roundabout where the tunnel and longer route rejoin, there's a parking area that faces directly across the water to Akureyri. In sunshine, the city's superb fjord-side setting and mountain backdrop is stunningly on display. Then again,

we've also seen it with a storm approaching, as a timely reminder of this northern city's exposure to the elements. Pick out the distinctive concrete church spire, or check to see if there is perhaps a cruise ship in harbour. And then return to the road to head for the city itself.

Akureyri

Akureyri (p194) is one of Iceland's most dynamic cities, a place whose inhabitants are passionate advocates for their city. With its long waterside paths, water activities, good restaurants and small pedestrianised centre, it's an agreeable place that rewards those who get out and explore on foot. It's also a major hub for travel in the north, the kind of place where you can come in from the wild, enjoy a decent meal, sleep in a comfortable bed and stock up on supplies before you venture out again.

BEST PLACES TO SLEEP

Akureyri has Northern Iceland's largest selection of places to stay (p197) with some truly excellent choices. The other good option, albeit on a detour off the Ring Road, is Húsavík, although accommodation there tends to fill up fast in summer and is often more expensive than in Akureyri. Húsavík possibilities include Kaldbaks-Kot (p193) or the Fosshótel Húsavík (p193). If you plan on whale watching, you could base yourself in Akureyri, leaving yourself a one-hour commute to reach Húsavík's harbour. But if you can, spend at least one night in Húsavík, where you'll enjoy a quieter experience and wake to superb views out beyond the harbour.

Ljósavatn

EXPERIENCE ★

Watch Whales off Húsavík

Among Iceland's best wildlife-watching experiences, a whale-watching tour is one of the biggest draws for travellers in the north. Three-hour boat tours head out in a variety of forms into Skjálfandi, a bay rich in krill, plankton and fish that draw whales, white-beaked dolphins and seabirds, particularly in summer.

HOW TO

Nearest stop: Mývatn North Lookout; between Laugar and Goðafoss (Rte 845); or Ljósavatn (Rte 85).

Getting here: The three possible routes from the Ring Road to Húsavík are close to Mývatn North Lookout (the partly gravel Rte 87; 57km, one hour), between Laugar and Goðafoss (Rte 845; 40km), and just east of Ljósavatn (Rte 85; 47km). Most travellers stay in Akureyri (one hour) or Húsavík itself. You can also do a tour en route to Akureyri.

When to go: The main whale-watching season runs from June to September, with mostly humpbacks. Blue whales are elusive, but your best chance is April and May, or October to December.

Tip: There's free parking behind the warehouses at the far southern end of the harbour.

Boat Options

There's no sight in nature more thrilling than watching a humpback whale surface, spout, groan and then dive again, its tail (flute) thrust into the air. Now imagine doing this without any engine noise as the backing track.

We're surprised it's taken this long, but some operators (North Sailing is one) now offer a tour in a 'silent' electric-powered boat. Yes, it's not the fastest boat in the Húsavík fleet, but it gets to all the same places the others go and it befits this natural spectacle to watch and listen without chugging motors.

Most other boats are wooden former fishing vessels, although a few have been converted from former whaling operations – nice! You'll be crammed in with plenty of other paying punters, but boat captains and guides are pretty good at manoeuvring the boats so that everyone gets a look.

The other option is the noisier Rigid Inflatable Boats (RIBs) that race across the bay. They get you there quickly, but that's their only advantage. And for us, such an experience is the antithesis of the slow, gentle movements of the whales themselves.

Puffin Island

Some companies offer a trip to **Puffin Island**, a summer nesting ground of these engaging, much-loved little birds, as an add-on to the usual three-hour

Whale-watching tour

excursion. The island is close to the shore, north of Húsavík.

You will almost certainly see puffins on the standard whale trips, but usually only a handful, compared with thousands coming and going from the cliffs on the dedicated tour.

The Whale Museum

Back on shore, don't miss the **Whale Museum** (whalemuseum.is; adult/child 2200kr/free), just above the northern end of Húsavík's harbour. This excellent exhibition has 11 whale skeletons, including what is believed to be one of only four complete blue whale skeletons in existence.

Staying Overnight

Húsavík is a charming place to stay – options include the cosy timber cottages of **Kaldbaks-Kot** (husavikcottages.com) or the **Fosshótel Húsavík** (fosshotel.is) with stylish contemporary rooms in charcoal accents. Whether or not you stay overnight, **Fish & Chips**, down by the docks, does exactly what it says on the label with good-value fish (usually cod) and chips. For a sit-down meal, **Gamli Baukur** (gamlibaukur.is) does everything from pasta and seafood to organic lamb.

WHALE TOURS

North Sailing (northsailing.is) and **Gentle Giants** (gentlegiants.is) are the two largest operators, both with 70- to 90-passenger boats and offices overlooking the harbour. Friends of **Moby Dick** (friendsofmobydick.is) is a smaller operator with personalised tours led by a marine biologist and a boat that takes about 40 passengers. Warm overalls are provided (which you pull on over your own warm clothing). North Sailing, Gentle Giants and **Húsavík Adventures** (husavikadventures.is) also offer tours on RIBs.

CITY GUIDE:
Akureyri

Akureyri and Eyjafjörður

Welcome to the beautiful 'Capital of the North' – with 18,000 inhabitants, this is Iceland's largest town outside the capital region. The oldest part of Akureyri, charming Innbærinn, lies close to the fjord, but the town now stretches almost all the way up to the mountain above.

WORDS BY
EYGLÓ SVALA ARNARSDÓTTIR
Eygló is a travel writer from Iceland.

Arriving

Car Akureyri is approximately two-thirds of the way along the Ring Road if you're travelling anticlockwise from Reykjavík. There are two parking zones. It's easiest to use apps *easypark.is* or *parka.is* to pay for parking. There are also three pay stations.
Plane Domestic and international flights arrive at Akureyri Airport a few kilometres south of town. It has taxis, car rentals, and a bus serving international flights.
Bus Buses run to Akureyri from Reykjavík and other parts of the country (see *straeto.is*). The terminal is at Hof Cultural Centre.
Boat If you arrive by ferry to Seyðisfjörður, Akureyri is 3½ hours by car to the west.

HOW MUCH FOR A

Large draught beer 1800kr

Large ice cream at Brynja (p197) 860kr

Admission to Akureyri Art Museum (p196) 2300kr

Getting Around

Orientation Downtown is walkable and most attractions are near the town centre. The Forest Lagoon, Kjarnaskógur forest, Botanical Gardens and the swimming pool are five to 10 minutes' drive and the ski area in Hlíðarfjall is 15 minutes' drive.
Driving On busy days it can be difficult to find a parking spot in the centre of town – park further out and walk.
Bus Public buses are regular and free in Akureyri. For schedules, go to *straeto.is*.
Electric scooters Download the Hopp app sharing service for electric scooters in Akureyri.

Moving On

Plane You can fly to Akureyri Airport from the UK in winter and other destinations in summer. There are flights to domestic destinations, including frequent flights to Reykjavík.
Bus From the terminal at Hof Cultural Centre you can take the bus to a range of destinations including Egilsstaðir, Reykjavík.
Ferry From Árskógssandur (30 minutes' drive north), you can take the ferry to Hrísey, and from Dalvík (another 10 minutes north) to Grímsey (p210).

For bus schedules and trip planning, go to *straeto.is*.

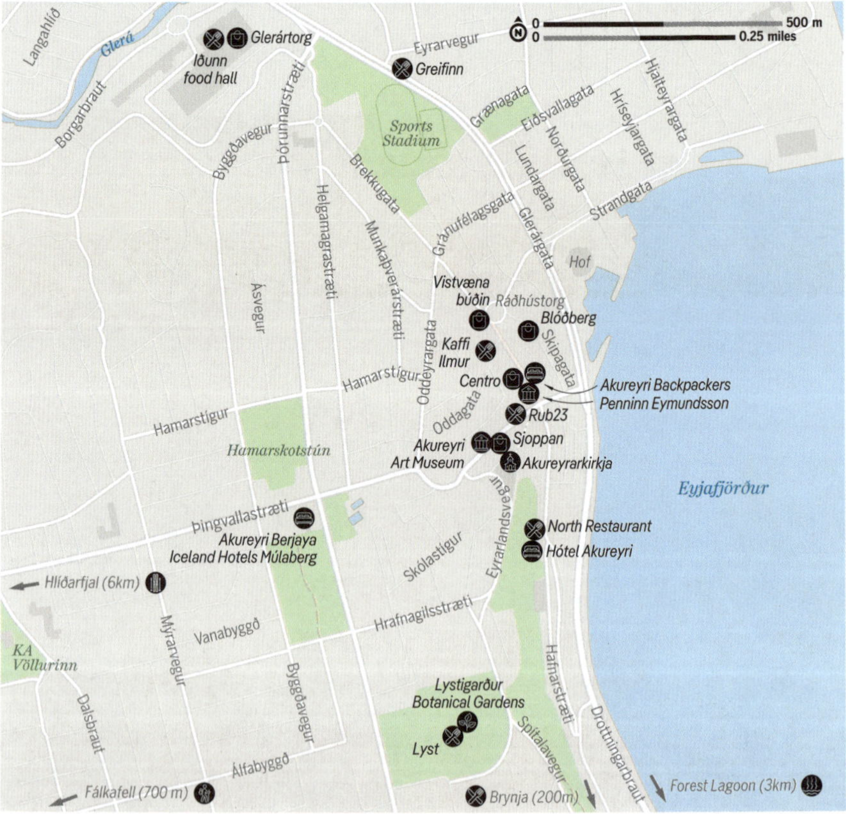

A DAY IN AKUREYRI

Walk along the shore to Innbærinn. Hike up to the **Fálkafell** scout hut or drive up to **Hlíðarfjall** ski resort for fjord views. Have breakfast at **Kaffi Ilmur** (kaffiilmur.com) in the town centre. Check out **Akureyri Art Museum** (p198), take in the stained-glass windows at **Akureyrakirkja** (akureyrarkirkja.is) and browse design store **Sjoppan** (p198).

Savour fresh seafood with a buffet lunch at **Rub23**, then head out to sea to wave at the humpbacks. Stroll through **Lystigarður Botanical Gardens** (lystigardur.akureyri.is) and see if you can spot some elves. Enjoy a slice of cake with your afternoon coffee at **Lyst** (lyst.is), or make the most of their happy hour.

Prepare for a flavour-packed evening at **North Restaurant**, based at historical **Hótel Akureyri**. Take a soak in the **Forest Lagoon** hot springs and marvel at the star-filled sky (or midnight sun) over the fjord. If you're not feeling sleepy, check out the vibe in the bars on **Hafnarstræti**.

Where to Stay

Akureyri's accommodation options range from forest camping and seaside apartments to mountain cabins and boutique hotels. Downtown, you'll find more luxurious and historical hotels, along with a hip hostel and cosy self-catering apartments. On the other side of river Glerá is a HI hostel. Near the swimming pool are hotels and guesthouses of different price ranges, some including breakfast. For groups, the Sæluhús apartments, cottages in Kjarnaskógur or Hlíðarfjall area are ideal.

BEST PLACES TO STAY

Akureyri Backpackers €€
Tune into the vibe of the Akureyri nightlife at this lively hostel.
akureyribackpackers.com

Hótel Akureyri €€€
Beautiful boutique hotel in the oldest part of town.
hotelakureyri.is

Akureyri Berjaya Iceland Hotels €€€
Classy and chic comfort near the swimming pool.
icelandhotelcollectionby berjaya.com

Hótel Hálönd €€
Just out of town up the mountainside. Enjoy simple comfort, on-site hot tubs and wondrous views.
hotelhalond.is

Where to Eat

The town centre has a selection of restaurants, including Asian, Middle Eastern, Italian, New Nordic and fusion. In Glerártorg mall, you'll find **Iðunn food hall** *(idunnmatholl.is)*, and on the opposite side of Glerárgata, **Greifinn** *(greifinn.is)*, a pizza institution (with popular pepperoni sausages). Locals love putting fries on everything – try the pizza with beef, fries and béarnaise. Or maybe the *bacalao* (salted, dried codfish), which is a treat.

AKUREYRI'S BEST-LOVED SPECIALITIES

North Iceland is where the *laufabrauð* was born, a crisp, deep-fried flatbread. It's served with smoked lamb at Christmas and is available in stores during Advent. In North Iceland, you'll find the original *óhrært skyr* under the KEA brand, best whipped with milk and sugar and served with cream and blueberries. Local fish processor Hnýfill makes delicious beech-smoked salmon (*beykireyktur lax*), best enjoyed on flatbread or rye bread. Available in **Nettó** supermarket.

The Akureyri hot dog with everything includes cocktail sauce and sometimes red cabbage. The special Akureyri hamburger has fries on top of the patty, as served at pit stop **Leirunesti** *(facebook.com/ Leirunesti; €€)*. Mix pineapple soda was invented in town, as was Lindu buff, a gooey chocolate bar. In Hauganes, a hamlet 30 minutes to the north, the Ektafiskur plant produces prime *bacalao*, served at their local **Baccalá bar** *(facebook .com/BaccalaBar; €€)*. Don't leave Akureyri without trying a milk-based ice cream at **Brynja** *(brynju.is; €)*, loved by locals in all seasons.

BEST PLACES TO EAT & DRINK

North Restaurant €€€
Michelin-starred chef highlights local ingredients; multi-course menu. Book ahead.
northrestaurant.is

Rub23 €€
Best sushi in town and juicy steaks in a renovated industrial building in Listagilið, Artists' Alley.
rub23.is

Akureyri Backpackers €€
Gastropub with lively atmosphere, offering hamburgers, nachos and lunch deals.
akureyribackpackers.com

Múlaberg €€€
Popular for its cocktails and happy hour on the terrace. Tempting small plates; varied mains.
mulaberg.is

Above: skiing near Dalvík

Play in the Snow

Visit Akureyri in winter to ski at **Hlíðarfjall** (hlidarfjall.is), a ski resort minutes from town, where there are lifts and slopes for skiers and snowboarders of all levels, ski school and equipment rental, cross-country tracks and opportunities for off-piste skiing. When there's sufficient snow, cross-country tracks are set up in Kjarnaskógur forest.

You can also try the other ski resorts in the North, in Dalvík, Ólafsfjörður, Siglufjörður and Sauðárkrókur, or even heli-skiing (skiiceland.is). At lake Mývatn, one hour to the east of Akureyri, there's an annual winter sport festival (vetrarhatid.com) with varied events including a horse show on ice and dog sledding.

CULTURAL AKUREYRI

Akureyri is an art-loving town. The ambitious **Akureyri Art Museum** (listak.is), on Listagilið (Art Street), showcases local and world-renowned artists, including Ragnar Kjartansson and Shoplifter. Among the best-known North Icelandic artists are abstract painter Óli G and Aðalheiður Eysteinsdóttir, whose wooden sculptures adorn the Berjaya Iceland Hotels. At Advent, her Christmas cat overtakes Akureyri town square.

A beautiful building in Innbærinn houses **Akureyri Theatre Company**, the only professional theatre in Iceland outside the capital region. A more modern construction by the harbour, **Hof Cultural Centre**, is home to the North Iceland Symphony Orchestra. Programs for both can be found at mak.is. Also check out **Græni hatturinn** (graenihatturinn.is), a music venue where established musicians and newcomers perform.

Visit the house-museums of children's book author **Nonni** (minjasafnid.is) and **Davíð Stefánsson** (minjasafnid.is), beloved national poet, to learn more about their lives and work. **Sigurhæðir** (facebook.com/flora.akureyri) is the home of Matthías Jochumsson, who wrote the national anthem. If you're visiting in summer, check the program of **Akureyri Art Summer** (listasumar.is), a two-month festival celebrating art in all its forms.

Left: Penninn Eymundsson

Browse the Shops

For a relatively small town, Akureyri is surprisingly urban. It has a shopping mall, **Glerártorg** (glerartorg.is), with international clothing brands, gift shops, toy stores, outdoor and sports shops and a food hall. While the mall is fine on a rainy day, the downtown stores are more interesting. **Vistvæna búðin** (vistvaena.is) carries a selection of ecofriendly products, from shampoo bars to bed linens. **Blóðberg** design boutique has beautiful woollen garments and blankets, ornaments and artwork. **Centro** (centro.is) is a fashion institution, **Penninn Eymundsson** (penninn.is) bookshop will fill your literary needs and don't forget tiny art store **Sjoppan** (facebook.com/sjoppanvoruhus) in Listagilið.

Fly Across Glerá River

The river Glerá splits Akureyri in two, flowing through a deep river canyon, into a dam and onwards to the sea. Children were once taught not to go near the canyon, but now you can safely fly across it with Zipline Akureyri for adrenaline-infused family fun.

HOW TO

Getting there: From downtown, it's a 30-minute walk or five-minute drive to the basecamp on Þingvallastræti 50, or take free bus A1 from the town centre to stop Dalsbraut/Stóragerði.

Tickets: 11,900kr for adults and 7900kr for children (eight-14 years old).

Other info: Runs May to September. Weight limit 30kg to 120kg. Details and bookings on *zipline.is/akureyri*.

Get ready for a thrilling ride, an adrenaline-packed adventure! **Zipline Akureyri** operates right in the middle of town – but the trees on the banks of Glerá river canyon will make you feel as if you're in a wild, wooded area.

Before you leave the ground, check in at the basecamp for safety gear and instructions. Your guides will walk you through the process of ziplining, then walk you to the starting point.

After receiving a thumbs up, take a jump (or sit down and let gravity do its work) and whoosh away across the canyon, dangling your feet over the water with butterflies in your stomach, the rushing river far below.

All over too soon? No worries – the tour has a grand total of five ziplines, zigzagging back and forth across the canyon. In between rides, you can take a short walk on the soft paths between the trees. By the end of it, you'll feel like a real flying pro!

Glerá River

Akureyri

The Ring Road from Akureyri to Hvammstangi has the unmistakeable feeling of turning towards Reykjavík, with its long and gradual arc to the southwest. But there's still so much to see. After the big city lights of Akureyri – it's all relative – these are long, empty roads lined with smaller, more intimate stops and attractions, with a whole world of possible detours breaking away off the Ring Road to the north.

Anthony Ham

Glaumbær (p206)
PALMI GUDMUNDSSON/SHUTTERSTOCK

Hvammstangi

247 KM
3-4 HOURS' DRIVE

THIS LEG:

- Akureyri
- Ytri Bægisá
- Öxnadalur Viewpoint I
- Öxnadalur Viewpoint II
- Varmahlíð
- Blönduós
- Þingeyrarkirkja
- Þrístapar
- Borgarvirki
- Kolugljúfur
- Hvammstangi

Driving Notes

Be wary of dense fog on the high passes as you climb out of Öxnadalur – just because it's sunny in Akureyri doesn't mean you won't be driving in dense fog at altitude.

Breaking Your Journey
Unusually for much of the Ring Road, you have two potential towns where you can pull over, fuel up and grab a snack – Varmahlíð (p206) and Blönduós (p210). Neither has much to choose from, but they at least provide an opportunity to stretch your legs and check the maps for what lies ahead.

Anthony's Tips

BEST MEAL The three-course dinner at Brimslóð Atelier (p205) in Blönduós.

FAVOURITE VIEW As you leave Akureyri to drive up Öxnadalur, one of the loveliest views in the north unfolds (p204).

ESSENTIAL STOP The turf houses of Glaumbær (p206) or the awesome natural power of Kolugljúfur (p212).

ROAD-TRIP TIP After Blönduós, maintain a moderate speed to avoid missing the minor roads.

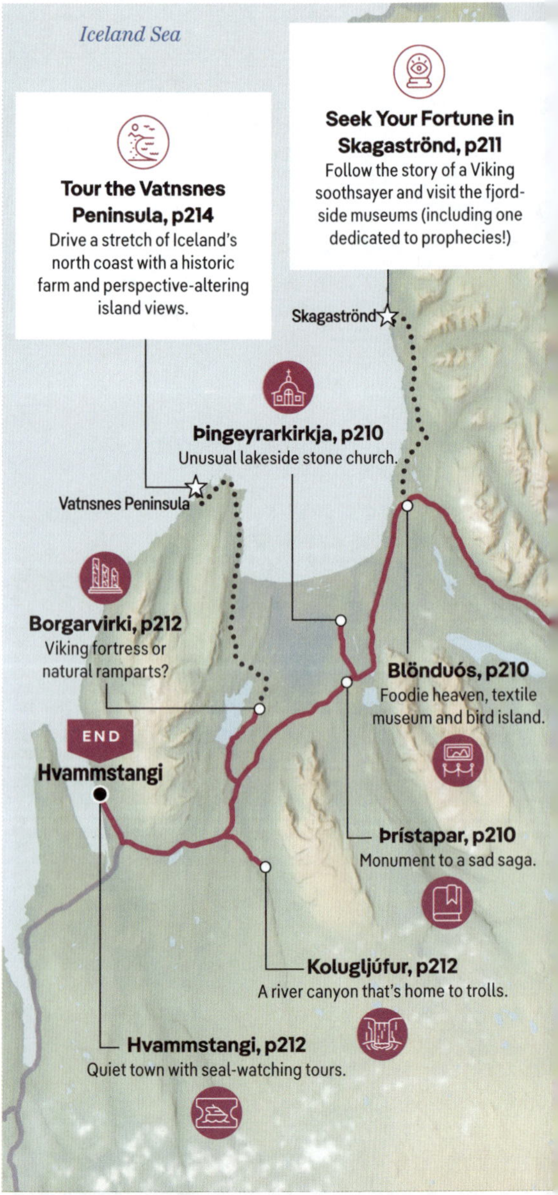

Iceland Sea

Tour the Vatnsnes Peninsula, p214
Drive a stretch of Iceland's north coast with a historic farm and perspective-altering island views.

Seek Your Fortune in Skagaströnd, p211
Follow the story of a Viking soothsayer and visit the fjord-side museums (including one dedicated to prophecies!)

Skagaströnd

Þingeyrarkirkja, p210
Unusual lakeside stone church.

Vatnsnes Peninsula

Borgarvirki, p212
Viking fortress or natural ramparts?

Blönduós, p210
Foodie heaven, textile museum and bird island.

END
Hvammstangi

Þrístapar, p210
Monument to a sad saga.

Kolugljúfur, p212
A river canyon that's home to trolls.

Hvammstangi, p212
Quiet town with seal-watching tours.

PREVIOUS STOP This leg of your Ring Road itinerary begins in Akureyri (p194), the largest town in Iceland's north.

Ytri Bægisá

As you leave behind the tree-lined outskirts of Akureyri heading west, nothing prepares you for what lies ahead – that is, unless you remember the view from the Eyjafjörður Viewpoint (p190) on the previous leg's approach to Akureyri.

As the road leaves the fjord's shore behind and you head inland, you're greeted by an extraordinary view that gets better with each passing kilometre. This is Öxnadalur, a wide, treeless valley that rises gently towards a panorama of conical mountains that layer in silhouette to the far horizon, somewhere deep in the highlands. There aren't many places to pull over and get out for photos – please don't just stop in the middle of the road, as some people do! – but it's possible to do so safely at the turn-off to the tiny hamlet (more just a collection of farm buildings) of **Ytri Bægisá**. This is close to where the valley splits into two, and the views are superb. It may be small, but what a place to live...

Öxnadalur Viewpoint I

After the valley splits, it begins to climb more consistently, slowly at first but inexorably towards the high mountain passes. Intriguing side roads disappear off down smaller valleys and deeper into the interior, while the valley walls, especially those on the western flank, get steeper. At this **viewpoint**, one of the rare proper parking areas set behind an equally rare wall of trees, you'll need to crane your neck to see the top.

Park your car, walk over to the banks of the small stream – the tiny remnants of the river and glacier that once carved this valley from the surrounding mountains – and look up. In the foreground, on the lower slopes opposite, a single farmhouse poses perfectly beneath the mountain wall. Atop the ridge, a particularly jagged series of needle-like outcrops resembles a dragon's back hewn from some old Norse saga. One of these is the 1075m spire

Mountains between Akureyri and Öxnadalur

Akureyri — 23km — Ytri Bægisá

Drive this section slowly – the turn-off to Ytri Bægisá is difficult to see.

Hraundrangi

of **Hraundrangi**, with the surrounding peaks of **Háafjall**. Together, they're among the most dramatic in Iceland.

Öxnadalur Viewpoint II

If you look up ahead, you could be forgiven for thinking that you're running out of valley as the road climbs ever higher. On the cusp of the final climb to the pass, a small **parking area** on the left is your chance to bid farewell to this remarkable section of the drive. The river valley wheels away to the south, keeping its secrets as it continues to its unknown source up in Iceland's interior highlands.

BEST PLACES TO EAT

Brimslóð Atelier, Blönduós $$$
Owners Inga and Gísli have published cookbooks and run food workshops. Their three-course dinner (bookings essential) showcases local ingredients and could be a trip highlight. Menus are seasonal. (brimslodguesthouse.is; from 7.30pm Mar-Nov)

Sjávarborg, Hvammstangi $$
At journey's end, Sjávarborg Restaurant is like an oasis in from the wilds. Fish and chips, local lamb, seafood soup and the occasional Asian influence. (sjavarborg-restaurant.is; 11am-11pm, shorter hours Oct-May)

Hlaðan Kaffihús, Hvammstangi $$
A simpler Hvammstangi offering, this harbour cafe does soup, panini, quiche and cakes, and more substantial dishes like lamb chops and local trout. (9am-9pm, from 10am Sun May-Aug)

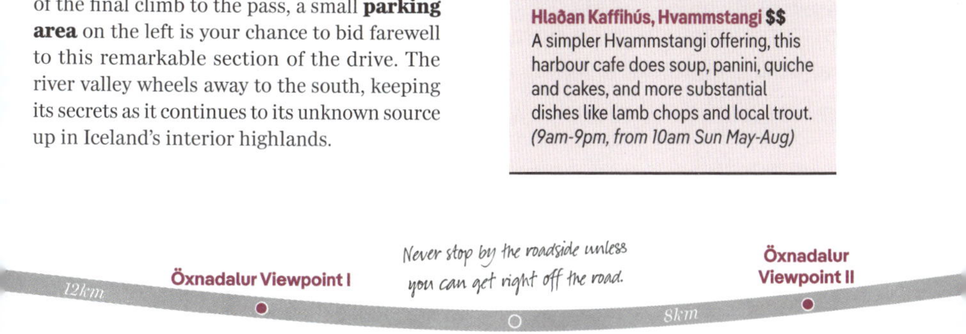

Never stop by the roadside unless you can get right off the road.

12km — Öxnadalur Viewpoint I — 8km — Öxnadalur Viewpoint II

The earlier views are more spectacular, but don't miss this one nonetheless. Turn off your engine, wait for any other vehicles to pass, and then take in the ringing silence and breathe in the crisp mountain air. Every drive should have a moment like this.

Varmahlíð

Home to fewer than 150 souls, **Varmahlíð** is a minor road junction, a service centre for passing vehicles, and an activities centre.

Most travellers know it as one of the best places in Iceland to go white-water rafting on the scenic Vestari Jökulsá or the roiling Austari Jökulsá. **Bakkaflöt** *(bakkaflot.com)* is one of the better operators – you'll find it south of Varmahlíð, down the paved Rte 752. A further 4km down the road, **Viking Rafting** *(vikingrafting.is)* does similar trips, as well as multiday trips down from the highlands and white-water kayaking.

The other major reason to stop here – and it's a good one – is to take in one of the hour-long shows at a horse farm. Ask at the **tourist information centre** *(visitskagafjordur.is)* or contact the farms directly. Best of all, the weekly (summertime-only) 'Horses & Heritage' evening program at **Lýtingsstaðir** *(lythorse.com)* encompasses facts and stories in a beautifully crafted turf house known as the Old Stable.

If you stay overnight, there's Hestasport Cottages (p213).

DETOUR: Glaumbær & Battle of Iceland

Just 8km north off the Ring Road down Rte 75, close to Varmahlíð, **Glaumbær** *(glaumbaer.is)* is one of the best examples of turf-roofed architecture in Iceland, and certainly in the country's north. This farm-museum shows how traditional buildings were joined by a passageway, an

Along the Way We Saw...

Along the way we stopped to sleep at Sauðá Guesthouse and fell in love. Icelandic horses moved out of the way to let me pass, and I sat, spellbound, dreaming of whales and the Westfjords. My night here, at the end of my exploration of the Vatnsnes Peninsula, was one of those where I pinched myself that I should be sleeping in such a magical place.

Anthony Ham

As you climb up to the pass and beyond, drive slowly in case of fog.

52km

Öxnadalur Viewpoint II

Varmahlíð

essential structure to enable the farm's inhabitants to move between the structures without having to venture out into the winter chill (for more on turf houses, see p216).

The buildings are filled with traditional furnishings, farm equipment and utensils, a reminder of just how cramped these quarters could be. Warm as they may have been, it would have been a *long* winter cooped up inside one of these structures.

Also here are two 19th-century houses – one is an old-fashioned tearoom serving cakes and traditional Icelandic tarts. Nearby is the grave of Snorri Þorfinnsson, the first person of European descent born in North America (in 1004).

A further 18km down Rte 75 from Glaumbær, the village of **Sauðárkrókur** is home to **1238 The Battle of Iceland** *(1238.is)*. It's impossible to travel around Iceland without an awareness of the sagas, but rarely are travellers afforded the opportunity to dive into one of the stories like they are here. The museum takes you back to the 13th century by recreating *Grettir's Saga*. It was a time when Iceland had no single ruler and life was governed by powerful local chieftains. In 1238, this descended into Iceland's first and only civil war, which ended with Iceland losing its independence.

The exhibition starts relatively slowly, telling the story of the battle through weapons, information panels and graphic illustrations. Then, just when you thought you were in a normal museum, you're launched into a virtual reality presentation where you find yourself in the midst of the Battle of Örlygsstaðir, which happened close to here. Remember that these were ancient battles, won in hand-to-hand combat, and finding yourself immersed in such a conflict can be thrilling and confronting in equal measure.

Glaumbær museum

Horse Riding in Hólar

The best detours are those that build on what has already captured your interest. Extending your trip north to the village of Hólar, near Skagafjörður, means taking your interest in horses to a whole new level.

HOW TO

Nearest stop: Varmahlíð

Getting here: Drive north of Varmahlíð along Rte 75, then keep on going. Hólar lies 11km east down Rte 767, off the eastern shore of Skagafjörður.

When to go: Year-round, although horse expeditions aren't possible in winter.

Tip: Combine this detour with Glaumbær and the Battle of Iceland (p206) and then use Sauðárkrókur as a base for the region. **Guesthouse Hofsstaðir** *(hofsstadir.is)* and **Gamla Posthúsið** *(ausis.is)* are excellent.

Hólar & Its Horses

Skagafjörður is riding country, and many of the operators out of Varmahlíð head out for multiday rides into the big-sky valleys in from the east coast of Skagafjörður. This is a perfect landscape for it – quiet, far from busy roads and considered by many locals to be the cradle of Icelandic horse heritage.

The tiny village of Hólar is akin to a pilgrimage destination for horse lovers. It's here that you find the **Icelandic Horse History Centre** *(sogusetur.is)*, an excellent museum dedicated to the Icelandic horse, set in converted stables. It's your chance to learn about those distinctive, shaggy-maned horses that you've seen in fields all along the Ring Road. They'll teach you about the five gaits of the Icelandic horse and detail the history of this small and stocky breed, which has been serving Icelanders since Viking days, known for its hardiness and its lively personality.

Hólar is slated to host the biennial National Icelandic Horse Competition (Landsmót Hestamanna), next scheduled for July 2026.

Christian Hólar

It may be tiny, but there's more to Hólar than its horses. The village was also one of Iceland's earliest centres of Christianity. At the village entrance is **Hólar Cathedral** *(kirkjan.is/holadomkirkja)* – one of Iceland's oldest churches. Although not the original built here – this version dates back to the

BUT WAIT, THERE'S MORE

To round out a remarkable array of sights for such a small place, just up from the church is Hólar University, known for its equine sciences program. It is flanked by the **Nýibær Turf House** *(entry free)*. And opposite the turf house is the small **Icelandic Beer Centre** *(facebook.com/bjorsetur.islands)*, which hosts regular beer festivals.

While there is camping and self-catering accommodation in Hólar *(visitholar.is)*, note that there are currently no supermarkets, cafes or restaurants, so bring in whatever you will need for snacks and meals.

From top: Icelandic horses; Hólar Cathedral

middle of the 18th century – it is steeped in antiquity. The first church here was built in 1050. The church still has cathedral status and its very own bishop, a legacy of the days when this was the centre of church power for all of North Iceland.

Its interior is filled with historical treasures, including a pre-Reformation altarpiece and a baptismal font dating to at least the late 17th century.

> ### ARCTIC ICELAND?
>
> People often assume that Iceland is an Arctic country, but only one tiny sliver of land on the island of Grímsey actually lies within the Arctic Circle. A 7980kg concrete sphere, the *Orbis et Globus* by Kristinn E Hrafnsson in collaboration with Studio Grandi, marks the actual spot where the Circle passes. It's a 45-minute hike north of the airstrip. So unless you are a runner, the best way to ensure you actually get to the real Arctic Circle is coming by boat (longer layover) or staying the night.
>
> To get here, there are daily flights in summer from Akureyri, or four to five weekly ferries from Dalvik.

Blönduós

With a pretty setting, **Blönduós** is a tight huddle of colourful houses along a windswept stretch of the North Iceland coast. With a couple of museums, a brilliant place to stay and eat, Brimslóð Atelier (p213), and the chance to actually stretch your legs with purpose on a bird-spotting island walk, it's a good place to break up the journey, whether overnight or just for an hour or two.

Start with the **Textile Museum** (*Heimilisiðnaðarsafnið; textile.is*), also known as the Icelandic Textile Centre; it's Iceland's only museum dedicated to this traditional craft. The building that houses it is worthy of attention – a striking creation, contemporary and cubist – while the museum contains exquisite embroideries and historical traditional clothing from different parts of the country. Everyone gets out their knitting needles for a festival in June.

Thus informed, head for **Hrútey**, the small island in the middle of the Blanda River, reached from town via a small footbridge. You'll share the island with a resident troupe of harlequin ducks.

Þingeyrarkirkja

A short distance from Blönduós, just off the Ring Road on Rte 721, Höp Lagoon is Iceland's fifth-largest lake. It's surrounded by low hills and is moderately scenic. But it's of most interest because of the **Þingeyrarkirkja** (*thingeyraklausturskirkja.is/en*), an imposing stone church and one of the largest in the Icelandic countryside. It replaced an earlier turf-roofed church, and it was the site of a Benedictine monastery as far back as the 12th century.

Using stone brought from cliffs 8km away, the church as you see it today was built in the 19th century by the locally famous stonemason Sverrir Runólfsson. Its walls are nearly a metre thick and held together by limestone. The interior has a brightly painted blue ceiling with golden stars, an alabaster altarpiece and an ornate baptismal font – definitely worth a look, if the door is open.

Þrístapar

Back on the Ring Road and not far away from Þingeyrarkirkja, **Þrístapar** occupies an important place in Iceland's history. It was on this site that Agnes Magnúsdóttir and Friðrik Sigurðsson were executed on 12 January 1830

Seek Your Fortune in Skagaströnd

There's something in the air in Skagaströnd, an ancient site of Viking divination and soothsayers. Perhaps not surprisingly, it has Iceland's only Museum of Prophecies...

HOW TO

Nearest stop: Blönduós

Getting here: Skagaströnd is 22km (20 minutes in a car) north of Blönduós, along Rtes 73 and 74. Alternatively, you could combine a detour here with an extended detour to Skagafjörður (p208).

When to go: Year-round.

Tip: On your way through Blönduós, be aware that Blönduós police district is famously diligent in monitoring speed.

Perched on the Skagi Peninsula's western rim and facing out to sea lies the increasingly artsy village of Skagaströnd. It's a fascinating place, very much at the mercy of North Iceland's powerful forces of nature.

The late-10th-century soothsayer, Þórdís, was one of the area's first residents. Her story – and other tales of Viking divination – are told at **Spákonuhof – the Museum of Prophecies**, where you can get your fortune told. The museum only opens in the brief June-to-August window.

Remarkably for such a small town, Skagaströnd has a second museum: the late-19th-century **Árnes Museum**, which occupies Skagaströnd's oldest house. If you didn't like what the fortune-tellers told you across the road, you can get a second opinion here.

For a final twist in the tale of Þórdís, legend has it that she buried treasure near the top of Spákonufell (639m), the mountain that dwarfs the village. She prophesied that it would be found by an unbaptised woman, to whom ravens will deliver the key...

From left: Þórdís figurine, Spákonuhof – Museum of Prophecies; Skagaströnd

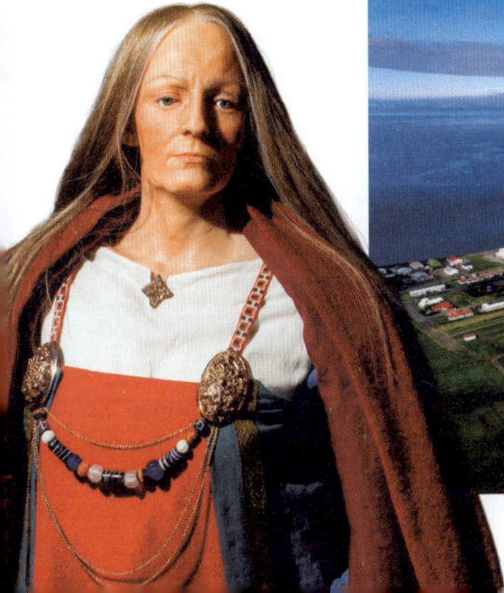

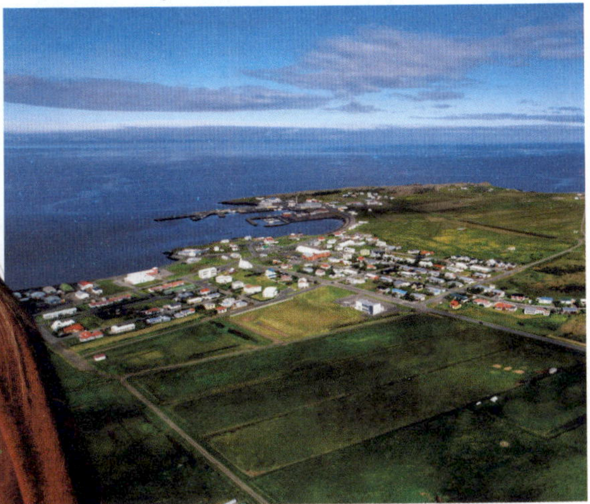

FROM LEFT: ARCTIC IMAGES/ALAMY, STEINNINN/WIKIMEDIA/CC BY 4.0

for two murders. It was the last execution to be carried out on Icelandic soil, and its story is told on panels at the site.

For a fictional recreation of the story, read the novel *Burial Rites* by Hannah Kent, which takes Agnes as its main character.

Borgarvirki

The mysterious old rock fortress of **Borgarvirki** is believed to be a defensive fortification from the early days of Iceland's human history, although it's actually a natural rock formation (an ancient 'volcanic plug' of columnar basalt) and sits 177m above the landscape. Keeping the ambiguity alive, the authorities 'restored' the site in the 1950s to resemble a Viking fortification, although the natural original needs no embellishment. Make of it what you will. And either way, it's a terrific spot for a scramble to stretch your legs and take in sweeping views.

Kolugljúfur

Another minor deviation, this time well signposted south off the main route, the canyon-falls combo of **Kolugljúfur** is a stunning spot. One of few such falls in the area, Kolufossar (named after the local trollwoman, Kola) and the ice-blue waters of the river Víðidalsá empty into the picturesque gorge in a series of parallel cascades over a number of steps that twist downward into the canyon below.

There's an observation deck, which has the best views. Take Rte 715 down the Víðidalur valley to get here.

Kolugljúfur

Hvammstangi

On a grey day, **Hvammstangi** can appear a bleak place, but it's lovely in the sunshine and borders some pretty spectacular country, not least among them the Vatnsnes Peninsula (p214). Its harbourfront is home to **Selasetur Íslands** *(selasetur.is)*, the Icelandic Seal Centre. Learn here about conservation, historical seal harvesting and folk tales about seals. You may be able to see conservationists at work – they might be taking DNA samples of various species or looking at the effects of tourism on local seal populations. Book with **Selasigling** *(sealwatching.is; 10,900kr per person)* for a guided tour of the museum and a boat trip to see the seals in their natural habitat.

In a warehouse building dating to 1909, **Galleri Bardusa** is a time capsule of Icelandic

Þrístapar — 25km — Borgarvirki — 21km — Kolugljúfur — 23km — Hvammstangi

You're not missing much if you take the Vatnsnes Peninsula detour (p214).

life. A craft store occupies part of the 1st floor, with gorgeous handcrafted items such as photo books, knitted children's slippers, artworks and more. The rest is a **Commercial Museum** *(adult/child 1,000kr/free)*, stuffed with items sold in the old Sigurður Davíðsson store here. Peer behind the original counter tops, with a cash machine and scales from the 1940s, at household goods from tea cups and medicines to beers, matches, canned goods and more. The 2nd floor holds jewellery, original make-up kits and perfume bottles – a wonderful peek into the past.

While you're in town, visit the excellent Sjávarborg restaurant (p205) and Hlaðan Kaffihús (p205). Sauðá Guesthouse, 15km north of town, makes for blissful overnighting.

BEST PLACES TO SLEEP

Brimslóð Atelier, Blönduós $$
Brimslóð Atelier is a fabulous, stylish seaside guesthouse where four rooms share two bathrooms and a chic lounge. Breakfast is a highlight. *(brimslodguesthouse.is)*

Hestasport Cottages, Varmahlíð $$
High on the hill above town, this cluster of seven high-quality self-contained timber cottages has views and excellent rooms of varying sizes. Horse riding and other activities are possible. *(riding.is/cottages)*

Sauðá Guesthouse, Hvammstangi $$
Three stylish double cabins with astonishing views across the water towards the Westfjords (watch for seals and whales). It's a fantastic choice 15km north of town, with lots of Icelandic horses in the surrounding fields.

Galleri Bardusa

Tour the Vatnsnes Peninsula

Shadowing the Ring Road is what's known as the Arctic Coast Way. It's a worthy rival for the affections of travellers, but you can get the best of both worlds by taking this detour that hugs the shoreline of the Vatnsnes Peninsula.

HOW TO

Nearest stop: Kolugljúfur or Hvammstangi.

Getting here: Rte 711 does a loop up and around the tip of the peninsula from the Ring Road; at its western end, it enters Hvammstangi. It's about 82km in total from the Ring Road to Hvammstangi and around the peninsula on Rte 711.

When to go: May to September, when road conditions are best.

Tip: Most of the route is well-maintained gravel – fine for a 2WD but keep control of your speed and generally drive carefully.

An Offshore Troll

Jutting out into the ocean as so many promontories do along Iceland's north coast, Vatnsnes Peninsula is starkly picturesque, a precursor to the deeply fissured coastline of the Westfjords. It's also a wildly beautiful place, wind-scoured and lonely with very few settlements – yet another Icelandic landscape where nature holds sway and the human footprint is small and fragile.

As you drive north on Rte 711 along the east coast of the Vatnsnes Peninsula, around 30km after leaving the Ring Road, take the turn-off at the sign for **Hvítserkur**. A gravel track takes you to a car park and a path to a viewing platform out to the craggy island outcrop. This 15m-high sea stack is one to add to your collection of weirdly wonderful Icelandic natural landforms.

According to local legend, Hvítserkur was a troll caught by the sunrise while attempting to destroy the monastery at Þingeyrar (p210). We think he looks like a huge stone beast drinking from the water, or perhaps even a misshapen elephant walking on water.

A Remote Farm

After rounding the peninsula's tip – no matter how hard you stare, no, you just can't quite see Greenland – the west coast faces out across a magnificent fjord to the snow-lined mountains along the Strandir coast of the Westfjords.

BEAR BAY

The waters of **Húnaflói** – a name that refers to the fjords on both sides of the Vatnsnes Peninsula – are often called Bear Bay. That's because on the rare occasions when polar bears land in Iceland aboard an ice floe from Greenland – there have been around 700 sightings since the 9th century – it often happens here. In 1518, eight people were killed at Skagafjörður by a polar bear. The last appearance of a polar bear in Iceland was in September 2024, at Höfðaströnd in the Westfjords, one bay around from Húnaflói. Polar bears are routinely culled by hunters or authorities when they appear.

Northern Lights over Hvítserkur

Down this west coast of Vatnsnes you'll find **Illugastaðir** farm, which is best known as the place where, in 1830, Agnes Magnúsdóttir and Friðrik Sigurðsson murdered two men, leading to their execution by beheading at Þrístapar (p210), a site south of Blönduós. Their graves are in the churchyard at **Tjörn**, further north along the peninsula.

At the farm, a 15-minute walk from the car park leads to a spot where you might see sunbaking seals. The farm closes from 1 May to 20 June due to eider duck nesting.

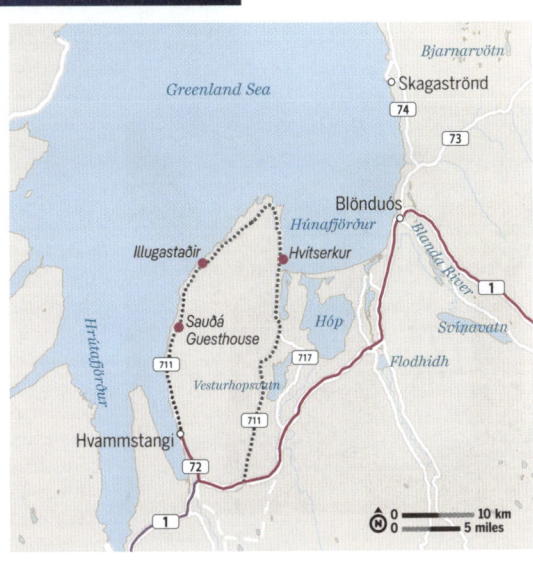

INSIGHT

Iceland's Real-Life Hobbit Homes

With lush grass roofs and walls hewn from packed-earth blocks, turf houses dot the Ring Road. Iceland's geothermal magic may overshadow these poignant vestiges of Viking settlement but, says Luke Waterson, these ancient dwellings have offered shelter for centuries in this rugged land, and have much to teach us today.

WORDS BY **LUKE WATERSON**
Luke specialises in adventure travel writing across the UK, Scandinavia and Latin America.

INTERMITTENTLY, AS YOU drive the Ring Road, your eyes do a double-take. If Iceland can seem like a real-life fairy tale of folklore and dramatic landscapes, then the grass-roofed, earth-walled houses sprouting along the route are surely where the fairy tale's characters live: buildings that appear straight out of the Shire itself.

In fact, these eccentric-looking, turf-covered structures, *torfbæir* in Icelandic, were Iceland's original homes. In the 9th century CE when Iceland was first settled, the island was a rough, tough place with one of Europe's harshest climates, limited forest cover and a prevalence of volcanic rock that was mighty hard to work with. Nor could much of Iceland be cultivated: even today, only one-fifth of it is farmable.

The first Norse inhabitants enterprisingly turned to what was available – sod, or the grass and layers of soil immediately beneath it – to construct their dwelling places, their storehouses, even their places of worship. Sod-built houses might not be unique to Iceland – there are examples across similar latitudes in Arctic Norway, Scotland's Outer Hebrides and Canada's Newfoundland – but here they remarkably remained the de facto building method until the 20th century. Some Icelanders lived in them until the 1990s, and many turf houses are still used as outbuildings.

Consequently, the art of building sod houses became particularly refined, and more examples exist in Iceland than elsewhere, as they remain deeply entrenched in Icelandic culture. JRR Tolkien, with an Icelandic nanny looking after his family and a fascination with Norse sagas, likely took *torfbæir* as inspiration for the

Glaumbær (p206)

LUKE WATERSON

houses of the peaceful, pint-sized hobbit race in his Middle Earth. Designer William Morris, the key figure in the Arts and Crafts movement that revolutionised Victorian design, had his imagination fired by *torfbæir* too, following sojourns in Iceland during the 1870s.

The typical *torfbæir* construction process entails first cutting blocks of packed earth into either *glaumbær* (rectangular building blocks the width of a wall) or *klömbur* (angled blocks that acted as clamps and strengthened structures). Exterior walls were built low, below a steeply pitched A-frame roof of beams made with highly sought-after timber, often sourced from driftwood, overlaid with turf to form most of the structure.

Houses were built side-to-side, thus minimising building materials. Besides the roof supports, the narrow wooden housefronts and the small amounts of stone stacked to weight down the structure, traditional *torfbæir* are totally turf-made. While chosen from necessity, turf had practical benefits: it provided insulation during bitter winter weather, and should the buildings get knocked down, they would be relatively easy to rebuild.

Torfbæir are considered romantic remnants of Icelandic history, embodying the island's Viking past and its colonisation against the odds. Many are preserved today as museums, conveying an atmospheric sense of what Iceland was like in previous centuries.

A great introduction to *torfbæir* is at Árbær Open Air Museum (p52), where Reykjavík's suburbs meet the Ring Road. A score of 19th- and 20th-century buildings, including turf houses and a pretty turf-roofed church, were transported here post-WWII from original locations around Iceland after concerns modern Reykjavík was losing its traditional heritage.

But it is the *torfbæir* that are still standing where they were first raised that provide the most profound sense of Iceland's past. Northern Iceland has many historic turf houses, most strikingly showcased at Glaumbær (p206), 8km off the Ring Road at Varmahlíð. These turf buildings were completed between 1750 and 1879, with sod-block construction evidencing exceptional workmanship: the site even gave its name to the *glaumbær torfbæir* building block. Explore the dim interiors to discover the typical rural Icelandic living conditions that changed little over a millennium. You can visit one of only six Icelandic turf churches at Saurbæjarkirkja, south of Akureyri, and Iceland's comeliest *torfbæir* buildings at Bustarfell Folk Museum off Vopnafjörður-bound Rte 85.

Keldur Turf House (p85), on Rte 264 near Hvolsvöllur in Southern Iceland, is generally deemed the nation's oldest *torfbæir* complex. Parts date to Iceland's early settlement. Ingjaldur Höskuldsson, a character in the colourful *Njál's Saga*, lived on the farm here in the late 900s and a subterranean farm passageway is believed to be 11th to 13th century in origin. The 20-odd structures include turf-roofed houses, lambing houses and a mill house, plus a wooden church built in 1875.

Iceland's *torfbæir* might appear to be relics, but they still have much to teach us today. They are perhaps the planet's ultimate green buildings – not merely in appearance, but in terms of their environmental impact and in the mileage required to transport materials to site. And they continue to inspire Icelandic architecture: Torfhús, northeast of Southwest Iceland's Laugarás geothermal lagoon (p75), offers state-of-the-art modern turf house accommodation.

> While chosen from necessity, turf had practical benefits: it provided insulation during bitter winter weather, and should the buildings get knocked down, they would be relatively easy to rebuild.

Hvammstangi

It may not be as dramatic as other parts of Iceland, but this quiet and underrated stretch of the Ring Road has a little taste of everything: volcano craters, horse farms, rushing rivers, waterfalls, fjords, fascinating museums and detours into wild western peninsulas for untouched natural beauty and endless adventure. The best bit? Driving this leg is a delight, as the Ring Road here is mostly free of traffic.

Jade Bremner

Glanni Waterfall (p224)
MAAO/SHUTTERSTOCK

Reykjavík

257 KM · 2½ HOURS' DRIVE

THIS LEG:

- Hvammstangi
- KIDKA Wool Factory Shop
- Norðlingafoss
- Sveinatunga
- Hvammskirkja í Norðurárdal
- Grábrók Volcano
- Glanni Waterfall
- Norðurá River
- Deildartunguhver
- Elf Village
- Borgarnes
- Esjurætur
- Mosfellsbær
- Reykjavík

Driving Notes

Get the tunes ready. While the scenery on this part of the road is not as gawk-worthy as other sections of the Ring Road, it's a pleasant, easy, stretch of asphalt. The route bends as it crosses fjords over long bridges and goes through tunnels before reaching Reykjavík.

Breaking Your Journey

Stock up on food and drink in Hvammstangi before leaving town. There are no major services on the Ring Road until around 120km south of Hvammstangi in the town of Borgarnes, then in Mosfellsbær, although certain sights will have toilet facilities. Plus, there are plenty of scenic picnic spots to enjoy, to break up the drive.

Jade's Tips

BEST MEAL In an atmospheric wooden house, Englendingavík (p223) gives you the feeling of an Icelandic family home.

FAVOURITE VIEW From the top of Grábrók crater (p223), with views into its bowl and to two other scoria cones.

ESSENTIAL STOP Walking the peaceful paths around Glanni Waterfall (p224).

ROAD-TRIP TIP Plan an extra day for a detour to the Snæfellsnes Peninsula (p228) – a diverse, remote landscape.

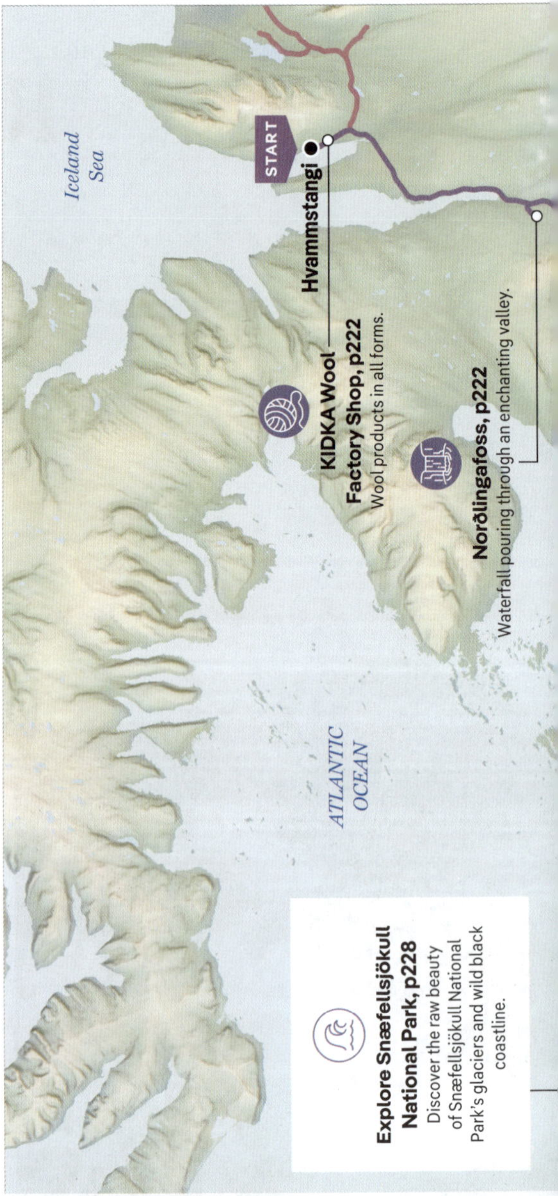

Iceland Sea

START — Hvammstangi

KIDKA Wool Factory Shop, p222 Wool products in all forms.

Norðlingafoss, p222 Waterfall pouring through an enchanting valley.

ATLANTIC OCEAN

Explore Snæfellsjökull National Park, p228 Discover the raw beauty of Snæfellsjökull National Park's glaciers and wild black coastline.

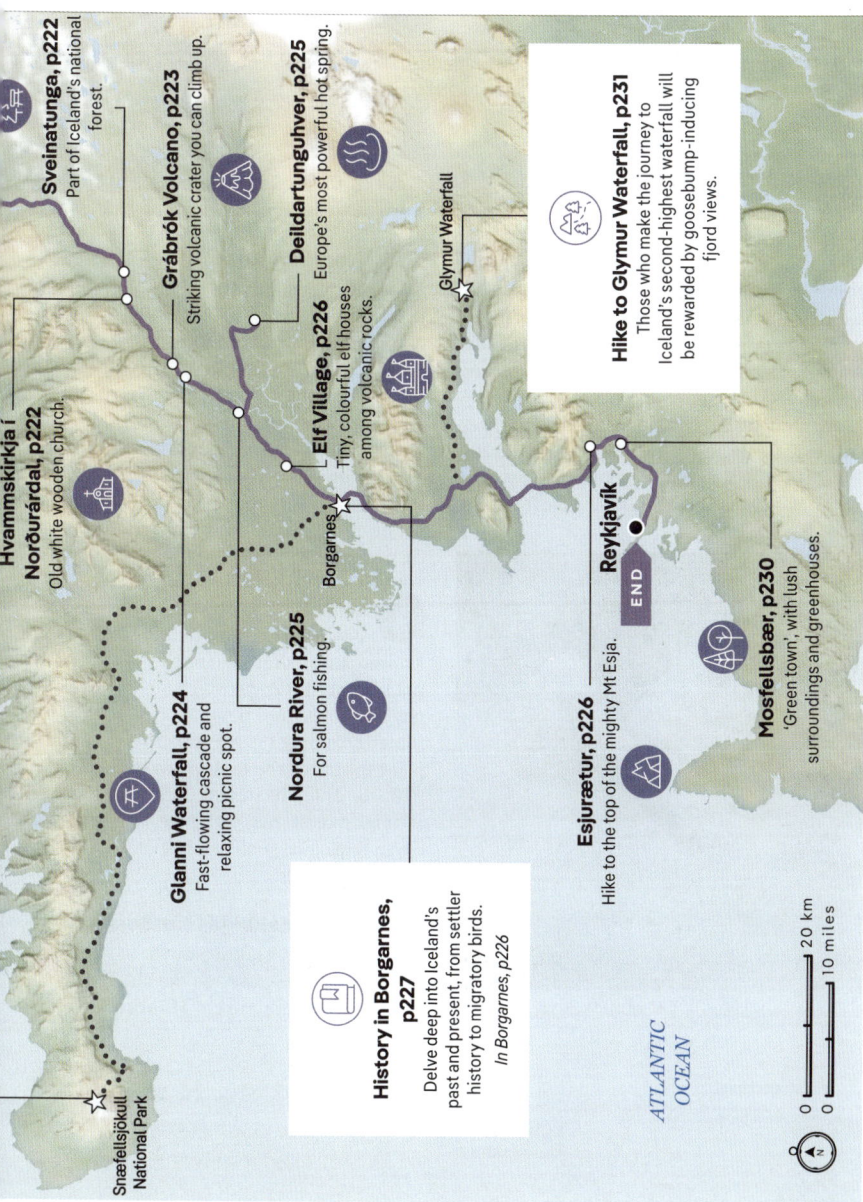

PREVIOUS STOP This leg starts in Hvammstangi (p212), an often bleak-looking town just off the Ring Road to the northwest, known for its nearby seal colonies.

KIDKA Wool Factory Shop

Just out of Hvammstangi is a woolly wonderland – the KIDKA Wool Factory Shop *(kidka.com)*. Wherever you travel in Iceland, you'll spot locals wrapped in Icelandic wool – the best of which is the traditional *lopapeysa* sweater. This wool is special: its outer layer *(tog)* is coarse and water-resistant, while the inner *(þel)* is soft and insulating, perfected over centuries in Iceland's harsh climate. It's also sustainable, with sheep roaming freely and wool processed naturally, supporting rural communities and craftspeople. At the shop, you can see this heritage in action, watching the production process and browsing cosy sweaters, hats, ponchos and blankets.

Norðlingafoss

Head around 40km south on the Ring Road through green fields (followed by a hop 2km west along Rte 586) to the less-visited but perfectly formed **Norðlingafoss**. This waterfall tumbles around 15m to 20m through an enchanting green and rocky valley into a serene pool. There are interesting formations around the falls, with red layers in some of the rocks. Paths lead around the falls, for different perspectives. Norðlingafoss makes for a great, easy-access picnic spot off the Ring Road.

Sveinatunga

Just off the Ring Road (1km north of Króksfoss/Norðurárdalur on the west side of the road) is **Sveinatunga**, which is part of Iceland's national forest and is open for visitors all year round. Spanning 186 hectares, this is a peaceful place to stretch the legs with a walk on gravel paths, and breathe in some fresh air as you pass through mossy areas with pine, birch and larch cover. It makes a good picnic spot, but there are no facilities here.

Hvammskirkja í Norðurárdal

Around 4.5km south of the Sveinatunga national forest is the old, red-roofed, white wooden church **Hvammskirkja í**

KIDKA Wool Factory Shop

Hvammstangi		KIDKA Wool Factory Shop		Norðlingafoss
	1km		40km	

Scenic drive skirting the waters of Hrútafjörður.

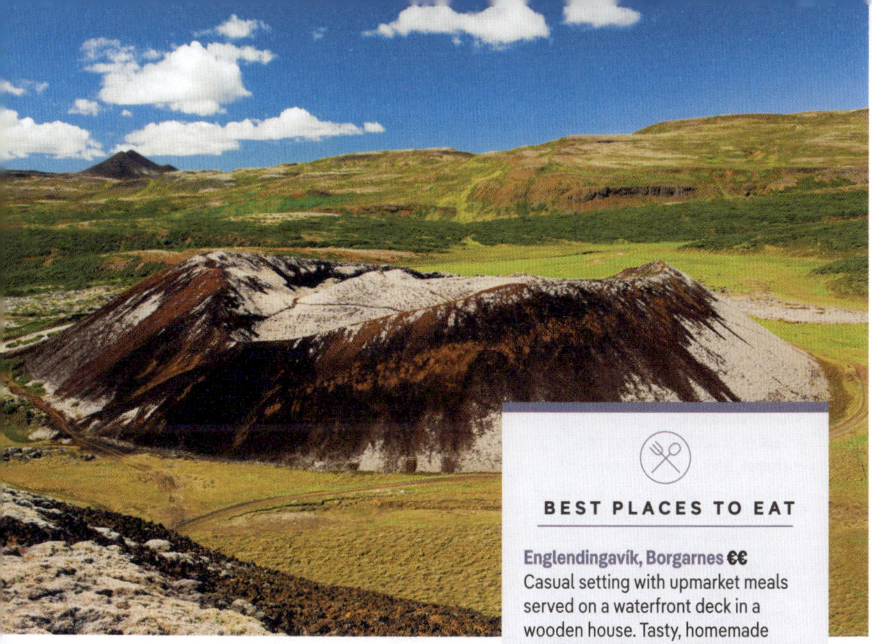

Grábrók

Norðurárdal, originally built in 1880 by Björn Þorláksson, a local blacksmith and farmer who later became a renowned architect. Its structure has been added to over the years to preserve it, but it is still a great example of simple, striking Icelandic design. The local community occasionally uses it for worship; visit during services for a peek inside.

Grábrók Volcano

Driving south, the landscape becomes more mountainous to the east and more volcanic to the west. Be sure to stop at one of the most striking volcanic craters in West Iceland, **Grábrók**, formed around 3000 years ago

BEST PLACES TO EAT

Englendingavík, Borgarnes €€
Casual setting with upmarket meals served on a waterfront deck in a wooden house. Tasty, homemade seafood and farm-fresh dishes. *(englendingavik.is; noon-9pm)*

Settlement Center, Borgarnes €€
Built into a rock face, this museum-adjacent spot serves traditional Icelandic and international eats (lamb, fish stew etc) in a light space. Popular lunch buffet. *(landnam.is/eng/restaurant; 10am-9pm)*

Erpsstaðir, Dalir €
Detour 20 minutes along Rte 60 to this legendary farm shop, selling delicious dairy products – butter, *skyr* (yoghurt-like dessert), caraway cheese and some of the creamiest ice cream you've ever tasted. *(erpsstadir.is; 1-5pm May-Sep)*

38km — Sveinatunga — 4.5km — Hvammskirkja í Norðurárdal — 13km — Grábrók Volcano

Road curves past rock outcrops with signs of volcanic terrain.

BEST PLACES TO SLEEP

Bjarg, near Borgarnes €€
Attractive set of linked cottages in a cosy, family-run old farmhouse (part of which has a turf roof) overlooking the fjord and mountains. *(facebook.com/bjargborgarnes)*

Hvammstangi Cottages & Hostel, Hvammstangi €€
A cluster of pleasant wooden cottages, and a campground just north of Hvammstangi. Each cottage has a bathroom and kitchenette. *(stayinhvammstangi.is)*

Helgugata Guesthouse, Borgarnes €€
Friendly guesthouse, with a shared lounge and terrace on the cliff overlooking Borgarnes and the blue fjord beyond. Good breakfast too.

during a fissure eruption. Combining natural wonder with cultural history, it makes for an unforgettable stop on the Ring Road.

Rising 173m above sea level, Grábrók lies in the Norðurárdalur valley, just off the Ring Road near the village of **Bifröst**. Part of the Grábrókarhraun lavafield, it is accompanied by two neighbouring scoria cones – Grábrókarfell and Litla Grábrók (also playfully known as 'Litla Grábrók Smábrók', or 'small panties'), both of which can be seen from the top of Grábrók. Bring your camera for the sweeping views of moss-covered craters, rugged lava flows and the surrounding valley.

The walk to the rim is relatively easy, with a wooden staircase and gravel paths showing the way. It takes about 40 minutes to climb up and circle the crater rim, a loop of roughly 1.5km, with the option to descend into the crater itself for a closer look. The site is free to visit and is a popular stop for travellers exploring the region.

At the base of Grábrók, visitors can also explore the **Old Brekka Corral**, which was built in 1872. This archaeological site reflects a centuries-old Icelandic tradition: rounding up free-roaming sheep in autumn and herding them into communal pens. The Brekka Corral remained in use up until 1922 and today offers a fascinating glimpse into Iceland's farming heritage.

Glanni Waterfall

Roughly 1.5km south of Bifröst, to the east of the Ring Road, is a short path leading down to the picturesque cascade of **Glanni Waterfall**, set in the Norðurárdalur valley, surrounded by lavafields formed by ancient volcanic eruptions. From a viewing platform, take in its fast-flowing cascade as it tumbles over rugged lava rock into the Norðurá River, famed for salmon fishing. Continue along the path south by the river for a gorgeous ramble by deep-green, moss-covered rocks to an area known as Paradísarlaut (or 'Paradise Hollow') – a tranquil, sheltered oasis with pools and enchanting turquoise ponds. The area is steeped in folklore; many believe it's home to elves and trolls.

Grábrók Volcano		Glanni Waterfall				Deildartunguhver
○	2.5km	○	○	12km	○	18km ○

Short, easy stretch leading to hidden falls.

Norðurá River

Norðurá River

Around 10 minutes' drive south of Glanni Waterfall, driving on the Ring Road past low-lying forests, a bridge to the east crosses the rushing **Norðurá River**, a tributary of the Hvítá, which runs all the way through the Borgarfjörður region. There are tranquil places along its banks to watch the waters flow, from sheltered pools and small streams to dramatic gorges. The river is also known for its abundant salmon – fishing fanatics can stay at a fishing lodge further north in **Rjúpnaási** *(nordura. is; prices vary by season, bookings essential)*, with views of the Laxfoss waterfall, near Glanni Waterfall. Guides transport anglers by 4WD vehicles to excellent fishing spots along the river.

Deildartunguhver

From the Norðurá River, continue on Rte 50 for a 15-minute detour off the Ring Road to Europe's most powerful hot spring, **Deildartunguhver**. Billowing clouds of steam rise from water bubbling at boiling point in great volume (180L per second). The bathing complex here, **Krauma** *(krauma.is; spa visits incl robe & drink from adult/child 7490/490kr)*, consists of five natural hot pots using mineral- and algae-rich waters from the hot spring. These are cooled down to different temperatures with natural glacial water from Rauðsgil. There's also a cold plunge pool on-site and a bistro with spa views, serving up Icelandic cuisine.

A dish at Krauma

Elf Village

Families will enjoy a quick but cute stop at **Elf Village** on the side of the Ring Road in the Hvanneyri area. A collection of tiny, hand-painted elf houses are scattered among volcanic rocks. In Icelandic folklore, elves or *huldufólk* (hidden people) are small mythical beings believed to live in rocks, lavafields and hillsides, creating a cultural bond with Iceland's rugged nature. Folklore warns against disturbing their homes, so visit quietly to avoid misfortune, and show kindness (it's believed to bring luck).

Borgarnes

Around 10 minutes' drive south of the Elf Village, on a long, straight stretch of the Ring Road bordered by green fields, is **Borgarnes**. It's a charming small town of around 3500 residents, with colourful wooden houses, modern facilities and views of the twinkling fjord and mountains beyond. Only 75km from Reykjavík, Borgarnes has a deep history relating to Iceland's Settlement Era – nearby fjord Borgarfjörður was the landing point of some of Iceland's first settlers. Cross the bridge to climb the hill on Brákarey island, then roam around the town's museums and galleries. If you have time, head to Snæfellsjökull National Park (p228). Fuel up at the restaurants – Englendingavík (p223) is one of our favourites – or stay overnight at Bjarg (p224) or Helgugata Guesthouse (p224).

Esjurætur

Reached by skirting snaking fjords and passing lonely farmhouses under big open skies on the Ring Road from Borgarnes, **Mt Esja** (914m) dominates the skyline some 15km from Reykjavík. This peak has the capital's favourite hiking spot. The **Esjurætur** hiking trails are a kind of natural outdoor gym for locals, but visitors come for the sweeping views at the top – on clear days it's possible to see Snæfellsjökull glacier from the mountain. At Esjurætur's car park you'll find route maps and coordinates (take a picture here) and handy advice on conditions, plus a cafe that's sometimes open for post-hike refreshments. Routes vary in difficulty and are marked with a boot-grading system: one boot means easy, three boots means tough. Most hikers walk 2.8km to **Steinn**, a rock formation viewpoint with breathtaking panoramas, before heading back. From Steinn, the path steepens significantly – experienced climbers can continue to the summit and sign the guestbook. Trails are well marked, but the weather changes quickly; check conditions before setting out.

Mt Esja

History in Borgarnes

This small town on Iceland's west coast has deep roots. The peninsula was once home to early settlers including Skallagrímur Kveldúlfsson, father of Viking poet-warrior Egill Skallagrímsson, whose saga is among the nation's most celebrated.

HOW TO

Nearest stop: Borgarnes is itself a stop on the route.

Getting here: Borgarnes is a small, walkable town – Borgarfjörður Museum and the Settlement Center are just a few minutes apart on foot, and you could easily visit both in one afternoon.

Tip: It's worth visiting the Settlement Center's excellent restaurant (p223), a striking venue cut right into the rock face.

Housed in a beautifully restored harbour warehouse, **Borgarnes' Settlement Center** (landnam.is/en; adult/child 3700/1200kr) explores Iceland's Viking heritage and the legendary *Egil's Saga*. Two dimly lit, atmospheric exhibitions use artefacts, models and audioguides to bring Iceland's discovery and early colonisation to life. Peruse the Egil's Saga Exhibition, telling the story of the warrior-poet Egill Skallagrímsson and his family's flight from Norway, their farm at Borg á Mýrum, and Egill's remarkable life of battles, raids and poetry. Each exhibition takes around 30 minutes to tour.

On the southern edge of town, the **Borgarfjörður Museum** *(Safnahús Borgarfjarðar; borgarbyggd.is; entry free)* is dedicated to preserving the heritage of the Borgarfjörður region, and offers a stop to learn about local culture. It houses exhibitions on local history, art, nature, traditional rural life, the natural environment and local literature, with a focus on the Icelandic Sagas. Recent exhibitions have included one on local female artists and gender equality and the Adventures of Birds, which explores the great adventure of migratory flight.

EXPERIENCE ★

From left: *Egil's Saga*; Borgarnes

Explore Snæfellsjökull National Park

Set off on an adventurous multiday detour into an area of raw beauty. The 170-sq-km park encompasses Snæfellsjökull glacier, lavafields and lava tubes to explore, and wild coastlines with black beaches and mystical formations.

Nearest stop: Borgarnes

Getting here: It's 132km (around two hours) from the Ring Road to the Snæfellsnes Peninsula along Rte 54 going west. Plan for at least an overnight trip to experience what the area has to offer.

When to go: May to October. Certain roads can be snowed in during the winter months, and sights are best experienced in the warmer months.

More info: Malarrif and Hellissandur villages each have a National Park Visitor Centre, or see *snaefellsjokull.is* for hiking trail maps and wildlife guides.

Snæfellsjökull

Jules Verne chose **Snæfell** as the setting for his novel *Journey to the Centre of the Earth.* The volcano once erupted so violently its peak collapsed into its own magma chamber, leaving a huge caldera. Today the crater holds the **Snæfellsjökull** ice cap (1446m), a popular summer hiking destination.

Saxhöll Crater & Sauðhóll

About 11.5km north of the Djúpalón exit on Rte 574, a marked turn-off leads to **Saxhöll Crater**, a roadside scoria cone that produced some of the lava here. A drivable track reaches the base, followed by a 300m climb to sweeping views over the vast Neshraun lavafields. Alternatively, hike south into the greener crater of **Sauðhóll**.

Vatnshellir

Around 1km north of Malarrif, this 8000-year-old lava tube lies 32m underground and extends through several caverns. With the guidance of **Summit Adventure Guides** *(summitguides. is;* adult/child 5400/2400kr) you can descend into the dark passages. Just 10 minutes east, Rauðfeldsgjá Gorge offers a short but atmospheric walk into a moss-covered cleft you can enter by hopping across rocks.

Djúpalón Beach, Dritvík & Malarrif Stacks

On the southwest coast, Rte 572 branches from Rte 574 to reach dramatic **Djúpalónssandur**. This black-sand beach features unusual rock formations (believed to be

> ### WHALE WATCHING AND SEABIRDS
>
> To the north of Snæfellsjökull National Park, the coastal areas around Grundarfjörður and Ólafsvík are prime territories for whale watching. From mid-February to September, **Láki Tours** *(lakitours.com; from 14,000kr per person)* runs boat trips to spot orca, fin, sperm, blue, minke and humpback whales. Meanwhile, from June to late August, tours from Grundarfjörður go to the basalt island **Melrakkaey**, home to endearingly comical puffins, one of Iceland's best-loved birds. Although they spend most of their days at sea, they come to land for four or five months per year to breed.

Gatklettur

an elf church and a troll woman). Further along Rte 574 there are also two brackish pools and the rock arch **Gatklettur**, which is often set against pounding, frothy-white waves below. Down on the beach, try lifting the four stones traditionally used to test fishermen's strength. Continue north across the rocky headland to see striking sea stacks, thought by some to be a troll church, before reaching the black-sand beach at **Dritvík**. From the 16th to 19th centuries this was Iceland's busiest fishing station, with up to 60 boats based here, though today only ruins remain at the edge of the lavafield.

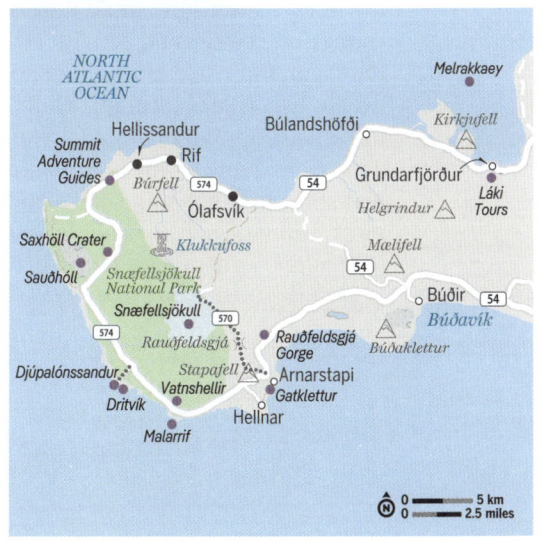

Mosfellsbær

As you drive 10 minutes from the Mt Esja trailheads, the route remains rural but you'll notice significantly more cars (you're only 10km northeast of Reykjavík). **Mosfellsbær** (moss-fell-town) is the last stop on your journey before you return to Reykjavík. According to *Egil's Saga*, the Viking Age war poet, sorcerer, berserker and farmer Egil Skallagrimsson is buried near Mosfellsbær, with lots of silver treasure. Today, Mosfellsbær is more commonly known for being 'the green town', thanks to its lush surroundings and many greenhouses. It was also home to Iceland's Nobel prize-winning writer Halldór Laxness. His former home 6km east of town is now a **museum** (p66) dedicated to his life story. Other points of interest include the **Lágafellslaug swimming pool** (sundlaugar.is; adult/child 1150/200kr) with three hot tubs, a 25m outdoor pool, a shallow children's pool and a water slide, plus nearby **Úlfarsfell** (Wolf's-Fell), a 296m mountain that provides hikes to soaring countryside and town views.

Cruising back into the city limits, Iceland's dramatic countryside behind you, feels like stepping out of a dream, a sobering snap back to modern civilisation. From here, it's a 45-minute drive to the airport, with memories from an epic road trip to last a lifetime.

Along the Way We Met...

MARTA MAGNÚSDÓTTIR Many visitors don't realise that in Iceland swimming and golf are hugely popular pastimes. We have some incredible pools – there's usually one in every town, no matter how small it is, thanks to the abundance of water and geothermal activity we have. In Snæfellsnes, where I'm from, there are four public pools! Visiting them is a great way to experience local life. Golf is also a hugely popular sport in Iceland, and golf courses are a lot cheaper, friendlier and accessible than in other European countries. Often you can just show up, rent some clubs and play a round against the most dramatic settings. My favourite is in Grundarfjörður *(gvggolf.is)* – just turn up and play.

Marta is the owner of coffee shop Valeria Kaffi, an author and former Iceland Chief Scout. @martamagnusdottir

Esjurætur — 6km — **Mosfellsbær** — 16km — **Reykjavík**

Traffic appears on the Ring Road closer to the capital.

Hike to Glymur Waterfall

A diverse, scenic, moderately challenging 7.5km trail to the second-largest waterfall in Iceland – tumbling some 198m into a striking valley.

HOW TO

Nearest stop: Borgarnes

Getting here: It's roughly 50 minutes' drive here from Borgarnes. Take a 20-minute detour off the Ring Road to the trailhead, leaving the Ring Road at Hvalfjarðarsveit and going east on Rte 47, then follow a gravel road to Botnsdalur for the waterfall car park.

When to go: June to October. Before then, the log for the river crossing hasn't been laid across the water, making it hard to complete the trail.

Tips: Instead of an out-and-back trail, there's also the option to make the route a longer circular trail through the valley (info boards in the car park show you where the trail goes).

The route starts beyond a gate on a fairly flat dirt trail through green pastures. Take the left fork with the Glymur sign on it, and enjoy views of green mountains in the distance (snow-tipped in winter). After around 1km to 2km of fairly flat, wide dirt paths you reach **Þvottahellir Cave**. This atmospheric natural lava tube (its name means 'Wash Cave') has a series of steps leading down to Botnsa River, and was once used by locals to dry clothes on rainy days. At the base of the cave, the river rushes for 10km along a deep canyon. Here hikers will find a tree trunk crossing. The trunk is placed across the river between June and October, to avoid it being swept away during floods in the rainier seasons. Hold on to the rope cable and cross the tree trunk, then follow the path along the river and up the hill for dramatic canyon and crevice views, soaring all the way to the 30km-long Hvalfjörður (Whale Fjord). Climb roughly 300m to clap eyes on Glymur Waterfall. This was once the highest cascade in Iceland, until overtaken by Morsárfoss in Vatnajökull National Park, which due to the melting Morsárjökull glacier now clocks in at 228m high.

EXPERIENCE ★

Glymur Waterfall

FROM LEFT: TOMASZ BIERNAT/SHUTTERSTOCK, IREK POD/SHUTTERSTOCK

 INSIGHT

Ring Road Roulette: A Family, a Motorhome and No Clue

In 2023, Thomas O'Malley and his family took on the Golden Circle and the south-coast stretch of Iceland's Ring Road. They faced muddy tracks, tantrums, torrential rain and toilet troubles, while discovering the surprising joys of life on the road.

WORDS BY **THOMAS O'MALLEY**
Tom lives in Scotland, Iceland's closest European neighbour, where he writes guidebooks for Lonely Planet, and takes his daughter on the occasional mountain hike.

THE RAIN LASHED sideways as I attempted to find reverse on our three-tonne juggernaut. Instead, we lurched forward into more mud. My pregnant partner clenched the armrests as though in turbulence. Just a few hours into our Iceland adventure and I was silently praying for deliverance. *Why, oh why, had I thought I could do this?*

We'd landed in Iceland mid-afternoon to moody skies, and had been shuttled to a grey industrial nowhere outside Keflavík: Campervan-ville. Back when I booked the trip, I scrolled through a list of vehicles and clicked on the full-blown, premium motorhome. *It's Christmas!* I thought. Now I was face-to-face with my folly. *How is it so long, on such spindly wheels?*

A bored man in a fleece raced through a back-of-a-napkin–type tutorial: 'Grey tank here, fridge to LPG when not on hook-up, toilet cassette's under the side-hatch, don't touch this'. I could feel a panic attack coming on. He emphatically warned me to check the wind forecast – *there's a wind forecast?* – every hour. Apparently, these things get blown clean off the road.

Back to the flooded field. Somehow, those old Icelandic gods helped nudge our bus on to hard ground, moments before we became one with the mire. Other motorhomes, it seemed, had sensibly parked nearby on a rectangle of tarmac. We followed suit. At last, I switched off the engine, hands trembling, and very quickly drank an entire can of duty-free Icelandic beer.

We transformed the living room to bedroom, which was quite fun, and closed the curtains.

The author's daughter at Skógafoss (p87)

Every little triangle of window had its own patch of fabric to keep out the perpetual June daylight. Finally, we lay down and listened to the rain hammering the roof. Suitably apocalyptic for such an ordeal, I thought, yet somehow soothing.

The next day we motored into Þingvellir National Park, which had huge parking spaces – thank you again, gods. Dark clouds added filmic drama to the landscape of black rocks and tectonic canyons. We ticked off the Golden Circle highlights. Our daughter loved seeing Geysir spurt into the air, while the epic Gullfoss falls, we noted, were no place for a pushchair.

We camped at the small seaside town of Stokkseyri, where I actually managed to plug in the motorhome. *Ha! This motorhome lark is easy!* I patted the side of our space shuttle, and smiled amiably at the man in the camper next to ours. These were van people. My people. He approached with a look of concern.

'You can't drain your grey water here.'

My what now?

It turned out the valve on our wastewater tank was open. This is not cool. Nor was the fact that our gas canisters hadn't been belted down. (I did wonder what that knocking was.) With a look somewhere between horror and pity, my new friend gave me the full motorhome lowdown. Then he did perhaps the kindest thing anyone has ever done. He emptied our toilet cassette.

After that, it all started to click. We traced Iceland's southern coast, collecting waterfalls like postcards: Seljalandsfoss (walked behind it), Skógafoss (climbed it), Kvernufoss (marvelled at its rainbows). We took a family photo in front of the Sólheimajökull glacier and gazed out from Dyrhólaey over black-sand beaches. We saw a puffin. We ate charcoal-coloured pizza. I even figured out how to reverse.

We made it as far as Jökulsárlón glacier lagoon, where we joined a boat tour past blue-tinted bergs. Nearby, at Diamond Beach, polished hunks of ice sparkled against black volcanic sand. My partner was delighted. This was everything Iceland had promised to be.

> I actually managed to plug in the motorhome. *Ha! This motorhome lark is easy!* I patted the side of our space shuttle, and smiled amiably at the man in the camper next to ours. These were van people. My people. He approached with a look of concern.

Our time almost up, we turned around, camping one night at the foot of Hvannadalshnúkur. The sun never set, even as I made a solo post-midnight hike to a nearby waterfall. Returning to the warm cocoon of the motorhome felt like coming home. *This vehicle is all a family like ours could ever need,* I thought. *Well, until the baby comes. Then maybe get a bigger one.*

We had arrived in Iceland anxious and clueless. We left tired, short on clean clothes, and completely in love with the country, the light, the landscape and our trusty house-on-wheels. Which didn't blow over once.

So, if you're wondering whether you should do a road trip with a toddler, a baby bump, a huge motorhome, or any combination of the above...*do it*. But, also, do some research before you go. Learn from your fellow campers. Stick to the tarmac. And bring beer. That midnight sun is waiting.

Toolkit

First Time
p236

Money
p237

On the Road
p238

Packing
p244

Where to Stay
p245

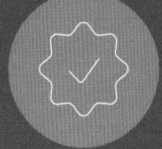
Responsible Travel
p246

Access, Attitudes & Safety
p248

Language
p249

Boat tour, Jökulsárlón (p128)

First Time

FIRST TIME TOOLKit

 For more information on starting the journey, see the Reykjavík City Guide, p36.

SIM CARDS
Mobile (cell) coverage is widespread, but there are some blackspots up in the hills and valleys. Purchase a local SIM card – Iceland telecom Síminn *(vefur. siminn.is/en/prepaid)* provides the greatest network coverage; Síminn's costs 3000kr (including either 10GB data, 50 minutes of international calls and 50 local texts) or 7000kr (unlimited local calls, texts and data plus 50GB of EU roaming data). E-sim cards increasingly work here.

Where to Arrive
Almost everyone arrives at Keflavík International Airport, 49km southwest of Reykjavík, and those driving the Ring Road often pick up a rental car at the airport and get underway immediately. There's also Akureyri International Airport (a couple of flights a week from London and Manchester), and the weekly ferry service from northern Denmark via the Faroe Islands to Seyðisfjörður. On the latter, you can bring your own vehicle.

Visas
Citizens or residents of the US, Australia, Canada, the UK, Japan, New Zealand, and EU and Schengen countries do not need a visa for visits under 90 days in any period of 180 days. Note that from 2026, non-EU nationals from these same countries will need to complete the online European Travel Information and Authorisation System *(etias.com)* before travelling.

Leaving Iceland
Keflavík International Airport can get overwhelmed at peak times when there never seem to be enough check-in machines or counters. It's usually quicker to use the former and then queue for bag drop. Travellers can request VAT refunds at the airport by submitting receipts and Tax Free forms signed by retailers.

Time Zones
Iceland has the same time zone as the UK (i.e. GMT/UTC), but there is no daylight saving time. This means that during the Northern Hemisphere summer, Iceland is one hour behind London, four hours ahead of New York and 10 hours behind Sydney. Iceland uses the 24-hour clock system.

WI-FI
Free wi-fi is almost universal and available at hotels, restaurants, attractions and public libraries; if you've forgotten to download that essential map or app and you're about to hike, most visitor centres (e.g. Skaftafell, or the cafe at Jökulsárlón) have strong, free wi-fi. Portable wi-fi devices are available to rent with some vehicles.

ELECTRICITY 120V/60HZ

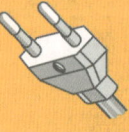

Type C 220V/50Hz   Type F 230V/50Hz

Money

Budgeting

Everything in Iceland is expensive, and this applies especially to what are likely to be your major expenses – food, accommodation, car rental and fuel. To save money on food, fill up at hotel breakfasts (if included in the cost of your room) and buy food for a picnic lunch at supermarkets. Accommodation in high season can double in price. You could easily spend €400 to €500 per person per day overall.

TIPPING

Although things are changing a little in the tourism industry, there is no culture of tipping in Iceland. As a result, tipping is never expected, and you won't be made to feel bad if you don't do it. This is partly because service and VAT taxes are always included in prices. Even so, in a restaurant, no-one will object if you round up the bill, thereby leaving a small tip as a reward for good service.

Cash or Card

You could travel around Iceland for weeks and never touch a kroner – credit or debit cards are king and Iceland is well on the way to becoming a cashless society, no matter how small the transaction. That said, there is always the option to pay in cash if you prefer. If you do need cash, there's an exchange counter in the arrivals hall, as well as ATMs in most medium-sized to large towns.

Euros or Kroner

Prices are sometimes quoted in euros, even though payment always takes place in Icelandic kroner (kr). Most often, the euro (and sometimes US dollar) equivalent is posted alongside the price of larger items. It's mostly a courtesy to foreigners so they can easily convert how much they're paying – €70 sounds a lot less scary than 10,000kr.

HOW MUCH IS
a day on the Ring Road?

Espresso	500kr
Parking at major attractions	1040kr
Museum ticket	2500kr
Golden Circle tour	10,000kr
Zodiac boat tour on Jökulsárlón lagoon	15,900kr
Northern Lights tour	9000kr
Entry to geothermal bathing spot	7500kr
Main course in Icelandic restaurant	4500–8000kr

Dos & Don'ts

- Do choose Icelandic kroner instead of your home currency if given the choice when paying by credit card – you'll save quite a bit on each transaction.
- Do the same at ATMs.
- Do consider travelling outside the summer season, when things are cheaper.
- Do carry an emergency stash of cash in case you lose your card.
- Don't forget to let your bank know you're going away.

On the Road

Road Conditions
Most main roads in Iceland, including the entirety of the Ring Road (Rte 1), are paved and well-maintained throughout. Except in the vicinity of Reykjavík, the Ring Road is a single lane in either direction, with few overtaking lanes. Secondary roads may start out paved, but often turn to gravel (such transitions are marked with the warning sign 'Malbik Endar'), albeit accessible to all types of vehicles. F roads are challenging roads, sometimes over mountain or through rivers, that should only be attempted by experienced 4WD drivers.

GPS TROUBLE

There are times when a GPS can lead you astray. For example, if you're driving from Höfn to Egilsstaðir, the GPS tells you to take Rte 95. What it doesn't tell you is that the road soon turns to gravel, then takes you up and over a mountain pass – not ideal when it starts to rain.

Maps
Google Maps and other programs like Mapy.com are generally reliable when it comes to Icelandic roads – be sure to download the necessary maps before leaving home for those moments when you're offline. Always carry a paper map as backup – we recommend the Michelin *Iceland* map (Map 750; 1:500,000). It has the requisite level of detail and fills in the gaps for those moments when the GPS is down. There's just something about paper maps...

Insurance
Do not visit Iceland without travel insurance. Apart from helping with emergencies, such as medical issues, flight cancellations and lost bags, a good travel insurance plan will cover the excess of any vehicle insurance you take out through the car rental agency. Given how expensive Iceland can be, the peace of mind of having such expenses covered is considerable.

HOW TO

DO ICELAND'S RING ROAD BY BIKE

Iceland's Ring Road is a major draw for cyclists, but there are no bike lanes – none at all. Cold, rain and wind can make for uncomfortable conditions and contingency planning is key. Bike rentals are available in Reykjavík and a handful of other towns. Off-road biking is also popular and many trails allow bikes.

FOTOKON/SHUTTERSTOCK

From left: Cyclist on the Ring Road; parking at Reynisfjara (p91)

PARKING

Most natural attractions don't have entry fees, but you will pay to park just about everywhere along the Ring Road. Usually the fee is 1000kr or 1040kr per day for standard vehicles. There is generally an on-site machine where you can pay by entering your vehicle's licence plate and credit card. Otherwise, you can pay online or through the app displayed at the site within 24 hours.

ROAD RULES

- Drive on the right
- Seat belts are required
- Blood alcohol limit is 0.05%
- Drive with dipped headlights on at all times
- Speed limits on most of the Ring Road: 90km/h
- Speed limits on gravel roads: 80km/h
- Speed limits in built-up areas: 30km/h to 50km/h (as signed)

Buying Fuel

Many smaller petrol stations are unstaffed, and even at those with someone in attendance, all pumps are automated. To fill, put your credit card into the machine's slot and follow the instructions. On newer touchscreens, you can press 'Full Tank', or input the maximum amount you wish to spend. Entering a maximum amount pre-approves your card for that capped amount, but you are only charged for the cost of the fuel put into your vehicle. Select the pump number you are using, fill your tank and then re-enter your card to get a receipt when finished.

Driving Licence

You can drive in Iceland with a driving licence from the US, Canada, Australia, New Zealand and most European countries. Although it's not legally necessary unless your licence is not in Roman script, we recommend that you also bring an International Driving Permit (normally issued by your home country's automobile association). Digital licences may be the future, but you must bring a physical copy of your licence – car rental companies will not accept digital licences on your phone or other device. It's a long way to come only to find you can't rent a car.

From left: Sheep crossing the Ring Road; campervan at Skógafoss (p87)

THE PROBLEM WITH SHEEP

Usually, Iceland's sheep are no danger to anyone, off in the fields and behind a fence. But not always – slow down if you see a sheep (or any animal) next to the road. They're known to panic at the approach of a car and can cross in front of you without warning.

One-Lane Bridges

All along the Ring Road, a flashing orange light announces the presence of a single-lane bridge (marked as 'Einbreið Brú'), i.e. one that can only be crossed by one vehicle in either direction at once. Slow to 70km/h and then 50km/h as you approach. Usually they work fine and everyone respects the rule that whoever arrives first, crosses first. However, sometimes it's not always possible to see the other end until you're already on the bridge and someone has to reverse off. The key is often to watch the other side on your approach to the bridge, not just when you arrive.

Speed Cameras

There aren't many speed cameras in Iceland, and certainly very few the further you get from Reykjavík. Most speed cameras are signposted in advance – there really is no excuse for speeding. The police can also catch you out – watch for where the Ring Road passes through a town, and the limit drops from 90km/h to 50km/h in just a few hundred metres. Speeding fines are significant, and vary depending on how far over the limit you are – from 23,500kr up to a whopping 83,310kr.

To Rent a Car

If you want to rent a standard 2WD car in Iceland, a driver must be at least 20 years old and hold a valid licence with no conditions attached. If you want to rent a 4WD, you need to be 23 to 25 years old (depending on the company).

WHAT KIND OF VEHICLE SHOULD I RENT?

2WD If you're staying strictly on the Ring Road and nearby detours, you should be fine with a 2WD vehicle (whether petrol, hybrid or EV). Most access roads to sites and even some hotels are gravel, but these are fine for 2WD vehicles, as are most gravel roads. On no account take your 2WD onto one of the F roads or mountain roads that leave the Ring Road and head into the Icelandic interior. Apart from the hazards of potholes and deep river crossings, you won't be covered by your insurance if you head down one of these roads and encounter difficulties.

4WD Renting a 4WD is a must if you plan on heading any meaningful distance off the main road. It can also be a good idea in winter when snow and ice on the roads can make for hazardous conditions, even on paved roads. Even though 2WD vehicles use winter tyres, a 4WD or AWD adds an extra layer of security. If you plan on taking F roads, even small 4WDs won't be enough – you'll need a high-clearance 4WD with proper tyres for backcountry roads.

Campervan Travelling the Ring Road in a campervan or RV is a longstanding tradition, and what you pay in rental costs, you save in accommodation. Most campervans are like mini-homes, but driving one requires care – most have low clearance, are wider than standard cars, and can be difficult to drive in high winds.

Van Life Halfway between a car and a campervan, the van (with mattress and kitchenette) is hugely popular along Icelandic roads. 'Van life' allows you to go off-grid, live in the elements (while protected from them) and self-cater. Note that you cannot park your van just anywhere – you must use campsites, which often have electricity hook-ups.

BRING YOUR OWN VEHICLE

You can bring your vehicle from Denmark (via the Faroe Islands) by taking the Smyril Line ferry from Denmark to Seyðisfjörður (p162). Book your passage well ahead, and carry with you all vehicle registration documents, proof of valid insurance (a 'green card' if your car isn't registered in a Nordic or EU-member country) and a driving licence. You'll need studded tyres in winter.

From left: Smyril Line ferry; Ring Road near Mývatn (p180)

Returning the Car

If returning your vehicle to Keflavík International Airport, timing is everything. Unless you're staying at the Aurora Hotel, within walking distance of the main terminal in the airport car park, try to time the return of your vehicle to just a few hours before your flight departs. Otherwise, you'll need to pay for a return bus or taxi to/from Reykjavík. If you have a day in the capital at the end of your trip, keep your car – paying for overnight parking at your hotel is cheaper than airport transfers.

In-Car Wi-Fi

It may be an added expense in an expensive country, but you can rent a portable wi-fi unit along with your vehicle. It's probably not worth it if you're staying in hotels, but if you're in a van or campervan and staying in campgrounds, it's a good way to stay connected. Prices vary according to the rental company and connection plan.

Tyre Trouble

The Ring Road may be paved, but the often-windy conditions can blow all sorts of debris (ice, gravel etc) onto the road. You'll also inevitably end up on a few gravel roads where sharp stones lie in wait. As a consequence, more travellers than you might think end up with a flat tyre. Not all rental vehicles provide a spare (!) – check when renting your vehicle – and if they do, make sure that your vehicle has a jack and all accompanying tools. For advice on what to do in the event of a flat tyre, see p243.

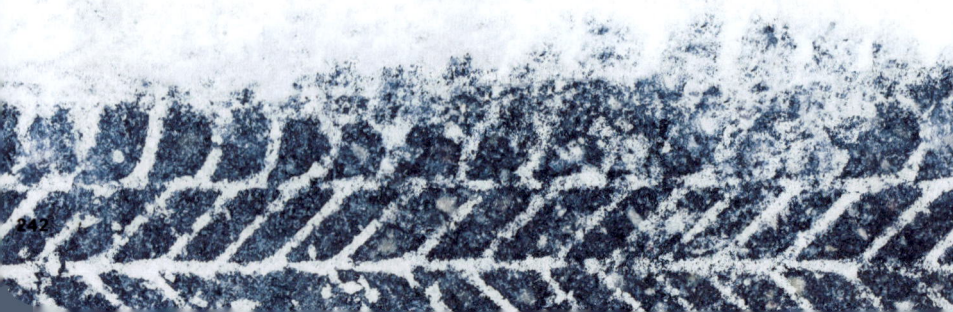

DRIVING PROBLEM-BUSTER

What if my car breaks down?

If your car breaks down, your first call should be to your car rental company – follow their instructions. Most offer insurance at the pick-up desk for roadside assistance – the implication being that you may be on your own if you don't pay it. Our advice would be to pay it – how much it would cost to get an Icelandic tow truck to pick you up 150km from the nearest town doesn't bear thinking about.

It's also worth noting that the Icelandic motoring association **Félag Íslenskra Bifreiðaeigenda** (FÍB; www.fib.is) is only open to locals. That said, if you have breakdown cover with an automobile association affiliated with ARC Europe you *may* be covered by the FÍB – check with your home association.

FÍB's 24-hour breakdown number is 511 2112. Even if you're not a member, it may be able to provide information and numbers for towing and breakdown services. It seems to depend on who you get on the phone – some travellers have reported receiving little help over the phone, and even less sympathy.

What if my car gets a flat tyre?

Assuming you have a spare (not all rental vehicles do) and have been provided with the necessary tools, change the tyre. Understand, however, that the spare tyre is only for temporary use on paved roads and you should drive no faster than 80km/h with it on your vehicle.

When you reach a town, ask if there's a tyre-repair workshop – most medium-sized towns have one. If it's reparable, the going rate seems to be around 8000kr. If it's not, contact your car rental company about your next move.

Packing

Clothing

Smart (and effortlessly) casual seems to be the mantra among locals. For all but the warmest of summer days, master the art of layering. On cold days, start with a warm underlayer, followed by wool or a warm fleece to keep the warmth in and a wind- and waterproof outer layer to keep rain and wind out, and a hat, gloves and sturdy walking shoes or hiking boots. Bring a nice set of clothes (jeans are usually fine) for eating out. And even in winter, don't forget your swimmers for geothermal hot springs.

Other Gear

- **Binoculars** – for spotting whales and birds
- **Umbrella** – rain is always possible
- **Adaptor** – Iceland uses two-pin European-style connections
- **Rain- or windproof jacket** – useful, even in summer
- **Sunglasses** – the sun can be bright, as are glaciers!
- **Sunscreen** – you'd be surprised...
- **Alcohol** – either bring your own or buy at duty-free on arrival
- **Lightweight sleeping bag** – if hiking to sleep in mountain huts
- **Hiking poles** – for slippery trails
- **Portable charger or power bank** – but check rules for carrying on airlines

FIRST-AID KIT

Most medications are readily available (if expensive) in Iceland, but take your prescriptions in paper form (including for glasses or contact lenses) for any important and/or regular medications just in case; better still, take enough with you for your whole trip (but still carry the prescriptions with you in case customs takes an interest). A basic first-aid kit could include painkillers (paracetamol and ibuprofen), an all-purpose antibiotic, band-aids and stretch bandages and a disinfectant cream such as Betadine. Mosquitoes can also be a problem in some lake areas – bring a mosquito repellent.

CLOCKWISE FROM TOP LEFT: VALKOINEN/SHUTTERSTOCK, TARZHANOVA/SHUTTERSTOCK, TERRACESTUDIO/SHUTTERSTOCK, NEW AFRICA/SHUTTERSTOCK, GOWITHSTOCK/SHUTTERSTOCK, TALE/SHUTTERSTOCK, LANDSCAPEMANIA/SHUTTERSTOCK, NEW AFRICA/SHUTTERSTOCK, ANTON STARIKOV/SHUTTERSTOCK, KOSOFF/SHUTTERSTOCK

TOILETRIES

Supermarkets have everything you need but they're likely to be more expensive than they are back home – bring your own, but just a minimum or your bags will be too heavy. Most hotels provide complimentary soaps and shampoos. There's an expanding range of high-end skincare products (lava face mask anyone?) with prices to match; good as gifts. Mostly you'll find these at the spa centres around the country, but shops in Reykjavík also stock them, as does duty free after you pass through security for international flights out of Reykjavík.

Where to Stay

Booking in Advance
Advance reservations are always recommended, particularly in summer. This is especially an issue along the south coast in the stretch of Ring Road between Vík and Höfn – in July or August finding a place to stay in Vík, or near Skaftafell or Jökusjárlón, can be a challenge. Many places will require that you pay in full upfront during summer, but this is less common at other times of the year.

High-Season Prices
Although Iceland can be busy at any time of the year, visitor numbers reach a whole new level in July and August, and many accommodation places set their prices accordingly. Particularly in the southeast, March prices, for example, can almost double by July. If you can avoid the high-season months (difficult if you're here to hike), you may end up saving a significant amount of money.

Accommodation Types
Many of Iceland's best hotels are located in and around Reykjavík, but there are a few high-end options along the Ring Road as well. Hostels and guesthouses tend to be more affordable, but you may need to share bathrooms; bring your own sleeping bag or sheets and you'll save money at some guesthouses, rural hotels, hostels and farmstays.

HOW MUCH FOR A...?

Hostel dorm
5000kr

Three-star hotel
25,000kr

Four-star hotel
40,000kr

HOW TO

CAMP IN ICELAND

Camping is an affordable way to see Iceland but is only allowed at designated campsites or private property with the owner's permission. It's only possible in summer (most campsites close in winter), and even then, bring plenty of warm clothes. Most campgrounds have shared ablutions blocks and should be booked in advance.

Responsible Travel

GOOD TO KNOW

Save the Moss Be careful when exploring: if you step on and damage precious moss (e.g. at Skaftáreldahraun, p107), it can take decades to regrow.

EVs & Hybrids Around half of new cars registered in Iceland each year are electric or hybrid, 11% of the total. The import of petrol and diesel cars will no longer be possible from 2030.

Don't Eat Whale With only about 2% of Icelanders reporting that they regularly eat whale meat, tourists keep the trade alive. Over 60 restaurants have pledged to stop serving whale.

Climate Change & Travel

It's impossible to ignore the impact we have when travelling; Lonely Planet urges all travellers to engage with their travel carbon footprint, which will mainly come from air travel. While there often isn't an alternative, travellers can look to minimise the number of flights they take, opt for newer aircrafts and use cleaner ground transport, such as trains. One proposed solution – purchasing carbon offsets – unfortunately does not cancel out the impact of individual flights. While most destinations will depend on air travel for the foreseeable future, for now, pursuing ground-based travel where possible is the best course of action.

The **UN Carbon Offset Calculator** shows how flying impacts a household's emissions:

The **ICAO's carbon emissions calculator** allows visitors to analyse the CO_2 generated by point-to-point journeys:

Stay on the Road

Icelandic roads can be narrow and rarely have hard shoulders. Avoid pulling over on natural features and in places without a hard shoulder unless it's an emergency – no matter how good the photo opportunity is. And even in a 4WD, off-road driving is never permitted as it can cause untold damage to fragile ecosystems. There's more than enough to see from the road itself and legitimate pullover spots.

Practical Steps

The orange Vakinn label shows that a tourism business meets the Icelandic Tourist Board's standards for ethical, professional and environmentally sustainable operations. There's a list of certified companies at *vakinn.is/en/certified-companies*. And when it comes to renting vehicles, you'll find lots of electric and hybrid car hire options from most rental companies, and charging stations are plentiful and widely distributed across the country. Some rental companies even include free charging.

Toilets & Waste

Travelling Iceland's Ring Road can require a level of bladder control – the distance between toilets can be surprisingly long. That said, most car parks at major attractions and all petrol stations have a handful of toilets – except in cases of dire emergency, avoid going to the toilet by the roadside and hold on to use the proper facilities. If your campervan has its own toilet, as most do, make sure that you dispose of any such waste only in designated areas – ask at your campsite or in petrol stations.

FROM LEFT: LALANDREW/SHUTTERSTOCK, MARIYANA M/SHUTTERSTOCK, MECHANIC3D/SHUTTERSTOCK

Overtourism

Around 2.6 million tourists visited Iceland in 2024 – that's five times the country's resident population. This creates massive pressure on local infrastructure and some Icelanders complain that prices and services (including the availability of housing) are increasingly aimed at tourists, rather than locals. Learn some words in Icelandic, visit outside the summer high season and take the time to speak with locals.

Responsible Hiking

Every year, Iceland's emergency services are forced into potentially dangerous (and expensive) manoeuvres to rescue foreign hikers who have become lost, or worse. With that in mind, it's important that every hiker takes responsibility for their own safety and that you try to minimise the potential risk for yourself and for others.

Do as much pre-hike research about the route as you can, and prepare accordingly, including what you're wearing and the maps you carry with you. Weather conditions can change suddenly, even in summer – keep an eye on *weather.is*. Inform a park ranger of your plans; leave a travel plan at *safetravel.is;* and whenever at a hut, write your plan in the guestbook.

Hiking at Selfoss (p61)

TRAVEL RESPONSIBLY

Water Bottles In this day and age, there really is no excuse for plastic water bottles. Iceland is known for its pure, clean water. Bring a reusable water bottle, or pick up a new one in Iceland, and refill it at the tap.

Fish, Not Beef Beef production is one of the largest drivers of climate change. Minimise the environmental impact of your holiday by opting for the fish of the day in this seafood capital of the world.

Shop Locally One of the things that makes Iceland so charming is its independent restaurants, bars and shops. Help keep these open by eating, drinking and shopping at locally owned businesses. Opt for locally grown produce labelled *'íslenskt'*.

When to Visit The peak summer months can put a lot of pressure on Icelandic businesses and the environment. Visit at other times of year to remove some of that pressure. You'll also save some money in the process.

Sign the Pledge Make an important statement by promising to be a responsible tourist while travelling in Iceland by signing the Icelandic Pledge *(global climatepledge.com/global/ iceland)*. You can also calculate the carbon footprint of your trip at *visiticeland.com/ carbon-offset*.

Access, Attitudes & Safety

SAFETY

The greatest risk to you while travelling in Iceland is most likely to come from either your own stupidity or recklessness. Every year, travellers die by setting out unprepared to hike into the wilderness or by climbing onto a glacier with neither a guide nor the correct safety equipment. Never climb onto a glacier with a guide. Always tell someone where you're going if you're hiking into remote areas. And make use of the excellent safetravel.is, both for advice, and to register your travel plans so that if people have to go looking for you, they know where to begin.

Travellers with Disabilities

As everywhere, accessibility is a work in progress in Iceland, but lifts and accessible bathrooms are now the norm in modern buildings, and ramps are increasingly common. Many businesses along Laugavegur, Reykjavík's main shopping street, have ramps, thanks to Ramp Up Reykjavík – 450 have been added with plans for 1500 ramps by March 2026.

Online resources include Wheel Map *(wheelmap.org)*, for searching and marking wheelchair-accessible places; Sjálfsbjörg *(sjalfsbjorg.is/english)* for short-term mobility equipment rental and curated lists of accessible hotels, restaurants and transportation services; and *WheelchairTraveling.com,* for destination-specific travel content for wheelchair users.

LGBTIQ+ Travellers

Iceland is widely considered to be one of the world's most LGBTIQ+-friendly countries. The country was among the first to give same-sex couples equal access to adoption and IVF. Both Icelandic Parliament and the Church of Iceland support same-sex marriage, defined as a union between individuals. Reykjavík is the beating heart of the Icelandic gay scene, and hosts two fabulous LGBTIQ+ festivals. Some 100,000 people celebrate **Reykjavík Pride** *(hinsegindagar.is; August)* in Reykjavík every year, a number equal to 70% of Reykjavík's population. And for bears and their admirers, there's **Reykjavík Bear** *(reykjavikbear.is)* in late August.

HOW TO — TRAVEL WITH CHILDREN

Iceland is very family-friendly. Some hostels and guesthouses offer family rooms or connecting rooms. Campsites have discounted rates for children, and some include playgrounds. You'll find lots of kid-friendly fare like hot dogs, hamburgers and chicken nuggets across the country, and many restaurants have kids menus. Most restaurants have a bathroom with a changing table.

Children under six must use a car seat– make sure you reserve one when booking. Baby seats for children up to three tend to be cheaper than child seats for older children. Breastfeeding is such a non-issue here that an Icelandic government official once addressed parliament while breastfeeding her six-week-old, and it was no big deal.

Language

Icelandic is a Germanic language of the same family as German, English and the Scandinavian languages (excluding Finnish). It stems from Old Norse and has changed remarkably little since the Saga Age.

HANDY WORDS

Excuse me. Afsakið. *af·sa·kidh*

Please. Vinsamlegast. *vin·saam·leh·gast*

Thank you. Takk/ Takk fyrir. *tak/tak fi·rir*

Yes. Já. *Y-ow*

No. Nei. *neigh*

Good bye. Bless. *bles*

Pronunciation Guide

Words and names take on different forms due to declension, and some include the special characters 'eth' (Ð or ð) and 'thorn' (Þ or þ). A few tips:

- The Icelandic 'j' sounds like the English 'y'.
- The character 'Þ' is pronounced 'th' like 'then'.
- The character 'Ð' is pronounced 'th' like 'the'.
- 'Reykjavík' is pronounced 'Rayk-yah-veek'.
- The letter 'r' is rolled.

English Spoken

Most Icelanders speak English and many people in the tourist industry are migrant workers with English as the common tongue. Icelanders won't expect you to uderstand their language, but they invariably appreciate it when visitors make an effort to learn a few words.

Greetings & Good Manners

How are you? Hvað segir þú gott? *kvadh say-yir thoo got*

Fine. And you? Allt fínt. En þú? *alt feent en thoo*

My name is... Ég heiti... *yekh hay·ti ...*

Do you speak English? Talarðu ensku? *a·lar dhoo ens·ku*

I don't understand. Ég skil ekki. *yekh skil e·ki*

Directions & Navigation

Where is...? Hvar er...? *kva·r eh·r*

Where's the (hotel)? Hvar er (hótelið)? *kvar er (hoh·te·lidh)*

What's your address? Hvert er heimilisfangið þitt? *kvert er hay·mi·lis-·fown·gidh thit*

Can you show me (on the map)? Geturðu sýnt mér (á kortinu)? *ge·tur·dhu seent myer (ow kor·ti·nu)*

Eating & Drinking

What would you recommend? Hverju mælir þú með? *kver·yu mai·lir thoo medh*

Cheers! Skál! *skowl*

Do you have vegetarian food? Eruð þið með grænmetisrétti? *er·udh thidh medh grain·me·tis·rye·ti*

breakfast morgunmat *mor·gun·mat*

lunch hádegismat *how·day·yis·mat*

Accidents, Emergencies & Illness

Help! Hjálp! *hyowlp*

Go away! Farðu! *far·dhu*

I'm lost. Ég er villtur/ villt. (m/f) *yekh er vil·tur/vilt*

Call...! Hringdu á...! *hring·du ow...*

a doctor lækni *laik·ni*

the police lögregluna *leukh·rekh·lu·na*

Where are the toilets? Hvar er snyrtingin? *kvar er snir·tin·gin*

Index

Journey legs **000**
Map pages **000**

4WD rental 241

A

accessible travel 248
accommodation 245, *see also* camping, *individual regions, individual legs*
Akureyri 191, 194-9, **196**
　accommodation 197
　food 197
　itineraries 196
　shopping 198
　transport 194
Akureyri to Hvammstangi 200-15, **202-3**, *see also* Reykjahlíð to Akureyri, Hvammstangi to Reykjavík
　accommodation 202
　food 202, 205
　highlights 202
　route 202-3
Almannagjá 66, 68
archaeological sites
　Hella 82
　Old Brekka Corral 224
　Stöð 149
Arctic Circle 210
art galleries, *see* museums & galleries
artworks & sculpture 147
　Áfangar, Richard Serra 42
　Akureyri 198
　Eggin í Gleðivík, Sigurður Guðmundsson 147
　Eysteinsdóttir, Aðalheiður 198
　List í ljósi art festival 162
　Ocean of Memories 157
　Tvísöngur, Lukas Kühne 20, 162
ATMs 237

B

Bakkagerði 162-3
bathrooms 246
beaches
　Dritvík 229
　Fauskasandur 144-5
　Fellsfjara (Diamond Beach) 127, 130, 132, 138
　Meleyri 148, 150
　Reynisfjara 91
　Sólheimafjara Beach 90
beer 150, 161, 209
bicycle travel 238, *see also* mountain biking
Bifröst 224
birdwatching 16, 17
　Bakkagerði 163
　Djúpivogur 147
　Sigurgeir's Bird Museum 186
　Snæfellsjökull National Park 229
Blautakvísl 104-6
Blönduós 210
Blue Lagoon 54-5
boat tours 13
　Fjallsárlón 123
　Húsavík 192-3
　Jökulsárlón 128
　Snæfellsjökull National Park 229
boat travel 242
Borgarfjörður Eystri 162-3
Borgarnes 226
breakdowns 243
Breiðdalsvík 148, 150-1
Breiðdalur 148
budgeting 237, 245

C

campervans 232-3, 241
camping 245
　Fossárdalur 146
　Geysir 71
　Þingvellir National Park 68
canyons
　Brúarhlöð 74
　Fjaðrárgljúfur 108
　Jökulsárgljúfur 178-9, **179**
　Kolugljúfur 212
car travel 238-43
　car trouble 243
　driving licenses 239
　insurance 238
　rentals 240, 241
　rules 239

cathedrals, *see* churches & cathedrals
caves, *see also* ice caves
　Gígjagjá 104
　Grjótagjá 187
　Hella 82, 135
　Loftsalahellir 91
　Rutshellir Cave 85
　Stóri-Hellir Cave 59
　Vatnshellir 228
　Yoda Cave 104
　Þvottahellir Cave 231
children, travel with 232-3, 248
churches & cathedrals
　Hallgrímskirkja 38
　Heydalir church 148
　Hofskirkja 122
　Hólar Cathedral 208
　Hvammskirkja í Norðurárdal 222-3
　Reykjahlíð village church 181
　Skálholtsdómkirkja 76
　Steingrímsson Memorial Chapel 109
　Vík í Myrdal Church 91
　Þingeyrarkirkja 210
　Þingvallakirkja 68
cities 18-21
climate 246
clothing 244
costs 237, 245
craters & pseudocraters
　Kerið 77
　Magni 88
　Modi 88
　Rauðhólar 52
　Sauðhóll 228
　Saxhöll Crater 228
　Skútustaðagígar 188
　Vindbelgjarfjall 188
credit cards 237
currency 237
cycling 238, *see also* mountain biking

D

Dettifoss 178-9, **179**
disabilities, travellers with 248
diving 68

Djúpivogur 145-6, 147
drinks, see beer, water
driving, see car travel
driving licences 239
Dyrhólaey 90-1

E

Egil's Saga 95, 227, 230
Egilsstaðir 159, 160, 161
Egilsstaðir to Reykjahlíð 170-81, 172-3, see also Stöðvarfjörður to Egilsstaðir, Reykjahlíð to Akureyri
  accommodation 172, 180
  food 172, 175
  highlights 172
  route 172-3
electricity 236
Elf Village 226
environmental issues 246-7
equipment 244
Eskifjörður 158
etiquette 248
events, see festivals & events
Eyvindarholt DC-3 aeroplane wreck 85-6

F

family travel 232-3, 248
farms
  Efstidalur II 70
  Finnsstaðir 159
  Flúðasveppir 67
  Freysnes 120
  Guesthouse Skálafell 122
  Hof 95
  horse farms 206
  Hrafnkelsstaðir 164
  Illugastaðir 215
  Keldur 85
  Krumshólar 95
  Lýtingsstaðir 206
  Möðrudalur 176
  Óseyri 148
  Sandfell 121-2
  Sel 114
  Skaftafell 111
  Sólheimar Eco-Village 76
  Svínafell 120
  Þingvallabær 68
Fáskrúðsfjörður 156
ferry travel 242

festivals & events
  Akureyri Art Summer 198
  Blue Church Summer Concert Series 162
  Bræðslan 163
  Food & Fun Festival 28
  Iceland Airwaves 40
  Innipúkinn Festival 40
  Jazz Festival 40
  List í ljósi 162
  Sumar á Selfossi 61
  Þorrablót 28
fishing
  Norðurá River 225
  Ölfusá River 61
Flúðir 75
folklore 94-6
food 26-9, 39, 161, 197, see also *individual legs, individual regions*
food festivals 28
forests
  Hallormsstaðaskógur 164
  Haukadalur 71
  Selskógur 159
  Sveinatunga 222
fuel 239

G

galleries, see museums & galleries
gay travellers 248
geological features
  Blábjörg 146
  Borgarvirki 212
  Dimmuborgir 187
  Dverghamrar 109
  Gatklettur 229
  Hjörleifshöfði 104
  Hljóðaklettar 179
  Hvítserkur 214
  Kirkjugólf 109
  Reynisdrangar 91
  Saxa Sea Geyser 156
  Steinn 226
  Streitishvarf 148
  Vatnshellir lava tube 228
geothermal areas
  Bjarnarflag 181
  Deildartunguhver 225
  Geysir 71
  Haukadalur 70
  Hveradalir Geothermal Area 56, 138
  Hveragerði Geothermal Park 56, 58

Hverir 180
Strokkur 71
geothermal energy 56
Geysir 71
glacier lagoons
  Fjallsárlón 123
  Jökulsárlón 127, 128-9
glacier walking
  Fjallsárlón 123
  Jökulsárlón 13, 129
  Sólheimajökull 92-3
glaciers & ice caps 8-13
  Breiðamerkurjökull 123
  Eyjafjallajökull 88, 92
  Heinabergsjökull 130
  Hoffellsjökull 130
  Kvíárjökull 122-3
  Langjökull 68
  Morsárjökull 115
  Mýrdalsjökull 92
  Skaftafellsjökull 113
  Snæfellsjökull 228
  Sólheimajökull 90, 92-3
  Svínafellsjökull 120
Glerá River 199
Goðaland 89
Golden Circle 62-77, 64-5, see also Reykjavík to Selfoss, Selfoss to Vík
  accommodation 64, 77
  food 64, 67
  highlights 64
  route 64-5
golf
  Geysir 71
  Ondverdarnes 59
GPS 238
Grettir's Saga 207
Grímsey 210
Guðmundsson, Guðmundur Arnar 162

H

Harpa 38
Helgustaðanáma 158
Hella 82, 137
hiking 247, see also glacier walking
  Esjuraetur 226
  Fáskrúðsfjörður 148
  Fimmvörðuháls 88-9
  Fjaðrárgljúfur 108
  Geysir 71

hiking (continued)
  Glymur 231
  Hengifoss 164
  Hverfjall 187
  Nýgræðuöldur 126
  Reykjavík 41
  Skaftafell 114-15
  Skaftafellsjökull 113
  Sólheimajökull 92-3
  Sólheimasandur Plane Wreck Trail 90
  Svínafellsjökull 120
  Vindbelgjarfjall 186, 188
  Þórsmörk 84
history
  Borgarnes 227
  Ring Road development 44-6
  Saga history 94-6, 121
  Settlement history 125
Höfn 130-1
Höfn to Stöðvarfjörður 140-51, **142-3**, *see also* Skaftafell to Höfn, Stöðvarfjörður to Egilsstaðir
  accommodation 142, 149
  food 142, 145
  highlights 142
  route 142-3
horse riding
  Geysir 71
  Gulfoss 72
  Hólar 208
  Svínafell 120
  Þingvellir National Park 69
hot springs, *see also* geothermal areas, spas & health centres, swimming pools
  Blesi 71
  Blue Lagoon 54-5
  Deildartunguhver 225
  Gamla Laugin 75
  Hrunalaug 75
  Jarðböðin 181
  Kerlingarfjöll Hot Springs 56
  Krauma 225
  Laugarás Lagoon 75-6
  Laugarvatn 70
  Mývatn Nature Baths 181
  Nauthólsvík 41
  Reykjadalur Valley 58, 60

Sundlaugin Laugaskarði 58
Vök Baths 174
Hrútey 210
huldufólk 96, 226
Húsavík 192-3
Hvammstangi 212-13
Hvammstangi to Reykjavík 218-31, **220-1**, *see also* Akureyri to Hvammstangi, Reykjavík to Selfoss
  accommodation 220, 224
  food 220, 223
  highlights 220
  route 220-1
hverabrauð 70
Hveragerði 56, 58
Hverfisfljót 110
Hvolsvöllur 85

I

ice caps, *see* glaciers & ice caps
ice caves
  Fjallsárlón 123
  Jökulsárlón 129
Icelandic gods 94-6
Icelandic language 249
Ingólfshöfði 124-5
insurance, travel 238

J

Jökuldalur 174
Jökulsárgljúfur 178-9, **179**
Jökulsárlón 127, 128-9
Jónatan, Hans 146

K

kayaking 128
Kirkjubæjarklaustur 109
Kjarval, Jóhannes S 162
Kristnitökuhraun 53, 56

L

Lagarfljót 164-5, **165**
lakes
  Lagarfljót 164-5, **165**
  Laugarvatn 67, 70
  Ljósavatn 190
  Mývatn 180, 181, 186
  Systravatn 109
  Þingvallavatn 66
Laki eruption 105
language 249

Laugar 188
lavafields & sand deltas
  Djúpalónssandur 228-9
  Kambaskriður 148
  Kristnitökuhraun 53, 56
  Mýrdalssandur 106
  Skaftáreldahraun 107
  Skeiðarársandur 110-11
legends 94-6
LGBTIQ+ travellers 248
lighthouses
  Dyrhólaey Lighthouse 91
  Hafnarnesviti Lighthouse 156
  Hvalnes 144
  Streitishvarf 148
Litla Hof 122

M

Magnúsdóttir, Agnes 210, 212, 215
markets 75
Melrakkaey 229
Mjóifjörður 160
Möðrudalur 176
money 237
Mosfellsbær 66, 230
mountain biking 60
mountains
  Háafjall 205
  Herðubreið 176
  Hraundrangi 205
  Hrossaborg 180
  Hverfjall 187
  Mt Esja 226
  Úlfarsfell 230
  Vífilsfell 52
  Vindbelgjarfjall 186, 188
museums & galleries
  1238 The Battle of Iceland 207
  Akureyri Art Museum 198
  Árbær Open Air Museum 52
  Ásmundarsafn sculpture museum 40
  Bobby Fischer Center 61
  Borgarfjörður Museum 227
  Borgarnes' Settlement Center 227
  Breiðdalur Geology Centre 151
  Commercial Museum 213
  Davíð Stefánsson house-museum 198
  Drill Core Library (DCL) 151
  Galleri Bardusa 212-13
  Geothermal Exhibition 56
  Gljúfrasteinn Laxness Museum 66

Hakið Visitor Centre 69
Icelandic Beer Centre 209
Icelandic Horse History Centre 208
Kjarvalsstaðir gallery 40
Langabúð 145-6
Lava Centre 83
Lava Show 91
Matthías Jochumsson house-museum 198
Nonni house-museum 198
Perlan - Wonders of Iceland 41
Petra's Stone Collection 149
Randulffssjóhús 158
Reykjavík Maritime Museum 38
Selasetur Íslands 212
Sigurgeir's Bird Museum 186
Sigurhæðir 198
Skaftárstofa Visitor Centre 107-8
Skaftfell 162
Skálholtsdómkirkja 76
Skriðuklaustur 164
Snæfellsstofa 164
Sólheimar Eco-Village art gallery 76
Textile Museum 210
Volcano Express 38
Wartime Museum 158
Whale Museum 193
Wilderness Center 165
music 40, 198
Mýrdalsjökull 88
myths 94-6

N

national parks
  Snæfellsjökull National Park 228-9, **229**
  Vatnajökull National Park 111, 115
  Þingvellir National Park 68-9, 96
Neskaupstaður 158, 160
Njál's Saga 85, 111, 121, 217
North Iceland 169-231
Núpsvötn 110

O

Ölfusá River 60-1

P

packing 244
parking 239
parks 59, *see also* national parks
Perlan - Wonders of Iceland 41

petrol 239
picnic areas
  Hljóðaklettar 179
  Hverfisfljót 110
  Km99 Picnic Area 110
  Ljósavatn 190
  Meleyri 150
  Norðlingafoss 222
  Núpsvötn 110
  Sveinatunga 222
planning 30-1, 32-3, 244
polar bears 215
pseudocraters, *see* craters & pseudocraters
puffins 16, 134
  Borgarfjörður Eystri 163
  Húsavík 192-3
  Ingólfshöfði 124-5
  Melrakkaey 229

R

rafting
  Hvítá river 74-5
  Varmahlíð 206
Rauðhólar 52, 134
reindeer 159
rental cars 240, 241
responsible travel 246-7
Reyðarfjörður 157-8
Reykjadalur Valley 58
Reykjahlíð 181
Reykjahlíð to Akureyri 182-93, **184-5**, *see also* Egilsstaðir to Reykjahlíð, Akureyri to Hvammstangi
  accommodation 184, 191
  food 184, 188
  highlights 184
  route 184-5
Reykjavík 36-43, **38**
  accommodation 39
  city card 40
  festivals & events 40
  food 39
  itineraries 38
  transport 36
Reykjavík to Selfoss 48-61, **50-1**, *see also* Selfoss to Vík, Golden Circle, Hvammstangi to Reykjavík
  accommodation 50, 56
  food 53
  highlights 50
  route 50-1

road conditions 238, 240
road rules 239
Route 35 59
routes 30-1

S

safe travel 248
Saga history 94-6, 121
Sagas
  Egil's Saga 95, 227, 230
  Grettir's Saga 207
  Njál's Saga 85, 111, 121, 217
sand deltas, *see* lavafields & sand deltas
Sauðárkrókur 207
sculpture, *see* artworks & sculpture
seals 14, 16, 17, 130, 212
Selfoss 61
Selfoss to Vík 78-93, **80-1**, *see also* Reykjavík to Selfoss, Vík to Skaftafell
  accommodation 80, 86
  food 80, 83
  highlights 80
  route 80-1
Seyðisfjörður 162-3
Sigurðsson, Friðrik 210, 212, 215
SIM cards 236
Skaftafell 111-12, 113, 114-15, **115**
Skaftafell to Höfn 116-31, **118-19**, *see also* Vík to Skaftafell, Höfn to Stöðvarfjörður
  accommodation 118, 122
  food 118
  highlights 118
  route 118-19
skiing 198
Skógar 87
slow travel 166-7
Snæfellsjökull National Park 228-9, **229**
Sólheimar Eco-Village 76
Sólheimasandur plane wreck 90
solo travellers 166-7
Southeast Iceland 99-165
Southwest Iceland 35-93
spas & health centres
  Krauma 225
  Laugarás Lagoon 75-6
  Laugarvatn Fontana 67, 70
  Rehabilitation & Health Clinic (Hveragerði) 58

253

speed cameras 240
Stöðvarfjörður 149
Stöðvarfjörður to Egilsstaðir 152-65, **154-5**, see also Höfn to Stöðvarfjörður, Egilsstaðir to Reykjahlíð
 accommodation 154, 158
 food 154, 157
 highlights 154
 route 154-5
Stokksnes 144
Strokkur 71
Sveinsdóttir, Petra 149
swimming pools, see also hot springs, spas & health centres
 Breiðdalsvík 150
 Lágafellslaug swimming pool 230
 Laugarvatn 70
 Seljavallalaug Swimming Pool 86-7
 Sundhöll Selfoss 61
 Sundhöllin 38
 Sundlaugin Laugaskarði 58
 Vök Baths 174

T

textiles 210, 222
theatre 198
time 236
tipping 237
toilets 246
Tómasdóttir, Sigríður 73
tourism 44-6, 166-7, 247
tours
 boat tours 13, 123, 128, 192-3
 glaciers 13, 129
 horse riding 69
 seals 212
 whale watching 17, 192, 193, 229
 wildlife 17, 124-5
towns 18-21
travel insurance 238
travel seasons 30-1, 245
travel to/from Iceland 236, 242
travel with children 232-3, 248
travellers with disabilities 248
trekking, see hiking
turf-roofed structures 20, 216-17
 Árbær Open Air Museum 52

Journey legs 000
Map pages **000**

Drangurinn 85
Glaumbær 206-7
Hofskirkja 122
Keldur 85
Nýibær Turf House 209
Sel 114

V

van rentals 241
Varmahlíð 206
Vatnajökull National Park 111, 115
Vatnsnes Peninsula 214-15, **215**
Viðey Island 42-3
viewpoints
 Akureyri Lookout 190-1
 Bishop's Cairn Viewpoint 177, 180
 Eyjafjörður Viewpoint 190
 Km97 Lookout 175
 Km99 Picnic Area 110
 Mývatn Lookout 180-1
 Mývatn North Lookout 186
 Námafjall 180
 Öxnadalur Viewpoint I 204-5
 Öxnadalur Viewpoint II 205-6
 Stokksnes 144
Vifilsfell 52
Vík 91
Vík to Skaftafell 100-15, **102-3**, see also Selfoss to Vík, Skaftafell to Höfn
 accommodation 102, 112
 food 102, 109
 highlights 102
 route 102-3
visas 236
volcanoes 22-5
 Grábrók 223-4
 Laki 105
 Lava Centre 83
 Lava Show 91
 Volcano Express 38
 Þríhnúkagígur 57

W

waste disposal 246
walking, see glacier walking, hiking
water (drinking) 247
waterfalls
 Ægissíðufoss 82
 Beljandi 148
 Brúarfoss 70
 Búðarárfoss 158

Dettifoss 178-9, **179**
Drífandi 86
Fjaðrárgljúfur 108
Flögufoss 148
Glanni Waterfall 224
Gljúfrabúi 86, 132
Glymur 231
Goðafoss 188, 189
Gullfoss 72-3
Hengifoss 164
Hlauptungufoss 70
Klifbrekkufossar 160
Kolufossar 212
Kvernufoss 87-8
Litlanesfoss 164
Miðfoss 70
Nauthúsafoss 85
Norðlingafoss 222
Nykurhylsfoss 146
Öxarárfoss 68
Rjúkandafoss 174-5
Seljalandsfoss 86, 134
Skógafoss 87, 138
Skútafoss 144
Svartifoss 114
Systrafoss 109
Urriðafoss 82
weather 30-1
West Iceland 169-231
whale watching 14, 17
 Húsavík 192-3
 Snæfellsjökull National Park 229
wi-fi 236, 242
wildlife 14-17, 159, see also birdwatching, polar bears, puffins, reindeer, seals, whale watching

Y

Ytri Bægisá 204

Z

ziplining
 Akureyri 199
 Hveragerði 60
 Vík 91

Þ

Þingvellir National Park 68-9, 96
Þórsmörk 84
þríhnúkagígur volcano 57
Þrístapar 210, 212

Notes

Notes

Notes

THIS BOOK

Destination Editor
James Smart

Coordinating and Production Editor
Vicky Smith

Assisting Editors
Anne Mulvaney, Charlotte Orr

Image Editor
Ania Lenihan

Cartographers
Vojtech Bartos, Daniela Machová, Bohumil Ptáček

Cover Illustration
Matt Saunders

Illustrated Map
James Gulliver Hancock

Photographer
Daniel Dorsa

Product Development
Anne Mason, James Smart, Marc Backwell, Katerina Pavkova

Series Development Leadership
Darren O'Connell, Piers Pickard, Chris Zeiher

Thanks
Sofie Andersen, Amy Lynch, Kate Mathews, Jenna Myers, Pia Peterson, Saralinda Turner

All rights reserved. No part of this publication may be copied, stored in a retrieval system, or transmitted in any form by any means, electronic, mechanical, recording or otherwise, except brief extracts for the purpose of review, and no part of this publication may be sold or hired, without the written permission of the publisher. Lonely Planet and the Lonely Planet logo are trademarks of Lonely Planet and are registered in the US Patent and Trademark Office and in other countries. Lonely Planet does not allow its name or logo to be appropriated by commercial establishments, such as retailers, restaurants or hotels. Please let us know of any misuses: lonelyplanet.com/legal/intellectual-property.

Mapping data sources:
©Lonely Planet, ©OpenStreetMap, ©Natural Earth, ©GEBCO, ©Esri, ©NASA Earth Observatory, ©USGS-ASTER and the GIS User Community